CHRIST IN
ANCIENT AMERICA

CHRIST
in
ANCIENT AMERICA

ARCHAEOLOGY AND THE BOOK OF MORMON VOLUME II

By
MILTON R. HUNTER, Ph. D.
of the
FIRST COUNCIL OF THE SEVENTY
CHURCH OF JESUS CHRIST OF LATTER-DAY SAINTS

VOLUME II

Published by
DESERET BOOK COMPANY
44 EAST SOUTH TEMPLE
SALT LAKE CITY, UTAH

FIRST EDITION

First Printing, April, 1959
Second Printing, January, 1960

Printed in U.S.A.
DESERET NEWS PRESS
SALT LAKE CITY, UTAH

FOREWORD

Christ in Ancient America by Dr. Milton R. Hunter of the First Council of the Seventy is a book of tremendous interest and value for those who would know firsthand the traditions and folkways of the early inhabitants of North, Central, and South America as well as know the truth contained in the Book of Mormon concerning these peoples.

This book follows the procedure that Dr. Hunter has pursued in all of his writings: He has built testimony in a most unusual way. From little-known books—largely inaccessible to the average layman—he has assembled material that reads so fascinatingly that those who once begin the book will be unable to lay it aside.

Dr. Hunter piles evidence on evidence from incontestable sources that the Book of Mormon record is indeed true wherein it states that Christ visited the Western Hemisphere. The persistent, although somewhat distorted, stories of the "White and Bearded God" among the inhabitants of Mexico, Yucatán, Central and South America cannot help indicating that the legends were based on truth. In fact, some of the archaeologists have proved that Christ or at least some of his apostles must have come since there is so much similarity between the Christian and the Indian knowledge.

Dr. Hunter feels, and those who have followed his career agree, that part of his mission at least is to find these materials which bear directly on the promise of the Book of Mormon, which is a witness for Christ ". . . to the Lamanites, who are a remnant of the house of Israel, and also to the Jew and Gentile. . . ."

Through Dr. Hunter's painstaking research, he bears his own testimony to the truthfulness of the gospel and encourages the building of such testimony in the hearts and minds of all who read his works.

Dr. Milton R. Hunter, according to Dr. G. Homer Durham, has "two fundamental qualities that have motivated his life: first, his unswerving faith in and devotion to the Church and its people;

second, that gifts enhanced by a thirst for knowledge and higher education do not depend for their expression on an easy ideal environment."

Dr. Hunter, in all of his work, first as a seminary and institute teacher and associate director; second, as a member of the priesthood quorums; and, third, as a member of the First Council of the Seventy, has always placed his Church first; and in order better to serve the Church, he has continued his study and research. He has been blessed in having a wife, Ferne Gardner Hunter, and a family who co-operate completely in his endeavors.

To most people the idea of giving up the comforts of home to trudge through the trackless jungle trails, enduring the hardships of primitive accommodations, the dangers of sickness and of attack from wild animals, the ferociousness of hostile natives would be unthinkable. Dr. Hunter has not only endured them, he has sought them out—if there were a remote chance that by so doing he could advance the knowledge of Latter-day Saints concerning the truthfulness of the gospel.

In all of his writings this has been Dr. Hunter's goal: To build faith in others. Innumerable articles and books have flowed from his facile pen in his earnest endeavor to depict the growth of Mormonism and to illustrate through archaeology, history, and biography as well as by reinforcing the standard works of the Church, the forcefulness of Latter-day Saint religion.

Christ in Ancient America adds its strength to the building of faith and testimony among Latter-day Saints.

March 21, 1959
Salt Lake City, Utah

MARBA C. JOSEPHSON

Associate Managing Editor
The Improvement Era

ACKNOWLEDGMENTS

It is the purpose of the writer to present in this book a correlation of archaeological and anthropological findings, as well as Indian traditions, with the claims made by the Book of Mormon in regard to Christ's resurrection, his appearance to the ancient Americans, and the marvelous work he did among them. All of the evidences presented contribute to sustaining the fact that Jesus did arise from the grave, breaking the bands of death for mankind, and that, as the God and Savior of the entire human family, he performed a phenomenal work in ancient America.

This volume expresses my personal views and findings. While I assume the complete responsibility for its contents, I am deeply indebted to many people for their helpful suggestions and assistance.

I express my deepest gratitude to the First Presidency of the Church and to President Joseph Fielding Smith for affording me opportunities to visit Mexico and Central America on mission tours and on other occasions—opportunities which enabled me to study and photograph the ruins and relics at numerous archaeological sites and museums.

C. N. Shelton, President of the TAN Air Lines, and his brother, Ralph V. Shelton, Vice-President, provided me the opportunity of visiting Peru and Bolivia, and of studying the archaeological ruins and artifacts there. For this unusual courtesy I offer sincere thanks. I am also grateful for the collection of archaeological photographs of South America that Ralph V. Shelton gave me.

Special recognition is extended to Paul R. Cheesman of Miami, Florida, for his wholehearted co-operation and for supplying me with a number of photographs of the Andean region.

For their hospitality and for taking me to many archaeological sites, I express sincere appreciation to President and Sister Frederick S. Williams of Lima, Peru. Also, I extend gratitude to Robert and Alwina Hulme of LaPaz, Bolivia, for their hospitality and kindness.

President and Sister Edgar L. Wagner of the Central American Mission extended numerous kindnesses to me on two mission tours. I express to them wholehearted appreciation. On several visits to Mexico I enjoyed the most genuine hospitality, consideration, and kindness from the late President Claudious Bowman and his good wife, Sister Bowman. Also, Major and Sister Joseph E. Vincent have been most kind in taking me to archaeological ruins and entertaining me in Oaxaca.

Deep appreciation is expressed to Stanford J. Robison for graciously permitting me to publish a number of the outstanding drawings of Maya stelae made by his late wife, Huberta Berg Robison. These drawings are exceptional in beauty and accuracy.

I extend appreciation to Elder Harold B. Lee and Elder Richard L. Evans, both of the Council of the Twelve, for reading the portion of this book which previously appeared in the *Improvement Era* and offering numerous and helpful suggestions. To Elder Bruce R. McConkie, my close associate on the First Council of the Seventy, I express gratitude for the encouragement, suggestions, and help that he has generously extended to me. Others of the General Authorities have encouraged me to continue this project.

I am grateful for the co-operation and the suggestions received from the members of the *Improvement Era* staff, especially Doyle Green, Marba C. Josephson, Elizabeth J. Moffitt, and Verl F. Scott, and appreciate their graciousness in allowing me to reprint Hofmann's "Jesus the Christ" as the frontispiece of this book. Sister Josephson not only read the entire manuscript and offered many valuable suggestions but she also read the proofs and wrote the foreword. I extend sincere thanks for all that she did.

I also express special appreciation to J. Fred Evans of Council Bluffs, Iowa, for providing me with several important books on archaeology and an abundance of information which he has collected in this field.

I sincerely acknowledge my deep obligation for the helpful suggestions of Alva H. Parry, manager of the Deseret Book Company, Thomas S. Monson and S. Ross Fox of the Deseret News Press, for giving unstintingly of their time and counsel in arranging for the printing and publishing of the book. All of the men at the Deseret News Press co-operated wholeheartedly in the production of this volume.

I am grateful for the work done by Evelyn Brough and Diane Reid, my secretaries, who typed the manuscript, and to Velma Harvey, who extended much help and co-operation in this project.

I owe a special debt of gratitude to my wife, Ferne G. Hunter, who co-operated wholeheartedly in helping to bring this volume into existence. To her I express sincere gratitude and appreciation. The fullest credit for the completion of this book rightfully goes to her. Without her help the book would not have been completed and published.

March 23, 1959

Salt Lake City, Utah

MILTON R. HUNTER

CONTENTS

ILLUSTRATIONS

HOFMANN'S JESUS THE CHRIST
Frontispiece reprinted by permission of the editors of the *Improvement Era*.
This courtesy is deeply appreciated.

CHAPTER 1

QUETZALCOATL—THE "WHITE AND BEARDED GOD"

INDIANS' UNIVERSAL TRADITION OF A "WHITE AND BEARDED GOD"*

When the Spanish *conquistadores* and Catholic fathers first arrived on the shores of Mexico, Central America, and the various countries of South America, and when the English and French colonizers and missionaries first penetrated the vast wildernesses of Canada and the United States, they received from the Indian tribes scattered over the Western Hemisphere various versions of a tradition of a "White and Bearded God" who had in the distant past visited their ancestors, taught them their culture, and mysteriously disappeared, but who would eventually return to them. This "Fair God" we shall discuss under the title of Quetzalcoatl (Ket-säl-kö-ät'l) by which he was known to the Aztec Indians of Mexico and their Toltec predecessors; however, he was known by various other names in the traditions of a number of other Indian tribes of North and South America.

Although the traditions from the various Indian groups regarding the "White Bearded God" do not agree in details, there being a variety of versions, yet in the principal points these Indian traditions from Canada in the north to Chile in the south have a close resemblance to one another. Dr. Daniel G. Brinton, an American scholar who made an extensive study of this subject during the latter part of the past century, devoted the greater portion of one of his books, *American Hero-Myths*, to this subject. The following is one of his summary statements:

The native tribes of this Continent had many myths, and among them there was one which was so prominent, and recurred with such strangely similar features in localities widely asunder, that it has for years attracted my attention, and I have been led to present it as it occurs among several nations far apart, both geographically and in point of culture. This myth

---

*Note: In Volume I of *Archaeology and the Book of Mormon*, we used the term "White Bearded God," which caused a certain amount of misunderstanding. Some of the readers interpreted that phrase to mean that he was a God with a white beard, while the writer was attempting to convey the idea that he was *a deity who had a white skin and wore a beard*. In order to rectify any misunderstanding, this ancient deity will be referred to in this volume by either of the following names: "White and Bearded God," or "White Bearded God." He will also be called the "Fair God."

Fig. 2:   JADITE HEAD REPRESENTING QUETZALCOATL
This head is in *Musée de l'Homme*, Paris, France.

is that of the national hero, their mythical civilizer and teacher of the tribe, who, at the same time, was often identified with the supreme deity and the creator of the world. It is the fundamental myth of a very large number of American tribes, and on its recognition and interpretation depends the correct understanding of most of their mythology and religious life.

The outlines of this legend are to the effect that in some exceedingly remote time this divinity took an active part in creating the world and in fitting it to be the abode of man, and may himself have formed or called forth the race. At any rate, his interest in its advancement was such that he personally appeared among the ancestors of the nation, and taught them the useful arts, gave them the maize or other food plants, initiated them into the mysteries of their religious rites, framed the laws which governed their social relations, and having thus started them on the road to self-development, he left them, not suffering death, but disappearing in some way from their view. Hence it was nigh universally expected that at some time he would return. . . .

Whenever the personal appearance of this hero-god is described, it is, strangely enough, represented to be that of one of the white race, a man of fair complexion, with long, flowing beard, with abundant hair, and clothed in ample and loose robes.[1]

During the past century the famous historian Hubert Howe Bancroft accomplished a gigantic task by collecting numerous Indian traditions and producing a history of the American Indians according to their traditions. His momentous historical contribution resulted in the publishing of thirty-six massive volumes, entitled *The Native Races*. After carefully collecting and studying the numerous Indian traditions regarding a "White Bearded God," Bancroft wrote the following conclusion:

Although bearing various names and appearing in different countries, the American culture-heroes all present the same general characteristics. They are all described as white, bearded men, generally clad in long robes, appearing suddenly and mysteriously upon the scene of their labors. They at once set about improving the people by instructing them in useful and ornamental arts, giving them laws, exhorting them to practise brotherly love and other Christian virtues, and introducing a milder and better form of religion; having accomplished their mission, they disappeared as mysteriously and unexpectedly as they came; and finally they are apotheosized and held in great reverence by a grateful posterity. In such guise or on such mission did [the "White Bearded God" under such names as] Quetzalcoatl appear in Cholula, Votan in Chiapas, Wixepechocha in Oajaca, Zamna and Cukulcan with his nineteen disciples in Yucatan, Gucumatz in Guatemala, Viracocha in Peru, Sumé and Pay-Tome in Brazil, the mysterious apostle mentioned by Rosales in Chile, and Bochica in Colombia.[2]

---

[1]Daniel G. Brinton, *American Hero-Myths* (Philadelphia, 1882), p. 27.
[2]Hubert Howe Bancroft, *The Native Races* (San Francisco, 1883), vol. 5, pp. 23-24.
Note: the foregoing names are pronounced as follows: Cholula—(Cho-loó-la); Chiapas (Chee-op'-us); Oajaca (Oaxaca)—(Wah-hah'-ka); Zamna—(Zahm'-na); Cukulcan (Kukulcan)—(Koo-kul-con'); Guatemala—(Gwä-tä-mä'la); Viracocha—(Vē-rä-kō'-cha); Sume—(Soo-may'); Bochica—(Bō-chee'-ka).

William Hickling Prescott, in his famous two volumes on *The Conquest of Mexico,* described Quetzalcoatl and the marvelous work that he performed anciently in Meso-America. Prescott wrote:

> A far more interesting personage in their [Aztec] mythology was Quetzalcoatl, God of the air, a divinity who, during his residence on earth, instructed the natives in the use of metals, in agriculture, and in the arts of government. He was one of those benefactors of their species, doubtless, who have been deified by the gratitude of posterity. Under him, the earth teemed with fruits and flowers, without the pains of culture. An ear of Indian corn was as much as a single man could carry. The cotton, as it grew, took, of its own accord, the rich dyes of human art. The air was filled with intoxicating perfumes and the sweet melody of birds. In short, these were the halcyon days, which find a place in the mythic systems of so many nations in the Old World. It was the *golden age* of Anahuac.[3]

Prescott described the "Fair God" as follows: "He was said to have been tall of stature, with a white skin, dark hair, and a flowing beard."[4] The famous historian gave an account of the departure of

------

[3]William Hickling Prescott, *The Conquest of Mexico* (Modern Library Edition, New York—First ed. Boston, 1843), p. 38-39.

Fig. 3:   CHURCH AT CHICHEN ITZA

—Photograph by Author

Quetzalcoatl from the ancient Americans, stating that he promised them that "he . . . would revisit them hereafter." Later in his book, Prescott wrote:

In a preceding chapter I have noted the popular traditions respecting Quetzalcoatl, that deity with a fair complexion and flowing beard, so unlike the Indian physiognomy, who, after fulfilling his mission of benevolence among them [ancient Americans], embarked on the Atlantic Sea for the mysterious shores of Tlapallan. He promised, on his departure, to return at some future day . . . and resume the possession of his empire. That day was looked forward to with hope or with apprehension, according to the interest of the believer, but with general confidence throughout the wide borders of Anahuac. Even after the Conquest, it still lingered among the Indian races, by whom it was as fondly cherished, as the advent of . . . the Messiah by the Jews.[5]

SOURCES OF INFORMATION REGARDING THE "WHITE AND BEARDED GOD"

The most important record regarding the "White and Bearded God" in ancient America is the Book of Mormon. This volume is an historical and religious record of the peoples who lived on this land from the time of the building of the Tower of Babel until A.D. 421. The account tells the story of three separate peoples—Jaredites, Nephites-Lamanites, and Mulekites—who migrated from western Asia and developed into great nations on the Western Hemisphere. The prophet-historians of these peoples recorded the religious teachings and history of their races as the events occurred, thereby making their accounts historically accurate.

The second source of evidence regarding the "Fair God" is found in the writings of Indian historians who wrote shortly following the Spanish conquest of the New World. These accounts were written primarily in Mexico—including Yucatán—and in Guatemala. These documents should give us reliable information, since the authors accounted the traditions of their forefathers which had come to them either in oral or written form.

A third source—an important and voluminous one—is the writings of the early Spanish chroniclers who recorded the history and religious beliefs and customs of the native Americans shortly after the discovery of the New World. These writers were usually Catholic priests who spent many years doing missionary work among the

---

[4]*Ibid.*, p. 39.
[5]*Ibid.*, p. 171.

Fig. 4: Pyramid of the Sun, Teotihuacan, Mexico

Indians. What they wrote they received directly from the aborigines, and became well informed regarding the religious customs, rites, practices, and traditions of the Indians. The fact that they received their information firsthand adds to the reliability of their accounts.

Archaeological discoveries and excavations have added an abundance of information to the recorded accounts previously mentioned; and so from these four sources we will tell our story of *"Christ in Ancient America."*

Ixtlilxochitl's Account of Quetzalcoatl

In the great central mesa of Mexico, the name by which the "White and Bearded God" was usually known was "Quetzalcoatl."

This is an Aztec name, and the name by which the "Fair God" will be designated in much of the discussion in this book. Indian writers and Catholic padres who did extensive missionary work among the Indians of Mexico and Central America shortly following the Spanish conquest have left us numerous accounts of the traditions of Quetzalcoatl.

One of the most authentic of the Indian writers was Ixtlilxochitl (Eesh-tleel-sho-cheetl'), a native American prince or chief who lived near the City of Mexico and wrote in approximately 1600 A.D. He wrote a history of his ancestors—who the writer believes were the Nephites and Lamanites—and of their descendants, the American Indians. His story began with the colonization of ancient America with three separate groups of people from Babel and western Asia, a story identical with that in the Book of Mormon. Ixtlilxochitl continued his story down to the Spanish conquest.

This Indian prince claimed that he produced his history from written documents which had come to him from his ancestors by right of his position as prince or chief in the royal family and also from the traditions he received from the old people.

Ixtlilxochitl's story of the people of ancient America is perhaps the most detailed and accurate of any of the ancient documents with the exception of the Book of Mormon. Of interest to us in discussing this subject is his very pertinent information regarding the appearance of Quetzalcoatl to his ancestors and the marvelous work accomplished by that "White Bearded God." To quote from the *Works of Ixtlilxochitl*:

And when the second group of colonizers, [the Toltecs] were in the height of their power, there arrived in this land a man whom they called Quetzalcoatl and others Huemac on account of his great virtues, considering him as just, saintly [holy], and good; teaching them by deeds and words the path of virtue and forbidding them their vices and sins, giving laws and good doctrine. And in order to refrain them from their pleasures and dishonesties, he instituted (established) fasting for them and [he was] the first who worshiped and placed the cross which they called Quiahuiteotl-chicahualizteotl and others Tonacaquahuitl, which means: God of rains and of health and tree of sustenance or of life.[6]

----

[6]*Works of Ixtlilxochitl*, cited in Milton R. Hunter and Thomas Stuart Ferguson, *Ancient America and the Book of Mormon* (Oakland, 1950), p. 203.

Fig. 5: PLUMED SERPENT'S HEAD AT BASE OF PYRAMID OF KULKULCAN, CHICHEN ITZA, YUCATAN, MEXICO

The Pyramid of Kukulcan was erected during the eleventh century A.D. in honor of Quetzalcoatl, known in Yucatán as Kukulcan. Observe the large head of the plumed serpent, a symbol of Quetzalcoatl. Ernest Caldwell is standing back of the serpent's head.

CATHOLIC PADRES' ACCOUNTS OF QUETZALCOATL

On the heels of the Spanish *conquistadores* came numerous Catholic padres, devoted advocates of European Christianity, carrying their messages to the American Indians. To them we are deeply indebted for much that is known today regarding the "White and Bearded God" who left such an astounding impression on the life and culture of ancient America.

Such Catholic padres as Bernardino de Sahagún (Sä-ha-goon'), Bartolome de Las Casas (Läs Cäss'-us), Juan de Torquemada (Tor-kay-mäh'da), and Diego de Landa (Län'da), in Meso-America and numerous others in the Andean region, all recorded much that they received from the Indians relative to the "White and Bearded God." They stated that he had suddenly appeared in ancient America, had taught the people many wonderful things and then had left just as

Fig. 6: JADE FIGURINE REPRESENTING QUETZALCOATL

This jade figurine and the jade beads, housed in the Guatemala National Museum, were taken from a tomb which archaeologists date in the early Christian centuries.

—Photograph by Author

suddenly as he had previously appeared. They all maintained that the Indians worshiped him as their Creator, God, Messiah, Savior, and Teacher. He is said to have given the ancient Americans their religion, their government, and their culture. He had promised those whom he taught, and their posterity, a blessed immortality on condition of their obedience to his teachings.

The accounts of these padres state that after this "Fair God" had done his benevolent work among the ancient Americans, he ascended to heaven to dwell with his Father, the head God. However, before leaving he promised the people that someday he would return to their posterity.

SAHAGUN'S COMMENTS ON QUETZALCOATL

Bernardino de Sahagún was born in Spain in 1499. He came to Mexico in 1529 and lived there until his death in 1590. He became a Catholic missionary of great renown among the Indians, and also a historian of marked importance. He wrote his scholarly work— *Historia de Las Cosas de Nueva España*—during the latter years of his life. His writings are among the most reliable and comprehensive reports concerning the ancient inhabitants of Middle America. Father Sahagún's history was lost and unknown for nearly three hundred years after it was written. Fortunately, it was discovered in a convent in Spain, and the first publication of it appeared in Mexico in 1829.

Lord Kingsborough published Sahagún's writings as volume eight of his *Mexican Antiquities* in 1848; and since then there have been numerous other Spanish-language editions. A part of his works has been published in English. From the time of the publishing of the first edition of his writings to the present day, scholars have regarded his writings with the deepest respect.

From the stories which had come to the Indians from their ancestors, Father Sahagún gathered the traditions of the sojourn and numerous accomplishments of Quetzalcoatl in America in ancient times. To quote his statements:

They [the Toltecs or descendants of the Nephites] worshipped only one Lord that they held as God, who was called Quetzalcoatl. . . . He did not want them to offer and give him in sacrifice anything except snakes and butterflies, and since the said Toltecas believed and obeyed him in everything, they were no less fond of divine things than their priest, and [they were] very fearful of their God.[7]

And these said Toltecs were apt in the Mexican language for they were not barbaric, although they did not speak it as perfectly as it is now used. They were rich, and because they were intelligent and capable they soon had riches, and they said their God and Lord Quetzalcoatl gave them said riches. And thus it was said among them that he who in a brief time becomes rich was a son of Quetzalcoatl.[8]

Quetzalcoatl was esteemed and loved as God and he was adored in the old times in Tula, and he had a very high *Cu* [temple tower] with many steps, which steps were very narrow—too narrow for an entire foot . . . and the vassals which he had were all skilled in mechanical arts and dextrous in the working of green stones called *chalchihuites*, and also for the working of silver and for the making of other things; and all these arts had their start and origin from this said Quetzalcoatl . . . and the said vassals of Quetzalcoatl

---

[7]Bernardino de Sahagún, *Historia de Las Cosas de Nueva España*, Libro 10, Capitulo 29, sec. 1.
[8]*Idem.*

Fig. 7:   BEARDED MAN AT OLD CHICHEN ITZA

Hebraic-like bearded man at Old Chichen Itzá, Yucatán, Mexico. Observe the quetzal feathers connoting that he was a worshiper of Quetzalcoatl.

—Photograph by Otto Done

were very rich and they lacked hardly a thing, there was no hunger, there was no lack of corn, and they did not have to eat *mazorcas* when small, and they heated their baths. . . .[9]

Thus the scholarly Sahagún characterizes Quetzalcoatl as the one God of the people of Tula, Tlapallan, or Bountiful.[10] He it was who blessed them with their culture and riches. The people built great cities and temple-towers in his honor.

Father Sahagún was regarded at first by the natives of Mexico as a representative of Quetzalcoatl. Hubert Howe Bancroft states that "Father Sahagún was also asked by everybody on his journey to Mexico City if he and his suite came from Tlapallan [Bountiful-land]." That region was the ancient Toltec-Nephite land where the "Fair God" had made his original New World appearance. Apparently the natives thought that the second coming of Quetzalcoatl would occur there.

TORQUEMADA'S COMMENTS ON QUETZALCOATL

Juan de Torquemada, a Catholic padre, arrived in Mexico from Spain about the middle of the sixteenth century. He spent the remainder of his life working with the Indians, and so he was able to gather many valuable traditions which had come down from their ancestors.

---

[9]*Ibid.*, Libro 3, Capitulo 3.

[10]Note: Ixtlilxochitl informs us that the headquarters of his ancestors or the capital city at 132 B.C. was *Huehuetlapallan*, which means "ancient Bountiful land." *Hue-hue* is from the Nahua (Mexican) tongue and means "old, old" or "ancient." Professor Marcos E. Bercerra of the Mexican Society of Geography, in his book on the native geographical names of the state of Chiapas, says that *Huehue-tlan* means "*bountiful place of the ancients*." He locates it in the state of Chiapas, Mexico.

Bercerra shows that many of the place names of Chiapas include this important name, *Tula* or *Tulan* or *Tlan*, meaning "*bountiful*" or "*abounding*." He uses the Spanish word *abundancia* to define it. *Abundancia* is defined "abundance, opulence, fertility, plenty. . . ."

[We may also mention] the ancient Maya term, *Tutul-xiu*, meaning "*abounding in plants*," the equivalent in Hebrew of *Zara-hemullah* or *Zarahemla*.

The famous Spanish-born Bernardino de Sahagún . . . says of ancient *Tulan*: "This city they called *Tullan*, which means place of fertility and abundance. . . ."

The French savant, H. de Charencey, points out that the root *Tul* means "*abundance, excess*," and that the Maya term *Tutul* (as used in *Tutul-xiu*) is a doubled "*Tul*": *Tul-tul*. The double use of the term makes it plural—this plural form being used for emphasis in the same fashion that *Hue-hue*, "old-old," means "very old" or "ancient." *Tutul* means "*very bountiful*."

The term *Tlapallan* sometimes appears in the old accounts as *Tulapan*, meaning "Bountiful-land capital." *Pan* is Maya for center or capital, as pointed out by Charencey. Thus, the name of the "seat of the kingdom," *Huehue Tlapallan*, means "Ancient Bountiful-land Capital." It was the capital or "seat of the kingdom" of the Tulteca-Olmeca [Nephite-Mulekite] settlers at the time of the council meeting of 132 B.C. *Tultecas* (*Toltecs*) means "Bountiful-people" or People of Bountiful-land."—Milton R. Hunter and Thomas Stuart Ferguson, *Ancient America and the Book of Mormon* (Oakland, California, 1950), pp. 149-153.

Torquemada gives considerable information about Quetzalcoatl, some of which he obtained from Sahagún and some which he took from Bartolome de Las Casas,[11] both Catholic missionaries and sixteenth century writers. However, much of his material he obtained directly from the Indians.

At times Torquemada confuses Quetzalcoatl with the tenth-century Toltec ruler, Topiltzin-Quetzalcoatl, who claimed a priesthood authority from the "Fair God." Many later writers have fallen into the same error. The following is quoted from Torquemada:

Fig. 8: BEARDED KUKULCAN
OR TOPILTZIN

Likeness of the white, bearded Kukulcan, tenth century Toltec ruler of Chichen Itzá, Yucatán, and priest of Quetzalcoatl, carved on a door jamb of the temple atop the Pyramid of Kukulcan at Chichen Itzá.

—*Photograph by Thomas Stuart Ferguson*

Concerning the God Quetzalcoatl, whom these Indian people had as God of the air, and the many things that they attributed to him.

Quetzalcoatl means plumage of serpent or serpent which has plumage, and these serpents, whose name these Indians gave to this their God, are in the Province of Xicalanco [in Campeche, a part of ancient Bountiful-land], which is at the entrance of the kingdom of Yucatán, as one goes from that (Province) of Tabasco [toward Yucatán.] . . . This Quetzalcoatl, according to true histories, was the Great Priest of the City of Tula [Bountiful]. . . . They say of him that he was a *white man*, large of body, wide forehead, large eyes,

---

[11]Bartolome de las Cases, *Apologetica Historica de las Indias* (written about 1550, 1909 edition), Capitulo CXXXII, pp. 327-328.

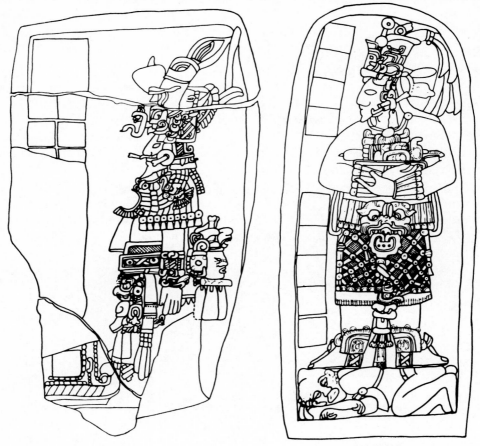

Fig. 9: STELA 27, YAXCHILAN, MEXICO

Fig. 10: STELA 4, NARANJO, GUATEMALA

Representations of Hebraic-like bearded Maya men wearing quetzal feathered headdresses and precious stones, symbols of Quetzalcoatl.

long and black hair, large and round beard. . . . they held him in great esteem, and reverenced him as a King in that City [Tula or Tollan or Tlapallan] . . . in spiritual and ecclesiastical matters this Quetzalcoatl was supreme, and as a Great Priest.

They say that in those times when he ruled over them that corn was very plentiful, and large pumpkins a fathom long, and very thick, and that the ears of corn climbed over them [the pumpkins] as over trees, so large and thick were they that one alone was enough of a load for a person, and all the other seeds were plentiful and tall. They sewed and harvested cotton of all colors—white, red, incarnadine, yellow, and many other and various colors, and in the same City of Tula many and diverse species of birds were raised, such as the Ziuhtototl, Quetzaltototl, Zaquan, Tlauhquechol, and many other fowl that sang sweetly and softly; there were cacao trees of all kinds; and his subjects were very rich, and they lacked nothing; they did not suffer hunger nor any decline; Quetzalcoatl did penance, piercing his legs, and drawing blood with which he stained the points of the maguey plant. . . .

. . . He never wanted nor permitted sacrifices of blood of dead men, nor of animals, but only of bread and roses and flowers and perfumes and other smells. He very efficiently prohibited and forbade wars, robberies, and deaths and other harm they inflicted on each other. They say that whenever they mentioned deaths or wars or other evils in front of him, he would turn his head and stop his ears in order not to see or hear them. Also, in him is praised the fact that he was very chaste and very honest, and very moderate in many other things.

This God was held in such reverence and devotion, and so reverenced with vows and pilgrimages in all these Kingdoms, on account of his prerogatives, that even the very enemies of the City of Cholula would promise to come in pilgrimage to fulfill their covenants and devotions, and they came secure [in safety], and the lords of the other provinces or cities had their chapels, oratories, and their idols and images, and only this one, among all the gods, was called in that city "Lord par excellence"; so that when they took an oath or said, "By our Lord," it was understood they referred to Quetzalcoatl, and not to any other god, although there were many others who were very esteemed gods. All of this was because of the great love they had for him and continued to have for him for the reasons mentioned. Also, it is true that the Lordship of this Quetzalcoatl was gentle, and he asked of them in service but light things as distinguished from painful things, and he taught them those things which were virtuous, prohibiting them those which were evil, noxious and harmful, teaching them also to hate evil things.

For this [i.e., for these reasons] it seems (and it will seem clear below) that the Indians who made and make human sacrifices were not following the will [of Quetzalcoatl]. . . .

. . . and among other doctrines he gave them, was to tell them that the inhabitants of the City of Cholula were to hold as certain that in future times there were to come by sea, from whence the sun rises, some white men, with beards like his, and that they would be lords of these lands and that they were his brothers. Thus, these Indians always expected that prophecy to be fulfilled, and when they saw the Christians, they immediately called them "son Gods" and "brothers of Quetzalcoatl," although after knowing them [the Spaniards] and experiencing their deeds, they did not hold them as heavenly, because the slaughter the Spaniards perpetrated in that City [Cholula][12] was outstanding (no other like it up to that time in the Indies nor, perhaps, in the other parts of the world).

This [Quetzalcoatl] was the God of the Wind, and his temple was round and very sumptuous. . . . the Indians applied the name to Quetzalcoatl, on account of his gentleness and tenderness toward everybody, not wanting the harsh and disagreeable things that others esteemed and prized. So that the God of Wind, who was among these Indians was Quetzalcoatl, . . .

. . . and it was held as true that he made the calendar. He had priests who were called Quetzalcohua, which means "the religious ones and Priests of the Order of Quetzalcoatl." He left a great memory of himself among these peoples, and they say that women who were sterile and barren, by making offerings and sacrifices to this God, would presently become pregnant. He was (as they say) God of the Winds, for they attributed to him the power

---

[12]Bernal Diaz del Castillo, in his work *The True History of the Conquest of Mexico* (1572), says 6,000 natives were put to death at Cholula by the conquerors.

Fig. 11: STONE STATUE OF
"FAIR GOD," OAXACA,
MEXICO

This Zapotec stone statue of Quetzalcoatl is in *Musée de l'Homme,*
Paris, France.

to command the winds to blow or to stop blowing. They also said that this Quetzalcoatl swept the roads so that the Tlaloc gods would come to reign. . . .

They say about this God Quetzalcoatl that while living in this mortal life [he] dressed in long clothes down to his feet, through modesty, with a cloak on top scattered with red crosses. . . . In the city of Tula he had a very sumptuous and large temple, with many *gradins* (steps), and so narrow that a foot could not fit on them. His image had a very ugly face, a long head, and very bearded. They had it lying down and not standing, and covered with cloth; and they say they did it in memory of the fact that he was to return again to reign; and in reverence to his great majesty they must have his figure covered; and having it lying down must have meant his absence, like him who sleeps and lies down to sleep, and that on waking up from that sleep of absence, he will arise to reign.[13]

QUETZALCOATL TRADITIONS BASED ON HISTORICAL FACTS

Certain skeptical writers have maintained that the whole Quetzalcoatl myth was a Spanish invention which they concocted to facilitate the conquest of Mexico and Peru and the victory of Christianity over the American natives. A German scholar, Paul Herrmann, ridicules such a concept. He states:

. . . how clumsy it all was, how small the propaganda value of this story to the cause of Spain! For if a militarily and culturally superior victor is to impose his gods on a subjugated people, he will naturally depict these gods as the quintessence of himself. But this is exactly what the Spaniards did not do—if they invented the story. On the contrary, Quetzalcoatl's appearance was so portrayed that the Aztecs could not fail to notice how little like the blond god the dark Spaniards were. The Aztecs were bound to conclude sooner or later that they could not be the sons of the Light God at all.

If the Spanish conquistadores did not portray the White Savior of the Indians after their own image, however, then he cannot be a Spanish invention and the myth must be Indian in origin. . . .

Carefully considered this leaves no other conclusion open than that the Light God Quetzalcoatl was a real person, that he was neither an invention of Spanish propaganda nor a legendary figment of Indian imagination. . . .[14]

Dr. Daniel G. Brinton, one of America's greatest students of Indian traditions and history, completely agrees with Dr. Herrmann's conclusion. Let us recall Herrmann's statement to the effect that the traditions of Quetzalcoatl are authoritative Indian traditions and history and not stories concocted after the arrival of the Spaniards. Referring to the entire Quetzalcoatl traditions in general and in particular to the fact that this ancient hero-god, according to Indian

---

[13]Juan de Torquemada, *Monarquia Indiana* (Madrid, Spain, 1723), vol. 2, pp. 40-50.
[14]Paul Herrmann, *Conquest by Man* (New York, 1954), pp. 171-172. Italics by author.

tradition, was "one of the white race, a man of fair complexion, with long, flowing beard, with abundant hair, and clothed in ample and loose robes," Dr. Brinton wrote:

> . . . This extraordinary fact naturally suggests the gravest suspicion that these stories were made up after the whites had reached the American shores, and nearly all historians have summarily rejected their authenticity, on this account. *But a most careful scrutiny of their source positively refutes this opinion. There is irrefrangible evidence that these myths, and this ideal of the hero-god, were intimately and widely current in America long before any one of its millions of inhabitants had ever seen a white man.*[15]

Recently Laurette Séjourné wrote an outstanding book entitled *Burning Water—Thought and Religion in Ancient Mexico*. Throughout her entire book she describes the various features of the Mexican religion which were in existence at the time of the conquest of Mexico by Cortes. She maintains that the Mexican religion had its origin

---

[15]Brinton, *op. cit.*, p. 27.

Fig. 12: DECORATED PILLAR OF TEMPLE AT EL TAJIN, MEXICO

Observe the carvings of serpents and quetzal feathers, symbols of Quetzalcoatl. The temple was erected a few centuries following the close of the Book of Mormon period by people who were perhaps descendants of Nephites and Lamanites.

—Photograph by Author

with what she terms the Toltec or Nahuatl culture. The Book of Mormon describes this culture and calls it Nephite. Laurette Séjourné strongly maintains that Quetzalcoatl was an actual historical character and that he was the founder of the Toltec or Nahuatl culture. To quote:

> A figure exists who, since he is inextricably linked with Toltec life, may give us a clue. This is Quetzalcoatl. His historical reality seems to be established without doubt, since his qualities as leader are many times mentioned.[16]

Recently the outstanding archaeologists of the world, whose interest is that of the American Indians, met at Paris in an International Congress of the Americas to exchange ideas on the most recent materials available relative to the history and culture of the Indians. Dr. Herbert Joseph Spinden, who for many years has been rated as one of America's foremost scholars on the Indians, gave one of the papers at this congress. In it he declared that *Quetzalcoatl was* "*. . . the greatest figure in the ancient history of the New World,* with a code of ethics and love for the sciences and the arts."[17]

The day is past when reputable students who deal with the subject of Quetzalcoatl attempt to throw suspicion on his historicity; but, on the other hand, they maintain that he not only existed in ancient America, but beyond a shadow of a doubt he was its greatest figure. In fact, Quetzalcoatl is now accepted as a deity—a god and not man.

---

[16]Laurette Séjourné, *Burning Water—Thought and Religion in Ancient Mexico* (London, 1956), p. 25.
[17]Herbert Joseph Spinden, *New Light on Quetzalcoatl* (Congreso Internacional de Americanistas, Paris, 1947.)

CHAPTER 2

QUETZALCOATL IDENTIFIED

TREMENDOUS INFLUENCE OF THE "WHITE AND BEARDED GOD"

The Catholic padres who faithfully dedicated their lives to missionary work with the American aborigines shortly following the discovery of the New World soon found that the "White and Bearded God"—regardless of what name he may have been called—had left a tremendous influence on the lives of the people of the entire Western Hemisphere. These Christian missionaries from the Old World were surprised, and at times even astounded, to find the American Indians teaching and practicing numerous high moral tenets and at the same time indulging in numerous crude and even barbaric pagan rituals. The more refined and higher moral practices were accredited by the native Americans as having been given to their ancestors by the "Fair God." Dr. Daniel H. Brinton reached the following conclusion regarding these more noble aspirations, religious beliefs, and practices of the aborigines:

> . . . whence comes the manifest and undeniable improvement occasionally witnessed—as, for example, among the Aztecs, the Peruvians, and the Mayas?
>
> The reply is, by the influence of great men, who cultivated within themselves a pure faith, lived it in their lives, preached it successfully to their fellows, and, at their death, still survived in the memory of their nation unforgotten models of noble qualities.
>
> Where, in America, is any record of such men? We are pointed, in answer, to Quetzalcoatl, Viracocha, Itzamna, and their congeners. . . .[1]

Later in his book Dr. Brinton described many of the chief characteristics and teachings of the "savior-gods" of the American Indians. Numerous different Indian tribes had their own traditions regarding the "White and Bearded God," each designating him by its own particular tribal traditional name; however, all of these ancient "Fair Gods" seemed to have taught similar doctrine to their respective peoples, and they themselves had similar moral qualities and standards. Evidence indicates that they were all perhaps the same individual, coming down, however, through Indian traditions under various names. The following pertinent quotation from Dr.

---

[1]Daniel H. Brinton, *The Myths of the New World* (Philadelphia, 1905), pp. 333-334.

Fig. 13: AZTEC STONE STATUE REPRESENTATION OF QUETZALCOATL

Brinton gives a concise description of the importance of the teachings given anciently by the "White and Bearded God" and the pronounced effect they had upon the lives of the American Indians:

> But in his highest divinity, he recognized a Father and a Preserver, a benign Intelligence, who provided for him the comforts of life—man, like himself, yet a god—God of All. "Go and do good," was the parting injunction of his father to Michabo in Algonkin legend; and in their ancient and uncorrupted stories such is ever his object. "The worship of Tamu," the culture hero of the Guaranis, says the traveller D'Orbigny, "is one of reverence, not of fear." They were ideals, summing up in themselves the best traits, the most approved virtues of whole nations, and were adored in a very different spirit from other divinities.

> None of them has more humane and elevated traits than Quetzalcoatl. He was represented of majestic stature and dignified demeanor. In his train came skilled artificers and men of learning. He was chaste and temperate in life, wise in council, generous of gifts, conquering rather by arts of peace than of war; delighting in music, flowers, and brilliant colors, and so averse to human sacrifices that he shut his ears with both hands when they were even mentioned.

> Such was the ideal man and Supreme God of the people who even a Spanish monk of the sixteenth century felt constrained to confess were "a good people, attached to virtue, urbane and simple in social intercourse, shunning lies, skilful in arts, pious toward their gods." Is it likely, is it possible, that with such a model as this before their minds, they received no benefit from it? Was not this a lever, and a mighty one, lifting the race toward civilization and a purer faith?

> Transfer the field of observation to Yucatán, and we find in Itzamna, to New Granada and in Namqueteba, to Peru and in Viracocha, or his reflex Tonapa, the lineaments of Quetzalcoatl—modified, indeed, by difference of blood and temperament, but each combining in himself all the qualities most esteemed by their several nations.

> They are credited with an ethical elevation in their teachings which needs not blush before the loftiest precepts of Old World moralists. According to the earliest and most trustworthy accounts, the doctrines of Tonapa were filled with the loving kindness and the deep sense of duty which characterized the purest Christianity. "Nothing was wanting in them," says a historian, "save the name of God and that of his Son, Jesus Christ."[2]

MANDAN INDIANS AND THE "FAIR GOD"

During the colonial period the Mandan Indians inhabited the whole area of the states North and South Dakota, Wisconsin, and Minneaots. White farmers settled this part of the United States about the middle of the last century, "shortly after the Mandan

---

[2]*Ibid.*, pp. 336-337.

Fig. 14: Tomb of Chacmool, Chichen Itza, Mexico

Observe the heads of the plumed serpent and also the carvings of serpents on the archaeological structure. These are symbolic representations of Quetzalcoatl, the "White and Bearded God."

had been wiped out by a smallpox epidemic."[3] When white trappers and explorers first discovered the Mandans, according to Dr. Paul Herrmann, a German scholar, these Indians held the following tradition regarding the "Fair God":

> Long before the first missionaries reached the Mandan, they are alleged to have known of a gentle, kindly god who was born of a virgin and died a death of expiation; they told of a miracle having close affinities with the feeding of the five thousand; they related the story of the first mother of mankind and her fall, of the ark, and of the dove with the green twig in its beak; they believed in a personal devil who sought to win over and subjugate to himself the world of men.[4]

Montezuma the "Savior-God" of the Pueblo Indians

The Pueblo Indians of Arizona and New Mexico worshiped a god named Montezuma who was similar to Quetzalcoatl. He is not to be confused, however, with the Aztec emperor of Mexico,

[3]Paul Herrmann, *Conquest by Man* (New York, 1954), p. 175.
[4]*Ibid.*, p. 178.

named Montezuma or Moctezuma, but is to be regarded as the
Pueblo Indians' version of the white Messiah or "savior-god." It
was claimed that Montezuma was born of a virgin mother of exquisite beauty and most charitable disposition. P. DeRoo, in Volume
I, page 106, of the *History of America before Columbus,* wrote:

> The many-sided culture-hero of the Pueblos, Montezuma, is the center of
> a group of the most poetic myths found in any ancient American mythology.
> The Pueblos believed in a Supreme Being, a Good Spirit so exalted and
> worthy of reverence that his name was considered too sacred to utter, as, with
> the ancient Hebrews, Jehovah was the unmentionable name. Nevertheless,
> Montezuma was the equal of this Great Spirit, and was often considered with
> the sun. Mr. Bancroft says, "Under restrictions, we may fairly regard him as
> the Melchizedek, the Moses, and the Messiah of the Pueblo desert-wander-
> ers. . . ."

ITZAMNA THE "FAIR GOD" OF THE ITZAS

When the Spanish Catholic priests first arrived in Yucatán, they
found that the Itzá-Mayas worshiped a "Fair God" who, in many
respects, was quite similar to Quetzalcoatl of the Valley of Mexico.
He was known by the name of Itzamna, being a deity held in the
highest veneration.

According to the Itzás' traditions, Itzamna was once a man who
had lived among their ancestors and had performed numerous benevolent deeds. The Maya codices, or sacred books, spoke of him as
a universal deity. Dr. Daniel H. Brinton described him as follows:

> Chief of the beneficent gods was Itzamna. He was the personification of
> the east, the rising sun with all of its manifold mythical associations. His name
> means dew or moisture of the morning. He was said to have come in his
> boat across the eastern waters. One of his titles was Lakin-Chan, the serpent
> of the East. . . .
>
> As light is synonymous with life and knowledge, he was said to have been
> the founder of the culture of the Itzás and Mayas. He was the first priest of
> their religion; invented writing and books. He named all of the localities in
> Yucatán and divided the land among the people.
>
> As a physician he was famous, not only knowing the magic herbs but
> possessed of the power of healing by the laying on of hands whence came his
> name *Kabul, the Skillful Hand,* under which he was worshipped in Chichen
> Itzá. For his wisdom he was spoken of as the royal or noble master of knowl-
> edge. In the Maya language, this is Yax-coc-ah-mut, which means that he was
> the first man of great fame.[5]

_____

[5]Daniel H. Brinton, cited in T. A. Willard, *Kukulcan the Bearded Conqueror* (Hollywood, California, 1941), p. 127.

T. A. Willard informs us that Itzamna was regarded as the light and life of the world, and so his universal symbol represented light and life. Let us quote some important extracts from Willard's discussion of Itzamna:

Father Bernardo de Lizana, one of the most devout priests of his time, stated in his history of Yucatán, written in 1633, that Itzamna was called

Fig. 15: STONE REPRESENTATION OF YOUTHFUL ITZAMNA

Certain writers maintain that this beautiful carving on one of the stelae at Quirigua, Guatemala, depicting a man's head, is a representation of Itzamna, the "Fair God," when he was a young man. This archaeological site had its beginnings near the close of Book of Mormon days.

Kabul, the Skillful Hand, with which he performed miracles, curing the sick by placing his hands on them. "He was a king, a priest, a legislator, a ruler of benevolent character, like Christ," wrote the historian. "He came from the east and founded the Itzá civilization." It was said Itzamna could revive the dead. . . .

Through various writings we are shown that Itzamna was one vital influence in implanting the ancient civilization of Yucatán so firmly that it spread out for hundreds of miles. Herrera, the celebrated Mexican historian, states in his work that "The one who first discovered the letters of the Maya language and who made the computations of the years, months and katuns . . . was Kinich-Ahau who was also called Zamna or Itzamna. . . ."

In *Documentos Ineditos Relaciones de Yucatán,* the reader will find many confirmations of the similarity between this [Itzá-Maya's] religion and that of the Christian doctrine. Itzamna was considered the Son and disciple of the one and only God, Hunab-Ku, upon whose altars were placed only fruit and flowers. Human sacrifice and other pagan practices were unknown to these people.

When the Mexican captain, Kukulcan [or Topiltzin] as the old writers called him, entered the country, he supplanted this Christ-like religion with an idolatrous one, and introduced human sacrifices and other abominations.[6]

The Catholic padre Bernardo de Lizana, referred to by Willard, wrote a book called *History of Yucatán and Spiritual Conquest* which was published in A.D. 1633. In it he gives us much information obtained from the Itzá Indians of Yucatán regarding the great god Itzamna. Among other things, he wrote:

In the city of Itzamal (now called Izamal) there are five very high pyramids, all ruined, on dry stone with their forces and supports which serve to raise the stones high. Today no complete edifices are seen, but the signs and vestiges are apparent. On one of them in the southern part, the ancients had a most celebrated idol which they called Itzamatul (Itzamna), which means he who receives and possesses the grace or dew or substance from the sky. And this idol had no other name because they say that he was a King and great Lord of this land, who was obeyed as the Son of God, and when they asked him what he was called or who he was, he would say nothing but these words, "I am the dew or substance of the sky and clouds."

This great King died and they raised altars to him and he was an oracle and afterwards it will be seen that they built another temple and for what. When this King, who was afterwards deified, lived, the people consulted him about the things that happened in some remote parts and he told them of present and future things. At the same time they carried their dead to him and he brought them back to life, and the sick got well, and for this he was greatly venerated and with reason, for if it were true that he was a Son of God, who only can give life to the dead and health to the sick, since it is impossible for an ordinary man, nor the demons, but only the same God, who is the lord of life and death.

_____

[6]T. A. Willard, *ibid.,* pp. 131-133.

Fig. 16: Stone Statue Representation of Quetzalcoatl

This pre-Columbian stone statue is housed in the museum at Chichicastenango, Guatemala, the headquarters of the Quiché Mayas since the Spanish conquest.

The people believed this, and did not know another god, and for this they said he resurrected and cured them.[7]

Bernardo de Lizana received from the Indians of Yucatán a tradition that Itzamna died and was buried in the City of Itzamal. His body was buried in three separate tombs. The following perti-

---

[7]Bernardo de Lizana, *History of Yucatán and Spiritual Conquest,* cited in Willard, *ibid.,* pp. 151-152.

nent information regarding Itzamna, the "Fair God" of the Itzá-
Mayas, and his father, Hunab-Ku, the supreme God, is quoted from
pages 148-149 of Willard's *Kukulcan the Bearded Conqueror*:

> . . . When his [Itzamna's] human form was divided into three parts, his
> "Skillful Hand" was buried in one pyramid; his head in another, and his body
> in the third. The sacred spots became the oracles or shrines to which people
> came from the directions of the four winds (a Maya expression) to worship
> the great and only god of the country of whom there was no image. [This God
> was the Heavenly Father.] His name, as we have said before, was Hunab-Ku,
> the father of Itzamna.
>
> Thus passed Itzamna, this reputed Son of God—perhaps our Christian God
> under another name, and the Itzás believed that his soul went to dwell with
> his heavenly father.

We can readily see by the foregoing Itzá-Maya traditions of
Itzamna that he can be identified as being the same god as Quetzalcoatl, the Messiah of the Indians of the Valley of Mexico, and also
the same god as Kukulcan, the benevolent deity of the Toltec-Mayas
of Yucatán following the Toltec invasion of that land during the
tenth century A.D. He was merely known among the Itzás by another name; however, he was the "White and Bearded God," known
universally by various names by the many different tribes of aborigines.

THE GOD WAKO

William Montgomery McGovern, an English explorer, recorded
the beliefs of a primitive tribe of Indians on the upper Amazon River
of South America regarding their god Wako. In his book, *Jungle
Paths and Inca Ruins*, pages 276-280, he wrote:

> Wako . . . was a combination of the ideas of tribal hero and high good
> god. . . . He . . . came to be regarded much as Christians regard the Supreme
> Deity.
>
> Wako created the earth, the sun, the moon, and lightning and thunder, . . .
> [and later he] created a woman. . . .
>
> Wako, I discovered, was reverenced above all as the giver of culture. It
> was Wako who taught human beings how to prepare the feather ornaments,
> and who told them how and when they were to dance. . . .
>
> According to my informants, *Wako suddenly appeared as a full-grown
> man among human beings,* first of all at Ipanoré, but subsequently at many
> other places. Wherever he appeared a cataract sprang up. Altogether Wako
> stayed on the earth a whole year. During this time he particularly instructed
> the members of each tribe how they were to prepare *kashiri* and *kaapi*. . . .

Fig. 17: BEAUTIFUL ZAPOTEC BUST

This beautiful figure is housed in Frissell's Museum, Mitla, Oaxaca, Mexico. The quetzal feathers on the headdress symbolize Quetzalcoatl.

. . . He therefore gave long instructions to all the assembled men and beasts as to what they were to do and how they were to behave. *He then ascended into the sky.* As he disappeared, he sent down a pounder, or drumstick, which has ever since been used by the Indians in honor of their lawgiver. . . .

Since Wako disappeared from the world, he has continued to exist somewhere in the high heavens, . . .

SIMILARITIES BETWEEN INDIAN TRADITIONS AND CHRISTIANITY

The Spanish Catholic missionaries who gathered traditions of Quetzalcoatl from the Indians, as well as practically every student who has made a study of the traditions, have commented on the numerous similarities between the Indian traditions and the teachings of Christianity. Miles Poindexter compares the Spanish priests' interpretation of Jehovah with the belief held by the Indians of Peru at the time of the Spanish conquest. To quote:

The Incas' idea of God as the Creator was almost identical with that of the Spanish invaders,—except that Viracocha of the Incas, as their ancestor and the beneficent Creator and preserver of all things, was a nobler conception, in some respects than the Jehovah of the Spanish priests; and the Amautas' conception, both of the age and of the method of creation of the world, was more enlightened than that of the Europeans. *Both conceptions were evidently from the same source. . . .*[8]

Dr. P. De Roo gives considerable evidence to sustain his hypothesis that Christianity was taught in ancient America and thoroughly instilled into the hearts of the American Indians. The Christian missionaries were surprised to find that the natives were familiar with numerous Christian doctrines when they were first contacted by the whites from the Old World. He states that ". . . most ancient and modern authors agree in saying that the Christian religion had been taught to the Indians in pre-Columbian days." To continue the quotation:

Bastian establishes this opinion by the numerous analogies he points out between the religious belief and practices of the Christians and those of American aborigines. Von Humboldt admits the parity to be so striking as to have given the Spanish missionaries a fine opportunity to deceive the natives by making them believe that their own was none other than the Christian religion. . . . Quite a number of ancient writers, such as Garcilasso de la Vega, Solorzano, Acosta, and others are equally explicit in asserting that several Christian tenets and practices were found among our aborigines. . . .[9]

William H. Prescott discussed a number of Christian doctrines and rituals of the Aztec Indians at the time of the Spanish conquest, such as repentance, confession, and baptism, and then he wrote:

. . . We are reminded of Christian morals, in more than one of their prayers, in which they use regular forms. "Wilt thou blot us out, O Lord, forever? Is this punishment intended, not for our reformation, but for our destruction?" Again, "Impart to us, out of thy great mercy, thy gifts, which we are not worthy to receive through our own merits." "Keep peace with all," says another petition; "bear injuries with humility; God, who sees, will avenge you." But the most striking parallel with Scripture is in the remarkable declaration that "he, who looks too curiously on a woman, commits adultery with his eyes."

These pure and elevated maxims, it is true, are mixed up with others of a puerile, and even brutal character, arguing that confusion of the moral perceptions, which is natural in the twilight of civilization. One would not expect, however, to meet, in such a state of society, with doctrines as sublime as any inculcated by the enlightened codes of ancient philosophy.[10]

---

[8]Miles Poindexter, *The Ayar-Incas* (New York, 1930), vol. 1, p. 175.

[9]P. De Roo, *History of America before Columbus* (Philadelphia, 1900), vol. 1, pp. 423-424.

[10]William H. Prescott, *History of the Conquest of Mexico* (Modern Library Ed., New York—First Ed., 1856), p. 41.

Fig. 18:   DECORATIONS OF QUETZAL FEATHERS AND SERPENTS ON THE TEMPLE
OF EAGLES, CHICHEN ITZA

Chichen Itzá is known as the "City of the Serpents," because of the extensive use of the serpent symbol there. Also, quetzal feathers, another symbol of Quetzalcoatl, appear on practically every monument and building in this Toltec-Maya city.

The facts of which Prescott and practically all other writers on ancient American cultures are not aware are that the true Christian religion was taught on the Western Hemisphere approximately 2,000 years ago, that the people regulated their lives by its doctrines and ordinances, and that such "pure and elevated maxims" as those mentioned by Prescott survived from that day. Completely in harmony with these facts, Dr. De Mier, in his discussion of the writings of Father Bernardino de Sahagún, the eminent and scholarly missionary who labored among the Indians of Mexico from 1529 to 1590, concluded:

> Not a single American missionary who has, until this day, left any writing has forgotten to notice the evident vestiges of Christianity, which had in former times penetrated even among the most savage tribes.[11]

As a result of coming in contact with numerous teachings so similar to those of Christianity, some of the early Catholic mission-

---

[11]De Mier, cited in P. De Roo, *op. cit.*, vol. 1, p. 229.

aries maintained that some of Jesus' apostles, perhaps Bartholomew
or Thomas, had brought Christianity to the Indians; however,
although the majority of the early Catholic fathers, such as Garcilasso
de la Vega, Solorzano, Acosta, Las Casas, and others, definitely
recognized the similarity between the Christian tenets and practices
and those found among the American aborigines, "they deny their
introduction by Christian teachers, giving, strange to say, to the
devil the honor of spreading the light of Christianity, in spite of
his hatred for it."[12]

Bancroft described Quetzalcoatl and his work as follows:

. . . Quetzalcoatl was a white, bearded man, venerable, just, and holy,
who taught by precept and example the paths of virtue in all the Nahua
cities, particularly in Cholula. His teachings, according to the traditions,
had much in common with those of Christ in the Old World, and most of
the Spanish writers firmly believed him to be identical with one of the
Christian apostles, probably St. Thomas.[13]

According to Bancroft, it was "during the Olmec period, that
is, the earliest period of Nahua power, [that] the great Quetzalcoatl
appeared."[14] Authorities place the height of the Olmec period
approximately at the time that Jesus Christ lived in Palestine, was
crucified, and resurrected. In the light of the Book of Mormon
account of the appearance of the resurrected Lord to the ancient
Americans, Bancroft's dating of Quetzalcoatl's appearance constitutes a significant fact which will be discussed later. Dr. P. De Roo,
a historian who during the past century made an extensive study
of Indian traditions, came to the following pertinent conclusion
regarding Bancroft's statement:

. . . If the vestiges of Christianity found in Central America date, as is
generally admitted, from Quetzalcoatl, it is evident that this missionary was
a person distinct from the apostle St. Thomas.[15]

Before concluding this brief discussion of "similarities between
Indian traditions and Christianity," let us refer once again to some
of the marvelous material collected by Dr. P. De Roo and the conclusions he reached as a result of his extensive research. In speaking
of the more enlightened nations of American Indians, he wrote:

---

[12]*Idem.*, p. 424.
[13]Hubert Howe Bancroft, *The Native Races* (San Francisco, 1883), vol. 5, p. 201.
[14]*Ibid.*, p. 200.
[15]De Roo, *op. cit.*, p. 424.

. . . but above all their earnestness and their accuracy evinced by their conformity with the general traditions of enlightened mankind and the conclusions of modern science, are proof sufficient that the remote ancestors of these tribes had attained a much higher degree of civilization than that of their fallen posterity, and that they had lived at no great distance from the biblical patriarch, who had preserved incorrupt the memory of man's primordial history and the truths of primeval divine revelation.

That these Indians, and probably several more congenial tribes, were Christians, in the broad sense of the word, at the time of their [the Europeans'] landing on American soil can scarcely be doubted. They knew and worshipped the one eternal spiritual, and unbiquitous God, who "caused" or created the heavens and the earth and all they contain; they knew of the happiness of our first parents eating the "fat fruit" of Eden, and of the "bad spirit" who brought them to sin, misfortune, and death; and, as they were acquainted with the circumstances of the dire tragedy, we may readily infer that they were not altogether ignorant of its most important particular: the promise of a Redeemer, which constitutes the deepest foundation of Christianity. . . .

[And later De Roo stated that] . . . it is almost certain that the Christian religion was preached at various times in America before Columbus' discovery; and while Christianity accepts all the fundamental tenets of Jewish dogmas and morals, and highly respects the typical liturgy of the Old Testament, there is no reason to disbelieve that the apparently Judaic vestiges may be explained by the fact of early Christian missions. The alleged similarities actually bear the imprint of Christian teaching to such an extent as to make the judicious Waldeck assert that, "If the Toltecs were Jews, they must have visited the Old World to obtain the Christian dogma apparent in their cult."

The vestiges of former Christianity in America, . . . have led the enthusiastic Lord Kingsborough, Brasseur de Bourbourg, and several more to believe that the American redskins are descendants of Israel, . . . Giordan, Meyer, Crawford, Juarros, Em. de Moraez, Ethan, Smith, Beatty, besides the Mormons, are of that same opinion. . . .

. . . Von Humboldt [maintained] . . . that Christian teachers had brought to the American races the light of civilization long before the Spanish and other conquistadores spread over them the gloomy shadows of servitude and extinction, and that whatever we find of social order and material progress among our most advanced Indian nations was probably the scanty remainder of a once flourishing Christian society. . . .

The history of Quetzalcoatl's missionary career offers many analogies with that of our Lord, who went about doing good, whom at one time the Jews wanted to make king, whom they denied and persecuted, and whom they worshipped after his death.[16]

QUETZALCOATL IDENTICAL WITH JESUS CHRIST

The identity of this "Fair God," described as a radiant, white, beautiful being, dressed in a long, white robe, has been a puzzle

---

[16]*Ibid.*, pp. 111-112, 196-197, 449, 558.

 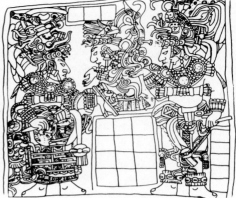

—Art work by Huberta Berg Robison

Fig. 19:   LINTEL 3, YAXCHILAN, MEXICO
Fig. 20:   LINTEL 14, YAXCHILAN, MEXICO

These beautiful lintels show the elaborate quetzal feather headdresses worn by the priests of Quetzalcoatl at Yaxchilan and also the extensive use which was made of jade and other precious stones by the Mayas within 200 years after the close of the Book of Mormon, and so these symbols of Quetzalcoatl were widely used throughout Meso-America not many years after the destruction of the Nephite race.

to the Catholic padres, to historians, archaeologists, anthropologists, and others who have studied these Indian traditions.[17] Numerous efforts have been made to identify him with certain historical characters, such as one of Jesus' apostles—perhaps Thomas or Bartholomew—or with the Savior himself.[18] Others have thought that Quetzalcoatl may have been a European Christian who had visited America perhaps a few hundred years before the arrival of Columbus.[19]

Dr. De Roo made this significant statement: ". . . Quetzalcoatl is often confounded with his Divine Master, whose doctrine and precepts he published and observed."[20]

A very vital question is, Who was Quetzalcoatl, the "White Bearded God" of Mexico, and the "Fair God" as he appears under a variety of names in Indian traditions?

---

[17]Daniel G. Brinton, *American Hero-Myths* (Philadelphia, 1882), p. 27; Bancroft, *op. cit.*, vol. 5, pp. 23-24; William H. Prescott, *Mexico and the Life of the Conqueror Fernando Cortes* (New York, 1898), vol. 1, p. 64, vol. 2, pp. 388-389.
[18]De Roo, *op. cit.*, p. 424.
[19]Thor Heyerdahl, *American Indians in the Pacific* (New York, 1952), pp. 219-345; Herrmann, *op. cit.*, pp. 170-172.
[20]De Roo, *op. cit.*, p. 427.

Laurette Séjourné comes so near giving the correct solution to the foregoing question that one may feel that she had almost discovered the long-sought answer for which scholars of American antiquity have so earnestly searched. In spite of their honest efforts to obtain that information, most of them do not know the true identity of Quetzalcoatl.

In 1830, which is much more than a hundred years ago, Jesus Christ gave to the inhabitants of the earth the answer to the question regarding the identity of the "White and Bearded God" of ancient America. However, a vast majority of the people of the world are still uninformed in regards to this problem, and so the purpose of this book is to present an abundance of evidence, and give sufficient explanations, so that those who desire may know who the "Fair God" of ancient America was.

Perhaps we can increase our understanding of this problem by quoting a marvelous statement from Laurette Séjourné:

> His [Quetzalcoatl's] essential role as founder of Nahuatl culture was never questioned by any of the historians of the sixteenth and seventeenth centuries, who always state that, just as our era began with Christ, so that of the Aztecs and their predecessors began—approximately at the same time—with Quetzalcoatl. His image, the plumed serpent, had for pre-Columbian peoples the same evocative force as has the Crucifix for Christianity. Later, in Tenochtitlán, he continued to be the object of the deepest veneration. Besides being invoked as the creator of man and his work, he was patron of two institutions which were the foundations of all Aztec social and religious life: the priesthood and the college of princes. Until the fall of the Empire the great pontiffs of the metropolis continued to call themselves "successors to Quetzalcoatl."
>
> Who, then, was this primordial figure, and why was his memory so ardently worshipped? As we know that during his reign . . . the social and religious views that dominated Meso-America for over fifteen hundred years were crystallized, we must think of him first as an organizer without equal.
>
> But whence did this statesman derive the power which enabled him to amalgamate and transfigure the cultural elements he had inherited from archaic times into so dynamically homogeneous a system? He must evidently have been possessed of some quite exceptional interior strength, and all that is known about him corroborates this view.[21]

It is marvelous how the Mexican archaeologist, Laurette Séjourné, *definitely designates Quetzalcoatl "as the founder of Nahuatl culture" and places that event at about the time Christ began the Christian era in the Old World;* and then she asked questions in the

---

[21]Laurette Séjourné, *Burning Water—Thought and Religion in Ancient Mexico* (London, 1956), pp. 25-26. (Italics supplied by the writer.)

last two paragraphs which certainly hint the correct answer, getting so near to it but even then not comprehending who Quetzalcoatl was.

Certainly the only person who has ever lived in this world who could have "crystallized the social and religious views which dominated Meso-America for over fifteen hundred years," that primordial figure who lived and did his unique work in the New World about the time that Christ began the Christian era in the Old World, that great statesman who possessed such power "to amalgamate and transfigure the cultural elements into so dynamically homogeneous a system" in ancient America, that religious genius who is supreme over all other religious teachers known, even so powerful that he could influence the cultures of all the native peoples of the Western Hemisphere so profoundly that "his memory was so ardently worshipped . . . for over fifteen hundred years," could have been none

Fig. 21: COFFIN LID, ROYAL TOMB, PALENQUE

The carvings on this lid from the royal tomb, Palenque, discovered by Dr. Alberto Ruz Lhullier in 1953, is considered one of the finest pieces of art yet discovered in ancient America. It dates approximately 200 years following the close of Book of Mormon history. Observe the quetzal feathers and other symbols of Quetzalcoatl.

other than Jesus the Christ, the Lord and God of this earth, and the Savior of the human family. Thus Jesus Christ and Quetzalcoatl are identical.

PRESIDENT TAYLOR IDENTIFIED QUETZALCOATL WITH CHRIST

The foregoing conclusion sustains the clear-cut and forceful statement given in 1882 by President John Taylor, the prophet, seer, and revelator of the Church of Jesus Christ. In that statement he answered the question regarding Quetzalcoatl's identity, giving the viewpoint of the Latter-day Saints which they have held throughout the history of the Church. In the words of President Taylor:

Modern revelation has restored another most important key to unlock the mystery of the almost universal knowledge of the Redeemer and of the plan of the atonement. It is found in the statement that Jesus, after his resurrection, visited at least the inhabitants of two distinct portions of the earth, which could not have been reached through the ministry of his Jewish Apostles. These two peoples were the Nephites on this land, and the Ten Tribes in their distant northern home. The knowledge that the Mexicans, and other aboriginal races of America had, at the time of their discovery by the Spaniards, of the life of the Savior, was so exact, that the Catholics suggested two theories (both incorrect, however) to solve the mystery. One was that the devil had invented an imitation gospel to delude the Indians; the other, that the Apostle Thomas had visited America and taught its people the plan of salvation.

The story of the life of the Mexican divinity, Quetzalcoatl, closely resembles that of the Savior; so closely, indeed, that *we can come to no other conclusion than that Quetzalcoatl and Christ are the same being.* But the history of the former has been handed down to us through an impure Lamanitish source, which has sadly disfigured and perverted the original incidents and teachings of the Savior's life and ministry. . . .

. . . in the traditions with regard to this especial God, we have an almost complete life of the Savior, from the announcement of his birth to his virgin mother, by an angel, to his resurrection from the grave. . . . The Book of Mormon alone explains the mystery. The account there given of Christ's ministrations amongst the forefathers of these peoples makes the whole thing plain. We understand, through that record, how and by what means they obtained this great knowledge, and can also readily perceive how the unworthy descendants of those whom the Savior visited, gradually add much childish rubbish to the original facts; making their story, like almost all other mythology, an unseemly compound of heavenly truth and puerile fable. But, in view of these facts, when all things are considered, it is almost a wonder that so much of the truth was retained to the days when America became known to Europeans.[22]

---

[22]John Taylor, *Mediation and Atonement* (Salt Lake City, 1882), pp. 201-203.

CONCLUSION

The abundance of historical evidence available thoroughly demonstrates the fact that the "Fair God" was a real historical person who visited the inhabitants of ancient America. This evidence is so completely in harmony with the beautiful story told in the Book of Mormon of Christ's appearance to the inhabitants of this land following his resurrection that, it seems to the writer, it leaves no room for doubt in the minds of those who thoroughly and without bias study this subject as to the identity of the "White Bearded God."[23] Quetzalcoatl, under a variety of names as presented in the traditions of the Indians of North, Central, and South America, is none other than Jesus Christ, the resurrected Lord, as was maintained by President John Taylor.

The story of the life and works of the Messiah and his revelations to the inhabitants of ancient America are beautifully presented in the records of those people, records which were revealed by an angel to the Prophet Joseph Smith; on the other hand, the accounts of Quetzalcoatl come to us in a distorted and corrupted form in Indian traditions; and yet sufficient truth was retained by the inhabitants of the New World to make it possible to identify the two persons as the same individual—Jesus the Christ, the Savior of the world.

----

[23]Note: In connection with this conclusion, study Moroni's promise—Moroni 10:1-5.

CHAPTER 3

RELIGION OF THE TOLTECS AND QUETZALCOATL

TOLTEC CULTURE INHERITED BY AZTECS

When Hernan Cortes and his Spanish *conquistadores* in February 1519 reached the fabulous Aztec city of Tenochtitlan where Mexico City now stands, they found a people who—according to Laurette Séjourné—had placed their roots in "*. . . a civilization which by that time had existed in Mexico for over fifteen hundred years*";[1] i.e., from about the time of the rise of Christianity in the Old World. Although the Aztecs were late comers to the Valley of Mexico— founding Tenochtitlan in 1325 A.D., they readily adopted much of the culture and religion of the people—known as Toltecs or Nahuas —whom they found there. Thereupon they carried forward in a corrupted form this much older and much higher civilization with its religious beliefs and practices. In the words of Laurette Séjourné:

> In tracing Aztec origins, *the chroniclers speak of the ancient Nahuas and attribute to them the foundation, at about the beginning of the Christian era, of the religious system that nourished Pre-Columbian Mexico up to the conquest, that is, for fifteen hundred years. . . .* Archaeological excavations have fully confirmed the accuracy of these texts, having unearthed in the ruins of the Nahuatl capital evidence of the same gods, the same rituals, the same symbolic language as in the last—ill-fated Tenochtitlan.[2]

TOLTECS, NAHUAS, OR NEPHITES

For an introduction to the ancient Toltec, Nahuatl, or Nephite culture perhaps we could do no better than to quote again from Laurette Séjourné's brilliant work on the *Thought and Religion in Ancient Mexico*.

The veneration shown by the proud Aztecs toward these ancestral Nahuas is certainly surprising. We might have supposed that, once lords of the universe, as it seemed to them, they would have taken full possession of the cultural heritage they had adopted, attributing it perhaps to some national hero. Nothing of the kind happened, *because they recognized that their entire system of knowledge came from those who were "the first inhabitants of this*

---

[1]Laurette Séjourné, *Burning Water—Thought and Religion in Ancient America* (London, 1956), p. 1.
[2]*Ibid.*, p. 21.

*land, and the first that came to these parts called the land of Mexico . . . those
who first sowed the human seed in this country.*"[3]

*Here we come face to face with this ancient people, whom all documents
without exception present as creators of the most important of the ancient
cultures. It is said that because of their supreme artistic talents they were
called* Toltecs, *a word which in Nahuatl means master craftsmen.*[4]

According to the Book of Mormon, the only authoritative history of the ancient Americans down to A.D. 421, the first people to
arrive on the Western Hemisphere following the flood were called
Jaredites. They came from the Tower of Babel under the direction
of a prophet named Mahonri Moriancumer. This people established
a mighty civilization in America, which lasted for more than 2,000

[3]*Ibid.,* p. 22. Séjourné quotes Fr. Bernardino de Sahagún, *Historia General de las Cosas
de Nueva España* (Editorial *Nueva España,* S. A. Mexico, 1946), vol. 2, p. 275. (Italics
were supplied by the writer.)

[4]Séjourné, *op. cit.,* pp. 21-22. Note: The *Toltecs* were also known as *Nahuas,* a name
perhaps derived from *Nephites.*

Fig. 22:   BEAUTIFUL PLUMED SERPENT'S HEAD, HIGH PRIEST'S TOMB,
            CHICHEN ITZA

This plumed serpent's head, symbol of Quetzalcoatl, and its mate shown later in the book, stand on top
of the pyramid known as the High Priest's Tomb.

—Photograph by Author

years. They finally destroyed themselves in a terrible war between the dates of B.C. 600 and the birth of our Lord Jesus Christ.

To replace the Jaredites and to raise up a holy people unto himself, the Lord directed a prophet named Lehi to bring another colony of chosen people to the New World. These immigrants left Jerusalem about B.C. 600. Throughout their history they were known as *Nephites* in honor of Lehi's very righteous son, Nephi, one of the greatest prophets who has ever lived. This name, *Nephites*, in the form *Nahuas*, was carried on by the Indians to the time of the coming of the Spaniards. Native historians such as Ixtlilxochitl also called the ancient American *Toltecs*, because of their numerous skills and industry. During the fourth century A.D., this intelligent, and—for many years—godly people, had dropped into extreme wickedness and apostasy from the true religion given them by Jesus Christ. As a result of their wickedness and in fulfilment of predictions made by the Master and his holy prophets, by A.D. 400 the Nephites as a nation were exterminated by the Lamanites. The latter group had been cursed by the Lord with a dark skin; this accounts for the color of the skin of the American Indians who are their descendants.

Fourteen years after the Nephites left Jerusalem, the Lord brought to the New World another group of people which are known in the Book of Mormon as Mulekites. About B.C. 200 the Mulekites merged with the Nephites and thereby lost their identity as a separate people.

It was the Nephite-Mulekite people, spoken of by the Catholic Padre Bernardino de Sahagún and Laurette Séjourné, who, about the beginning of the Christian era, developed *"the religious system that nourished Pre-Columbian Mexico up to the conquest, that is, for fifteen hundred years."* This culture, established by Christ, was handed down in a polluted, paganized, and badly adulterated form even to the coming of the Spaniards. The Nephites (Toltecs or Nahuas) were "the creators of the most important of the ancient cultures." It was their religion and their culture which held the controlling influence over the various Indian groups—both high and low cultures—of North, Central, and South America for hundreds of years. So strong and lasting was this influence that even the bloodthirsty Aztecs submitted to that culture as they inherited it and acknowledged the ancient Toltecs as its source. The Book of

—Photograph by A. R. Hall, Craig, Alaska

Fig. 23: Representation of Haida Indians' "Fair God"

This representation of the "White God" stands on top of an ancient totem pole north of Ketchikan, Alaska. Observe that the deity has an object in his hands which some people think represents a book. Many of the Haida Indians are white. They seem to be related to the Mayas of Yucatán and Guatemala.

Mormon should be conscientiously, thoroughly, and honestly studied by every person who is honestly attempting to learn all he can regarding the culture and history of the American Indians and their origin, since it is the only historical account of the ancient Americans written by eyewitnesses. It is pure source historical material.

CULTURE OF THE TOLTECS AS KNOWN BY SAHAGUN

The very reliable Catholic padre and famous missionary among the Indians, Bernardino de Sahagún (1499-1590), described the Toltec culture as he received information from the Indians of the Valley of Mexico during the first century of the Spanish conquest. Thus his reports would be firsthand and very reliable. To quote from this great Catholic historian:

. . . Whatever they [the Toltecs] turned their hands to was delicate and elegant, all was very good, remarkable and gracious, such as the houses they made very beautiful, highly decorated within, of a certain kind of precious stone very green with lime, and those so adorned had a lime highly polished which was a sight to be seen, and the stones also, fashioned and stuck together, that seemed like a kind of mosaic; with justice were they later called exquisite and noteworthy, because they possessed such beauty of workmanship and labour. . . .

. . . They were the inventors of the art of featherwork . . . and all that was done in ancient times was made with wonderful invention and great skill.

. . . the Toltecs had much experience and knowledge in the qualities and virtues of herbs, and they left docketed and named those now used for treating because they were also physicians and the best in the art . . . they were the first inventors of medicine.

. . . What they achieved in knowledge of precious stones was so great that, though these were buried in a larger one and below ground, by their natural genius and philosophy they would discover where to find them.

. . . So remarkable were these Toltecs that they knew all mechanical skills, and in all of these were unique and exquisite craftsmen, for they were painters, stone workers, carpenters, bricklayers, masons, workers in feather and ceramics, spinners and weavers. . . .

. . . They were so skilled in astronomy . . . that they were the first to take count of and order the days of the year. . . .

They also invented the art of interpreting dreams, and they were so informed and so wise that they knew the stars in the heavens and had given them names and knew their influences and qualities. So also they knew the movements of the heavens by the stars.

. . . These Toltecs were good men and drawn to virtue . . . they were tall, larger in body than those who live now. . . . They also sang well, and while they sang or danced they used drums and timbrels of wood . . . they played, composed and arranged curious songs out of their heads; they were very devout, and great orators. . . .[5]

IXTLILXOCHITL'S APPRAISAL OF THE TOLTECS

Next to the Book of Mormon, the *Works of Ixtlilxochitl*[6] give the most reliable and complete account of the history and culture of the early Toltecs (Nephites) and the Lamanites, the ancestors of the American Indians. Fernando de Alva Ixtlilxochitl wrote the history of the inhabitants of ancient America—the Jaredites who came from the Tower of Babel, the Nephites, Lamanites, and Mulekites, who came from Jerusalem—from written documents received from his ancestors and from oral traditions received from Indians who knew the traditions of their people. His first work was written about A.D. 1600 and his second about 1608.

The reliable historian, Hubert Howe Bancroft, states that "Fernando de Alva Ixtlilxochitl was a grandson of the last king of Texcoco, from whom he inherited all that were saved of the records in the public archives. His works are more extensive than those of any other native writer. . . ."[7] Bancroft also indicates that Ixtlilxochitl ". . . wrote honestly, compiling from authentic documents in his possession."[8] In 1944 Dr. George C. Vaillant, a distinguished archaeologist and authority on early cultures of Mexico, stated that Ixtlilxochitl ". . . was a descendant of the old Texcocan lineage, the ruling house, and had access to many of the ancient records of his people and left a full history."[9]

Ixtlilxochitl, an Indian native of Mexico, where he spent his entire life, ". . . was born about 1568; he was a student at the College of Santa Cruz in Tlateloco [Mexico]; . . . he was an interpreter in the court of justice of the Indians; and he died in 1648 at the age of eighty."[10] The quotations given from this native historian may be regarded as reliable and very valuable.

---

[5]Sahagún, *op. cit.*, vol. 2, pp. 276, 268, 269, 280, 281.

[6]Milton R. Hunter and Thomas Stuart Ferguson had the *Works of Ixtlilxochitl* translated from Spanish into English, and from this document wrote a book in which they compared its contents with the contents of The Book of Mormon. The book is entitled *Ancient America and the Book of Mormon*. It was published in 1950.

[7]Hubert Howe Bancroft, *The Native Races of the Pacific States of North America* (San Francisco, 1876), vol. 5, p. 147.

[8]*Idem.*

[9]George C. Vaillant, *The Aztecs of Mexico* (Baltimore, Maryland, 1944), p. 85.

[10]Alfredo Chavero, preface to *Obras Historias de Don Fernando de Alva Ixtlilxochitl* (1891 edition), vol. 1, p. 6.

Ixtlilxochitl refers to the ancient inhabitants of America as "Toltecs." The first group, who came from the Tower of Babel and who would correspond with the Jaredites of the Book of Mormon, he calls *early Toltecs, Ancient Ones,* or *Giants;* and the peoples who would be comparable to the Nephites and Mulekites, he merely calls *Toltecs.* They are also referred to in many early documents as *Nahuas.*

A number of quotations will be given from Ixtlilxochitl which will describe the appearance, beliefs, modes of living, culture, religious beliefs, and customs of these ancient Americans whom he calls *Ancient Ones, Giants,* and *Toltecs.* The footnotes not only tell where Ixtlilxochitl's quotations may be found, but they will also guide the readers into very closely related materials contained in the Book of Mormon—the most authoritative history in existence dealing with the great races which inhabited ancient America from the time of the building of the Tower of Babel to A.D. 421.

According to Ixtlilxochitl, the early Toltecs or Ancient Ones knew "many things from the creation of the world to its destruction. . . . And they say that the world . . . was destroyed by the deluge; . . . and how men began to multiply from a few that escaped this destruction within a Toptlipetlacalli, which almost means closed ark."[11]

And [the Toltec history tells] how afterwards men, multiplying, made a very tall and strong Zacualli, which means the very high tower, in order to shelter themselves in it when the second world should be destroyed.

When things were at their best, *their languages were changed* and, not understanding each other, they went to different parts of the world; and the Toltecs, who were as many as seven companions and their wives, *who understood their language among themselves,* came to these parts, having first crossed large lands and seas, living in caves and undergoing great hardships, until they came to this land which they found good and fertile for their habitation. . . .

. . . according as it appears in their histories, that the first king they had was called Chichimecatl, who was the one who brought them to this New World where they settled, who, as can be inferred, came from the great Tartary, and *they were of those of the division of Babylon,* as it is declared more at length in the history that is written.[12]

---

[11]*Works of Ixtlilxochitl,* cited in Milton R. Hunter and Thomas Stuart Ferguson, *Ancient America and the Book of Mormon* (Oakland, Calif., 1950), pp. 18, 22; Book of Mormon, "Preface"; Ether 1:1-4.

[12]*Ixtlilxochitl* cited in Hunter and Ferguson, *op. cit.,* pp. 24-25. (See also Ether 1:33-37; 6:12-16, 30; 1:40-43; 2:1-7, for the Book of Mormon account of these events.)

Fig. 24: PLUMED SERPENTS, MERIDA, YUCATAN

The plumed serpents, symbolic of Quetzalcoatl, are housed in the museum at Mérida. They were artistically made by craftsmen of the Toltec-Maya culture.

After living in America for many centuries, these early Toltecs, sometimes referred to as *Ancient Ones or Giants,* ". . . had many wars and dissensions . . . especially in all the land that is now called New Spain. *They were destroyed and exterminated by great calamities and punishments from heaven, for some grave sins that they had committed.*"[13]

Then Ixtlilxochitl discussed the second group of settlers, known in the Book of Mormon as Nephites, whom he definitely designates as Toltecs. To quote:

The Toltecs were the second settlers of this land after the decline of the giants. . . .

Tolteca means artisan and wise man, because the people of this nation were great artisans, as is seen . . . in the ruins of their buildings, in the towns of Teotihuacán, Tula and Cholula.[14]

_____

[13]*Ixtlilxochitl* cited in *ibid.*, p. 49. (See also Ether 13:13-26; 14:1-2, 21-25; 15:2, 13-33 for the Book of Mormon account.)

[14]*Ixtlilxochitl,* cited in *ibid.*, p. 57. (See also Jacob 1:14; Alma 3:11.)

Fig. 25: JADE FIGURINE OF
BEARDED MAN

This remarkable figurine of a Hebraic-
type bearded man was discovered by
Dr. Ruz in the Royal Tomb in Palenque in 1953. Perhaps the jade
figurine is a representation of the high
priest or ruler in whose tomb it was
found. Jade was a sacred stone symbolic of Quetzalcoatl, and so jade
objects were buried with the priests
and rulers, worshipers of the "White
and Bearded God."

Fig. 26: SIDE VIEW OF JADE
FIGURINE

Fig. 27: BACK VIEW OF JADE
FIGURINE

Figures 25, 26, and 27 are three different views of the same jade figurine.

. . . and they [the Toltecs] had knowledge of the creation of the world,
and how it was destroyed by the deluge, and many other things they had in
picture and in history. . . .[15]

[In B.C. 132] . . . all the land of this New World being in peace, all the
Tolteca Wisemen, astrologers, as well as men of other arts, got together in

---

[15]*Ixtlilxochitl,* cited in *ibid.,* p. 89. (See also 1 Nephi 5:10-12; Alma 10:22; 3 Nephi
22:9-10.)

Huehuetlapallan, seat of their kingdom, where they discussed many things, happenings and calamities that they had, and movements of the heavens since the creation of the world, as well as many other things . . . Among other things, they added the leap year in order to make the solar year agree with the equinox, and many other curiosities, as will be seen in their tables and rules for their years, months, weeks, and days, signs and planets, according as they understood them, and many other curiosities.[16]

The Toltecs were great architects and carpenters and were skilled in the mechanical arts, like silversmiths. They took out [mined] gold and silver and smelted it, and carved precious stones; they did the best thing of what there is in the world. . . .

[The Toltecs were] poets, philosophers, and orators, so that they used all the arts, the good as well as the bad. . . .[17]

And they were painters, the best in the land (world); and the women great spinners and weavers, weaving very gallant mantles of a thousand colors and figures—those which they (the men) wanted, and as fine as those of Castile; and they wove the cloth in many different ways, some that looked like velvet, and others like damask and satin; others like thin linen and others like thick linen, just as they (the men) wanted and needed. . . .[18]

These said Toltecs were good men and friends of virtue. They did not tell lies, and their way of speaking and greeting each other was *"Sir"* and *"Sir, brother . . ."* and *"Sir, older brother"* and *"Sir, younger brother."* Their speech, instead of swearing, was *"It is true,"* *"thus it is,"* *"it is ascertained,"* and *"yes"* for yea, and *"no"* for no. . . .[19]

These [Toltec] kings were high of stature, and white, and bearded like the Spaniards, . . .[20]

The foregoing quotations constitute only a small part of the numerous things that the Indian prince, Ixtlilxochitl, said about the Toltecs; however, the author feels that this is sufficient to permit the reader to gain a partial understanding of the high Nephite (Toltec) civilization that existed in ancient America during the early Christian centuries and the Jaredite civilization which existed earlier. For a more thorough understanding of that wonderful period in American history, one needs to turn to the Book of Mormon and read the marvelous story contained therein.

---

[16]*Ixtlilxochitl,* cited in *ibid.,* p. 147; Words of Mormon 16-18; Mosiah 1:1, 10, 18; 2:1-2, 5, 8; 25:1-19.
[17]*Ixtlilxochitl,* cited in *ibid.,* pp. 257, 291; 1 Nephi 18:25; 2 Nephi 5:14-17; Jarom 1:8; Helaman 6:9-11; 3 Nephi 6:4, 8, 11; Mosiah 11:8-11.
[18]*Ixtlilxochitl,* cited in *ibid.,* p. 315; Mosiah 10:5; Alma 1:29; 4:6; 46:11-12; Helaman 6:13; 1 Nephi 4:19; 10:8; 2 Nephi 4:33.
[19]*Ixtlilxochitl,* cited in *ibid.,* p. 323; 3 Nephi 12:33-37.
[20]*Ixtlilxochitl,* cited in *ibid.,* p. 240; 2 Nephi 5:20-21; Jacob 3:5, 8; 3 Nephi 2:14-16; 1 Nephi 13:15.

Fig. 28: Quechua Indian in Peruvian Andes

65

tograph is a reproduction of a painting which was the cover on the "Adventure Issue," *Ideals*, Vol. 15, No. 2, June,
8. The writer appreciates the privilege granted by the publishers of *Ideals* to reprint this beautiful photograph.

66   Fig. 29:   ANCIENT BALL COURT, COPAN, HONDURAS, WITH STELAE-STUDDED
          COURT IN BACKGROUND

Fig. 30:   ALTAR PANEL IN TEMPLE OF THE SUN, TIKAL, GUATEMALA

67

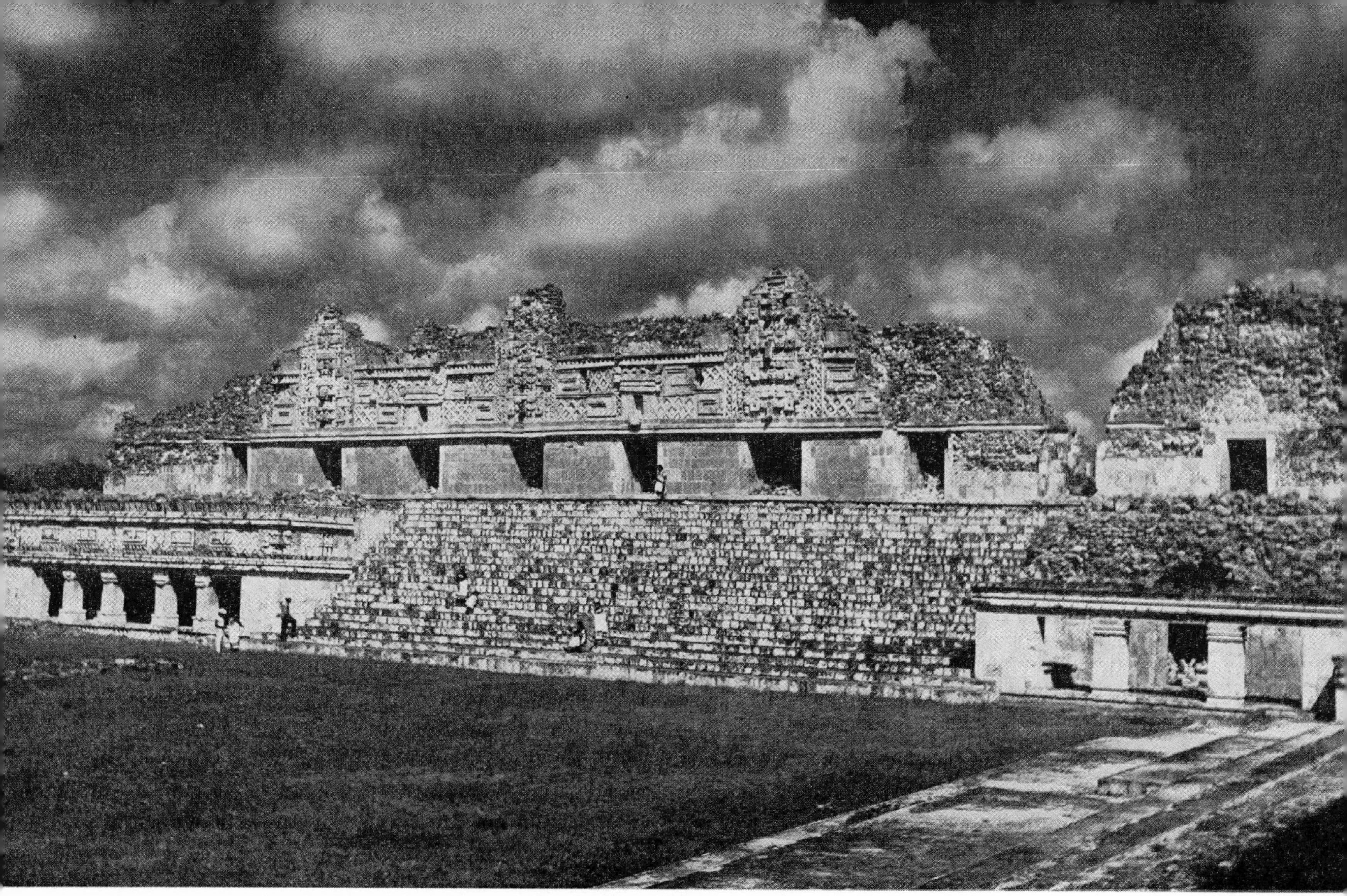

FIG. 31. TEMPLE OF VENUS, UXMAL, YUCATAN, MEXICO

−*Photograph by Otto Dome*

Fig. 32: Temple of Venus (left), Temple of Masks (right), Kabah, Yucatan, Mexico, with Jose Davila and the Writer Approaching the Archaeological Structures

Fig. 33: Maya Arch in Nunnery, Uxmal, Yucatan, and Three Maya Girls in Native Costumes

Fig. 34: Temple of the Masks, Kabah, Yucatan, Mexico

—Photograph by Otto Done

Fig. 25.—Northern Hotel, Yucatán, from Mr. C— N— S—

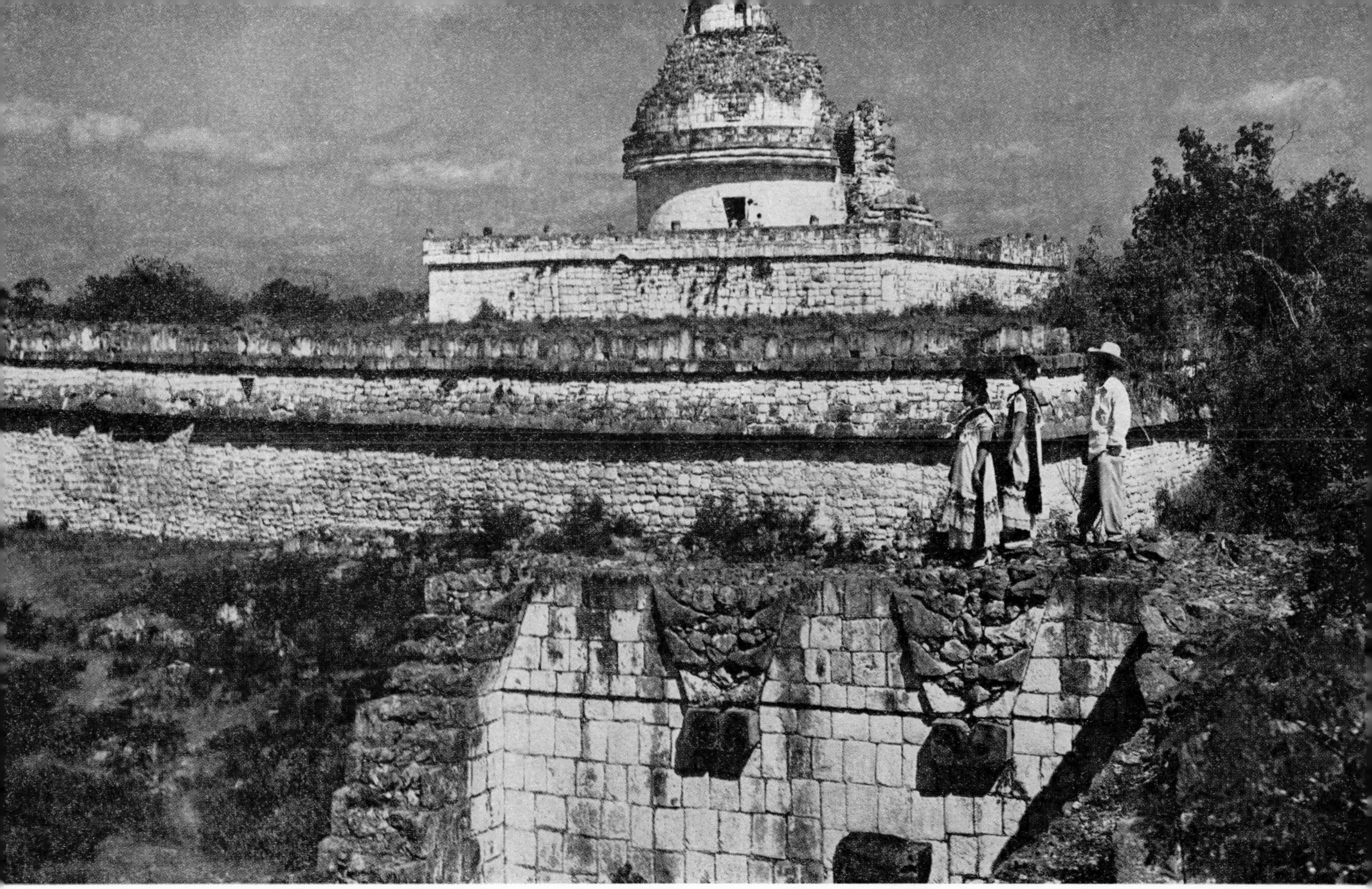

Fig. 36: Observatory, or El Caracol, Chichen Itza, Yucatan

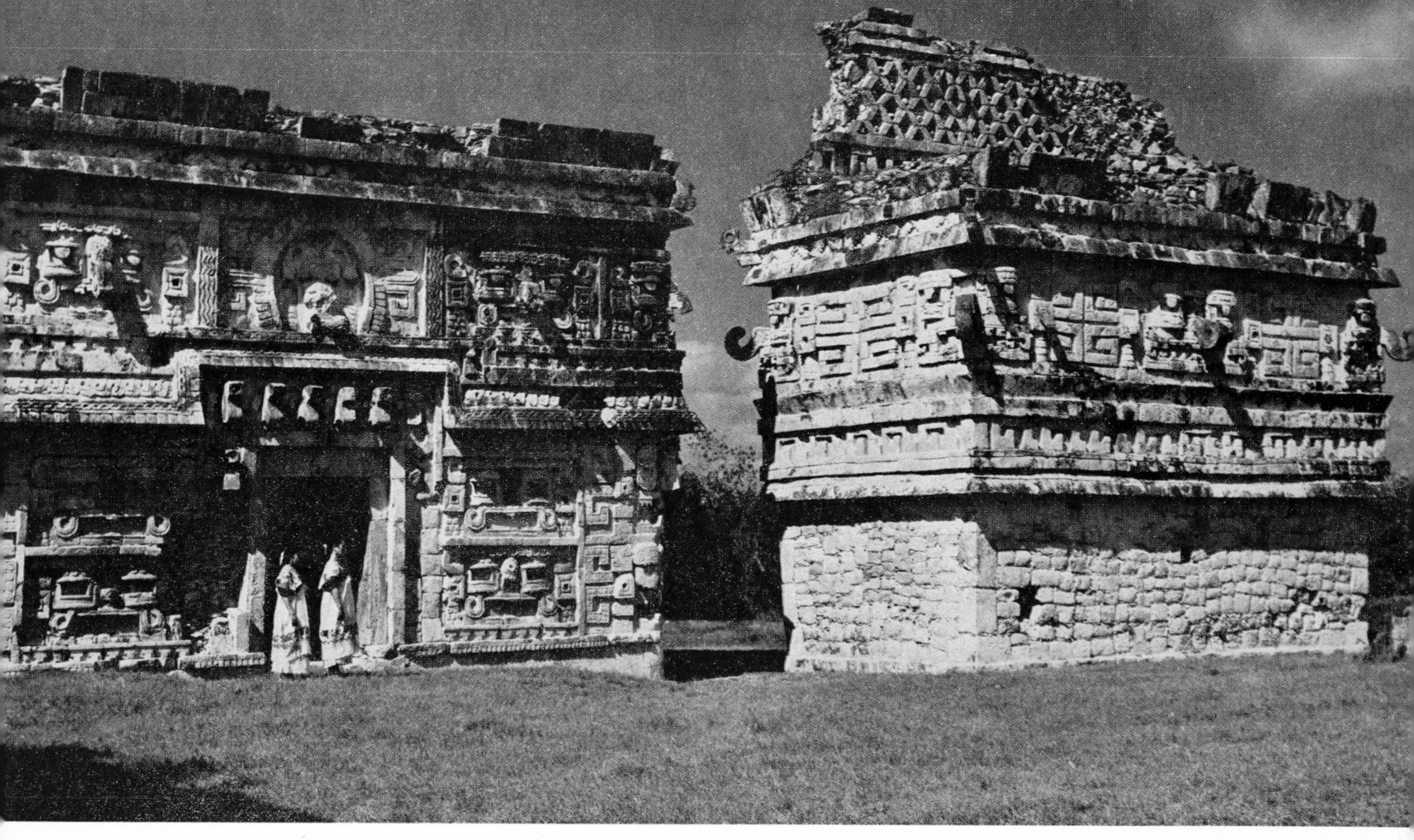

Fig. 37. NUNNERY AND CHURCH (REAR VIEW), CHICHEN ITZÁ

—Photograph by Otto Done

Fig. 38:   Temple of the Masks, Kabah, Yucatan

Fig. 39:   NUNNERY AND TEMPLE OF DWARF, UXMAL, YUCATAN

76   Fig. 40:   GOVERNOR'S PALACE, UXMAL, YUCATAN

This building is considered by many authorities to be the most beautiful archaeological structure in pre-Columbian America.

—Photograph by Otto Don

Fig. 34: TEMPLE OF THE MASKS, KABAH, YUCATAN, MEXICO

—Photograph by Otto Done

Fig. 35. Nayouxx Uxxxx Vxoxxx with Mxxx Cxxx xt Nxxxx Cxxxxx

80

—Photograph by Otto Done

Fig. 41: TEMPLE OF CHICHAN CHOB, OR RED HOUSE, CHICHEN ITZA, YUCATAN

Fig. 42: TEMPLE OF THE TWO LINTELS, OLD CHICHEN ITZA   77

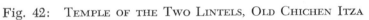

Fig. 43:   TEMPLE OF KUKULCAN, OBSERVATORY OR CARACOL, AND TEMPLE OF
          THE WARRIORS, CHICHEN ITZA

Fig. 44:   TEMPLE OF THE WARRIORS, CHICHEN ITZA, YUCATAN

—Photograph by Otto Done

Fig. 45: Two Young Maya Women Standing by Plumed Serpents Atop
the Temple of the Warriors, Chichen Itza, Yucatan

Fig. 46: Temple of the Warriors and El Castillo or Temple of Kukulcan, Chichen Itzá

The most important section of the *Works of Ixtlilxochitl* deals with the life and works of Quetzalcoatl. This part of his writings will be reserved for use at a later place in the book.

NEPHITE CIVILIZATION SUPERB

The descriptions of the Toltec (Nephite) culture given by Sahagún and Ixtlilxochitl enumerate some of the chief characteristics of the more highly developed Meso-American civilizations as far as the information had come down to them. But even these descriptions only partially tell of the sublimity, grandeur, and godliness of the remarkable Nephite (Toltec) culture and people that existed in ancient America during the early Christian centuries. The Mexican archaeologist Laurette Séjourné agrees with the foregoing statement, although it is very likely that she has never read the Book of Mormon which describes that marvelous ancient civilization. Truly the Nephites during that period established a "golden age" in world's history. Let us quote Laurette Séjourné:

> Yet, extensive as it may seem, the list does not tell of all the skills used in the creation of the great Tollan of legendary splendour. Though what Sahagún tells us is confirmed by archaeological findings, the illustrious historian, who was not privileged to look upon the ruins, is very far from giving us an idea of the prodigious creative power of their builders, which we shall see later for ourselves.[21]

Laurette Séjourné made the foregoing statement as a result of conclusions drawn from archaeological discoveries. Perhaps even she would be astounded if she had a full comprehension of the high culture attained by the ancient Nephites (Toltecs), especially during the first and second centuries following the resurrection of Christ and his appearance to the inhabitants of ancient America. Jesus the Christ, the Lord and God of the entire world, ushered in a period of peace and righteousness under which the people developed a culture—especially in religious activities—which perhaps no people has ever equaled in the history of the world, with the possible exception of the people who lived such godly lives during the days of Enoch that the City of Enoch and its inhabitants were taken to heaven. For nearly 200 years the Nephites maintained their superb culture, which was centered around religion, with Jesus Christ revealing to them divine truths and serving as their Lord and God.

---

[21]Séjourné, *op. cit.*, p. 23.

Finally wickedness crept in, and the Nephite culture declined, following the same road that all cultures eventually follow when the people refuse to accept Jesus as their Savior and Redeemer and openly defy his holy laws and commandments.

Let us have a brief glance at the Nephite culture as it is described in the Book of Mormon when it was at its height:

And it came to pass in the thirty and sixth year, the people were all converted unto the Lord, upon all the face of the land, both Nephites and Lamanites, and there were no contentions and disputations among them, and every man did deal justly one with another.

And they had all things common among them; therefore there were not rich and poor, bond and free, but they were all made free, and partakers of the heavenly gift.

And there were great and marvelous works wrought by the disciples of Jesus, insomuch that they did heal the sick, and raise the dead, and cause the lame to walk, and the blind to receive their sight, and the deaf to hear; and all manner of miracles did they work among the children of men; and in nothing did they work miracles save it were in the name of Jesus. . . .

And the Lord did prosper them exceedingly in the land; yea, insomuch that they did build cities again where there had been cities burned. . . .

And now, behold, it came to pass that the people of Nephi did wax strong, and did multiply exceedingly fast, and became an exceedingly fair and delightsome people. And they were married, and given in marriage, and were blessed according to the multitude of the promises which the Lord had made unto them.

. . . they did walk after the commandments which they had received from their Lord and their God, continuing in fasting and prayer, and in meeting together oft both to pray and to hear the word of the Lord. . . .

And it came to pass that there was no contention in the land, because of the love of God which did dwell in the hearts of the people.

And there were no envyings, nor strifes, nor tumults, nor whoredoms, nor lyings, nor murders, nor any manner of lasciviousness; and surely there could not be a happier people among all the people who had been created by the hand of God.

There were no robbers, nor murderers, neither were there Lamanites, nor any manner of -ites; but they were in one, the children of Christ, and heirs of the kingdom of God.[22]

MOTHER CULTURE—NEPHITE

We could conclude, therefore, with many of the outstanding archaeologists of the world—especially Mexican archaeologists—that

---

[22]4 Nephi 2-17.

the descriptions of the culture of the Toltecs given by Sahagún and Ixtlilxochitl deal primarily with the chief characteristics of the more highly developed Meso-American Indian civilizations that arose following the close of Book of Mormon history. These explanations, however, as has been pointed out, only partially describe the exceedingly high culture and superb religious pattern that existed among the Nephites following the resurrection of the Savior until approximately A.D. 200, and then disintegration began its ugly work.

It is a fact of marked significance of which every student of this subject should take cognizance, that many outstanding archaeologists and anthropologists, especially those of Mexico, maintain that the unusually great Toltec culture—meaning that which followed A.D. 400—as well as all the other marvelous Indian cultures of Meso-America and the Andean region, *were the outgrowth of an even greater civilization,* by some writers termed the "Mother Culture." After spending many years of research, Dr. Alfonso Caso, one of Mexico's most prominent archaeologists, made the claim that the accumulated evidence indicates that the *high Indian cultures found their origins in a much greater civilization—* " *. . . a most ancient culture, which is found at the bottom of the specialized cultures of central Mexico and northern Central America. . . ."*[23] As time passes more and more of the archaeologists are discovering the foregoing to be a fact. These discoveries and conclusions marvelously sustain the claims made by the Book of Mormon, a record written anciently by holy prophets and given to an American Prophet, Joseph Smith, by an angel sent directly from the presence of God.

There are many archaeologists, however, who still hold to the old erroneous theory that the high American Indian cultures gradually developed from primitive savagery. On this subject, Thor Heyerdahl points out that ". . . until very recent decades it has been the opinion of most followers of the contemporary school of anthropology that man, in all his local varieties, came to America as a savage barbarian, . . . Many have even inclined to the belief that, from an archaic culture based on primitive hunting and collecting, high-culture with all its diversified aspects developed out of savage mentality and activities, each tribe and nation beginning from the

---

[23]Alfonso Caso, cited in Sylvanus G. Morley, *The Ancient Maya* (Palo Alto, Calif., 1947), p. 42.

Fig. 47:   BALL COURT WALL AT CHICHEN ITZA

Wall elaborately decorated with plumed serpents and men wearing headdresses of quetzal feathers, symbols of Quetzalcoatl.

bottom, independent of other American cultures, and developing analogous features merely through the parallel inclinations of human nature."[24] He continues by pointing out that this theory is rapidly losing supporters, since it fails ". . . to find verification or support in archaeological material and excavations."[25]

As early as 1900, after discussing many of the more civilized tribes of the American Indians, Dr. P. De Roo stated:

> . . . the general traditions of enlightened mankind and the conclusions of modern science, are proof sufficient that the remote ancestors of these tribes had attained a much higher degree of civilization than that of their fallen posterity, and that they had lived at no great distance from the biblical patriarchs, who had preserved incorrupt the memory of man's primordial history and the truths of primeval divine revelation. . . .[26]

Dr. De Roo made the foregoing statement without knowing

---

[24]Thor Heyerdahl, *American Indians in the Pacific* (Stockholm, Sweden, 1952), p. 285.
[25]*Ibid.*, p. 128.
[26]P. De Roo, *History of America before Columbus* (Philadelphia, 1900), p. 111.

that Jehovah had given numerous revelations to both the Jaredites and the Nephites, revealing to the ancient Americans the entire gospel plan of salvation. In fact, it was under the direction of the Lord and divine revelation that the Jaredites came from the Tower of Babel to colonize the New World. Numerous very important revelations were received by the Jaredites' prophet-leader, Mahonri Moriancumer; for example, he stood in the presence of the Lord, even Jesus Christ, and saw him with his own eyes as one man sees another. The description of this glorious vision is found in the Book of Mormon:

> . . . behold, the Lord showed himself unto him, and said: Because thou knowest these things ye are redeemed from the fall; therefore ye are brought back into my presence; therefore I show myself unto you.
>
> Behold, I am he who was prepared from the foundation of the world to redeem my people. Behold, I am Jesus Christ. . . . In me shall all mankind have light, and that eternally, even they who shall believe on my name; and they shall become my sons and my daughters. . . .
>
> Behold, this body, which ye now behold, is the body of my spirit; and man have I created after the body of my spirit; and even as I appear unto thee to be in the spirit will I appear unto my people in the flesh.[27]

The Book of Mormon tells many instances wherein the ancient American prophets were as close to the Lord as were the biblical patriarchs and received as many—or more—divine manifestations and revelations as did the holy men of God on the Eastern Hemisphere. Certainly it could be said of them that they also ". . . preserved incorrupt the memory of man's primordial history and the truths of primeval divine revelation."

The following quotation from S. Linne, whose statement was made in 1939, is in perfect agreement with the opinions of many archaeologists today, especially those of Mexico:

> In the Valley of Mexico, the archaeologists have penetrated as far down as to the times of the primitive agriculturists, the so-called archaic culture. Here, already, we are confronted with the peculiar phenomenon characteristic of America, that the cultures appear suddenly, quite readily formed and without strong relations between each other. Subsequently they develop further, within the limits of a narrow margin, then disappear to be succeeded by others. A new stock with other artistic intentions but in many ways with corresponding modes of living, weapons, and tools, have taken possession of the land.[28]

[27]Ether 3:13-14, 16.
[28]S. Linne, cited in Heyerdahl, *op. cit.*, p. 285.

Naturally the correct answer is that America was colonized at various times with highly civilized peoples from other parts of the world. It is not known exactly how many migrations with high cultures migrated to the New World in ancient times; however, the Book of Mormon gives a detailed history of three definite and distinct migrations—the Jaredites who came from the Tower of Babel, the Nephites who came from Jerusalem A.D. 600, and the Mulekites who also came from Jerusalem A.D. 586. Each group of people

—Photograph by Author

Fig. 48: BONAMPAK MURAL

Observe the plumed headdresses, jaguar skins, and precious stones worn by the men depicted in the mural. Bonampak is dated approximately A.D. 600, less than 200 years after the close of the Book of Mormon.

brought the culture of its country to the Western Hemisphere; and so the beginnings of human life in the New World were represented by cultures fully developed and not by savage, primitive, nomadic hunters.

Dr. A. L. Kroeber, one of the world's outstanding anthropologists and for many years head of the department of anthropology at the University of California, points out that the cultures of Meso-

America and Peru were basically very similar; and then he positively declared that "in each case the culture meets us full blown."[29] Dr. Kroeber then called attention to the Indians' traditions of a white and bearded race of culture institutors and concluded that those people may have been responsible for the fact that the "other Culture" appeared originally in "full bloom" in the various countries of the New World preceding the rise of the numerous inferior Indian cultures.

Thor Heyerdahl of *Kon-Tiki* fame agrees with Dr. Kroeber in giving credit to a white race for establishing the high American culture anciently which served as the "Mother Culture" of all later Indian achievements. To quote Thor Heyerdahl:

> The specified traditions of light-skinned and bearded founders of culture were most prominent and complete among the Aztec, Maya, Chiocha, and Inca nations, that is, among the natives with the highest cultural standing in the New World, and we have also ample evidence to verify that these historic nations really did owe their cultural standing to other people with even more impressive high-cultures who had been active in just these same localities in earlier times. These original culture-bearers are known to us only through their archaeological remains, chiefly consisting of deserted ecclesiastical sites. It is noteworthy that all the known culture peoples concerned disclaim the honour of having constructed these monuments, or of having originated their own cultural standards, and give all the credit to foreign intruders remembered as having lighter skins than themselves, long beards, marked ecclesiastic interests and benevolent characters.[30]

If Thor Heyerdahl had just completed reading the Book of Mormon, he could not have given a more accurate statement of the ancient Nephites—with their high culture, holy prophets who received revelations from God and some occasional personal visitations from the Master, with their true gospel of Jesus Christ, and strong ecclesiastical interests.

Miguel Covarrubias, a Mexican writer and archaeologist, pinpoints the ancient "Mother Culture" as to the time of its sudden appearance more definitely than do most authors. To quote Covarrubias:

> . . . The tantalizing presence of a great and remote past in what is now uninhabited, impenetrable jungle is all the more puzzling because *most archaeologists now agree that many of these artistic masterpieces date back*

---

[29]A. L. Kroeber, *Cultural Relations between North and South America*, Proc. 23rd Int. Congr. Americanists, New York (New York, 1930).

[30]Heyerdahl, *op. cit.*, p. 285.

to the beginning of the Christian era. Appearing suddenly out of nowhere in a state of full development, they constitute a culture that seems to have been the root, the mother culture, from which the later and better-known (Maya, Totonac, Zapotec, etc.) cultures sprang.[31]

Let us recall the fact that another outstanding Mexican archaeologist, Laurette Séjourné, in her recent book—*Burning Water— Thought and Religion in Ancient Mexico*—is as definite as Covarrubias in placing a time for the establishment of the "Mother Culture" in ancient America. She states that ". . . *the chroniclers speak of the ancient Nahuas [Nephites] and attribute to them the foundation, at about the beginning of the Christian era, of the religious system that nourished Pre-Columbian Mexico up to the conquest, that is, for fifteen hundred years.*"[32]

Helen Augur, in her book *Zapotec*, discusses somewhat in detail this ancient "Mother Culture" of Meso-America. After having introduced the subject, she stated: "Meanwhile, simply for convenience, we shall call the unknown mother culture of middle America 'Complex X.' This term covers a whole set of important elements such as ceremonial cities with their stepped pyramids, a mastery of astronomy, and a written language; . . ."[33] This author made a number of other pertinent statements with which we should become acquainted. To quote:

> Middle America, in the centuries before the Christian era, is a complex of small puzzles and great mysteries. The men of early Monte Albán already had wide horizons. They were in touch with other cities in Oaxaca, with the pre-Maya in Guatemala, with nations living along the Gulf of Mexico, and with the peoples of the central plateau. We see great ceremonial cities rise over an expanding area, cities wondrous in their stepped pyramids, their carved jade and stelaes, their colossal stone heads, and even more amazing in the mental powers they reveal. There are three remarkable things about these cities: they all belong to the same unique, highly evolved culture; this culture is quite unlike that of other regions in the Americas; and it appears fully formed, without prelude. No transitional epics lie under the stones of Uaxactún or Monte Albán or La Venta; these magic cities might as well have dropped from the sky. As Dr. Caso remarked when we were discussing this enigma, "The Middle American culture is incredible, inexplicable—but there it is. We must accept it without being able, at the moment, to understand it."[34]

It is of marked significance that Helen Augur places the date for

---

[31]Miguel Covarrubias, *Mexico South—the Isthmus of Tehuantepec* (Mexico, 1946), p. 80.
    [32]Séjourné, *op. cit.*, p. 21.
    [33]Helen Augur, *Zapotec* (Garden City, N. Y., 1954), p. 146.
    [34]*Ibid.*, pp. 143-144.

the high culture having been established at Monte Albán at approximately B.C. 600. In giving the date 600 B.C., or earlier, she is in complete agreement with Dr. Herbert J. Spinden, one of America's greatest Maya archaeologists and scholars. Dr. Spinden, in discussing the Maya calendar, stated:

Now Mayan history does not reach back to the zero date which must be regarded as a theoretical beginning of Mundane Era. The earliest object with contemporary date is Tuxtla Statuette with May 16, 98 B.C. It appears, however, that the real historic beginning of the day count was 7.0.0.0.0., 10

—Photograph by Author

Fig. 49: REPLICA OF TIKAL CALENDAR STONE

The original calendar stone at Tikal was photographed by the writer in January, 1959. Observe the headdresses of quetzal plumes.

Ahua 18 Zac, August 6, 613 B.C. The Calendar of months was probably inaugurated in 580 B.C. when 0 Pop New Year's day coincided with the winter solstice.[35]

Helen Augur continues by stating:

Six centuries before Christ, before the Persian Wars and the Golden Age of Athens, centuries before the first dated Maya stone, the Indians of Oaxaca had already worked out the calendar which was eventually adopted all over Middle America. They built the earliest observatory so far found in the New World, and the only one of its kind. They were superb engineers, stone carvers, and potters, and they had a *written language.*[36]

She then pointed out that American students of archaeology and anthropology are still in doubt as to what people were responsible for this high "Mother Culture" which preceded all later marvelous Indian cultures. These quotations from Helen Augur and Dr. Spinden are of much interest and importance to members of the Church of Jesus Christ of Latter-day Saints, because they know who established this remarkable "Mother Culture." The date 600 B.C. corresponds almost exactly with the date that Lehi, accompanied by his family, with Ishmael and his family, left Jerusalem to begin their historic journey toward America, the "Promised Land."[37] The date of 613 B.C., given by Dr. Spinden as the date of the beginning of the Mayan calendar, could represent the time of departing of the progenitors of the Mayas to ancient America from the Holy Land. Nephi could have brought the ideal of the calendar with him and instituted a calendar from that date. Since Dr. Spinden maintains that the calendar of months was probably inaugurated in 580 B.C., that date could be the exact time that Nephi inaugurated the calendar for his people after the arrival of Lehi's colony on the Western Hemisphere. Since scholars have observed the close similarities between the Egyptian calendar and that of the Mayas and other peoples of Meso-America, that fact lends even more credence to the belief that Nephi was responsible for the American calendars. It is a well-known fact by those who are acquainted with the Book of Mormon that the Nephites brought much Egyptian culture with them to America, even writing some of their records in the Egyptian language.[38] Thus Nephi or one of his descendants could have used

[35]Herbert J. Spinden, *Ancient Civilizations of Mexico and Central America,* Handbook Series No. 2, American Museum of Natural History (New York, 1922), p. 136.
[36]Augur, *op. cit.,* p. 120.
[37]1 Nephi 17:13.
[38]Mosiah 1:4; 9:32.

the Egyptian calendar as the basis for creating a calendar for the people in the New World by making such alterations as eighteen months of twenty days each and five extra days instead of twelve months of approximately thirty days each as used in the Gregorian calendar. It is also important to note that both the Gregorian calendar, the one we have inherited, and the one used by the peoples of Meso-America made adjustments for the extra fraction of a day each year.

Fig. 50: Religious Ceremony at Chichen Itza

Plumed serpents and quetzal feathers, best-known attributes of Quetzalcoatl, are prominently displayed.

Conclusions

Members of the Church of Jesus Christ of Latter-day Saints and others interested in authoritative history of ancient America know through studying the Book of Mormon that following the flood to A.D. 421, three successive native cultures—Jaredite, Nephite, and Mulekite—flourished in the New World. The culture bearers of these three groups migrated from Asia—the first immigrated from the

Tower of Babel and the other two from Jerusalem—each group bringing to America highly developed cultures as inheritances from their native lands; and so it is not surprising to learn that such outstanding scholars as Dr. A. L. Kroeber, Dr. Alfonso Caso, and others, have found a "Mother Culture" underlying all Indian cultures, and have met in their archaeological and anthropological researches in each case the culture "full blown." If the Book of Mormon is as it claims to be, archaeologists should find a "high culture"—a "Mother Culture"—antedating any of the known Indian civilizations—and such is the case.

Furthermore, anthropologists, archaeologists, and historians, having marveled at the high status and superior qualities of the ancient "Mother Culture," are puzzled as to who its founder may have been. As we have already learned, some of the students of America's ancient civilizations maintain that a real historical character, known as Quetzalcoatl, was the founder of the "Mother Culture."

The Book of Mormon informs us that the "Fair God" was none other than Jesus Christ of New Testament fame and the God known to the Old Testament peoples as Jehovah. He it was who directed the migration of the Jaredites to America and who directed emigration of the Nephites and Mulekites from Jerusalem to the Western Hemisphere. It was he who revealed to all of those ancient peoples through personal visitations and through holy prophets his gospel or religion around which cultures developed. Furthermore, as a climax to the marvelous events of ancient times and as has already been pointed out, this same God following his crucifixion and resurrection in the Holy City, visited the inhabitants of ancient America and ushered in a reign of peace, righteousness, prosperity, and great cultural achievements.

Thus Jesus Christ gave to the ancient Americans—the Nephites-Mulekites (Toltecs or Nahuas)—their religion and culture; and then following the close of the Book of Mormon and the downfall of the Nephite nation, the Only Begotten's name was changed by the Lamanites and the descendants of the Nephites from Jesus Christ to Quetzalcoatl. It was by this name that the ancient "Culture Founder" was known to the Aztecs at the time of the Spanish conquest.

Chapter 4

CHRIST THE GOOD SHEPHERD

Good Shepherd of Ancient Israel

The Lord and God of the Old Testament, usually referred to by the ancient Hebrews as Jehovah and in the Meridian of Time as Jesus Christ, was designated by many of the ancient Hebrew poets and prophets as the "Good Shepherd." One of the most beautiful and perhaps the most widely known and deeply loved of the Psalms is number twenty-three. King David begins this thrilling hymn of worship with the following appealing sentence: "The Lord is my shepherd; I shall not want." Similar expressions of stirring praise and adoration to the "Good Shepherd" are found in some of the other Psalms.[1]

The prophets Isaiah, Zachariah, and Ezekiel symbolized the Lord as the "Great and Good Shepherd" and those who loved him and received his message as the sheep of his fold.[2]

Good Shepherd of the New Testament

When Christ was upon the earth teaching the gospel in the Holy Land, he called himself the Good Shepherd, just as the ancient prophets of Israel had referred to him in the Old Testament times. Perhaps the outstanding discourse given by the Master on this subject was recorded by John. Jesus pointed out clearly that the shepherd and the sheep will enter into the door, but thieves and robbers attempt to climb into the sheepfold by some other method. He described the tender care given the sheep by the shepherd who owned the flock, saying: ". . . he goeth before them, and the sheep follow him: for they know his voice";[3] and a little later in his discourse, Jesus said:

I am the good shepherd: the good shepherd giveth his life for the sheep.
But he that is an hireling, and not the shepherd, whose own the sheep are not, seeth the wolf coming, and leaveth the sheep, and fleeth: and the wolf catcheth them, and scattereth the sheep.

---

[1]Psalms 100:2-5; 95:1, 3, 6-7.
[2]Isaiah 40:10-11; Ezekiel 34:11-13, 1:30.
[3]John 10:4.

The hireling fleeth, because he is an hireling, and careth not for the sheep.[4]

After Jesus had said these things and made other important remarks regarding his position as shepherd and those who accepted him and his teaching as his sheep, many of the people who were listening to his discourse became angry. They were acquainted with the teachings of the Old Testament prophets who had predicted that Christ, their Messiah, would be the Good Shepherd, and so they said: "If thou be the Christ, tell us plainly."

Jesus answered them, I told you, and ye believed not: the works that I do in my Father's name, they bear witness of me.

But ye believe not, because ye are not of my sheep, as I said unto you.

My sheep hear my voice, and I know them, and they follow me:

And I give unto them eternal life; and they shall never perish, neither shall any man pluck them out of my hand.[5]

"OTHER SHEEP I HAVE"

A few months before Jesus' death, he announced to the people in Jerusalem that he anticipated visiting an isolated branch of Israel. To quote:

I am the good shepherd, and know my sheep, and am known of mine.

As the Father knoweth me, even so know I the Father: and I lay down my life for the sheep.

And *other sheep I have, which are not of this fold: them also I must bring, and they shall hear my voice;* and there shall be one fold, and one shepherd.[6]

Those of the Palestinian fold did not understand the parable or the comments made by Christ and so he did not explain in more detail. In the same chapter, John wrote:

This parable spake Jesus unto them: but they understood not what things they were which he spake unto them. . . . And it was at Jerusalem. . . .[7]

If Jesus were literally resurrected from the tomb in the Holy City, as Christianity definitely proclaims, there would appear to be nothing inherently illogical, unsound, or incredible in the Book of Mormon's claim that he appeared thereafter to the inhabitants of the New World. In fact, the statement quoted from the Gospel of John calls for a personal visit by the Christ to a branch of Israel in a place other than Palestine. The Nephite record verifies that statement; otherwise it remains unexplained.

---

[4]*Ibid.*, 10:11-13.
[5]*Ibid.*, 10:24-28; 1 Peter 2:25; 5:4; Hebrews 13:20-21.
[6]*Ibid.*, 10:14-16. (Italics supplied by the writer.)
[7]*Ibid.*, 10:6, 19-23.

Now if the New World were colonized by a branch of the house of Israel—a hook-nosed, bearded, white-skinned group of settlers from the eastern end of the Mediterranean Sea, as the documentary and archaeological sources indicate it was—what would be more probable than that Christ would visit such a people?[8]

8Milton R. Hunter, *Archaeology and the Book of Mormon* (Salt Lake City, 1956), pp. 46-54, 70-80, 182-282.

Fig. 51: CHRIST THE
      GOOD SHEPHERD

—*Painting by Loren Covington,
   Hurrican, Utah*

—*Courtesy of Loren Covington
   —Photograph by author*

It was Israel which anciently had attained to great heights of spiritual insight and ethical monotheism.[9] Was it not Abraham, Isaac, Jacob, Joseph, Moses, and other great prophets of that race with whom the Lord made covenants and declared that he would be their God and they would be his people? Also, since one of the purposes that Jehovah had in mind in leading the Nephites and the Mulekites to the New World was that they would record their religious history in order that it might be brought forth in the latter days to convince the house of Israel that Jesus the Christ is the Messiah and universal Savior, he certainly would visit that people to add to that testimony.[10]

Shortly after B.C. 600 Jesus Christ revealed to Nephi the fact that he would appear to the inhabitants of ancient America in the Meridian of Time. That ancient prophet saw in vision the earthly advent of the Messiah among the Jews, his missionary work, and his final rejection by them. He wrote, "And I, Nephi, saw that he was lifted up upon the cross and slain for the sins of the world."[11] He was also informed that the Messiah would be buried in a tomb, and after three days he would be resurrected and ascend into heaven. Nephi declared:

. . . after Christ shall have risen from the dead he shall show himself unto you, my children, and my beloved brethren; . . .
. . . the Son of righteousness shall appear unto them [the Nephites]; and he shall heal them, and they shall have peace with him, . . .[12]

In describing his vision, Nephi wrote:

And I saw the heavens open, and the lamb of God descending out of heaven; and he came down and showed himself unto them [the Nephites].
And I also saw and bear record that the Holy Ghost fell upon twelve others; and they were ordained of God [Christ], and chosen.
And the angel spake unto me, saying: Behold the twelve disciples of the Lamb, who are chosen to minister unto thy seed.[13]

Thus the ancient Americans from the time of their first prophet-historian, Nephi, were looking forward to the time when the resurrected Savior would appear to the inhabitants of this land and establish his Church and kingdom.

---

[9]William Foxwell Albright, *Archaeology and the Religion of Israel* (1941), pp. 4-5, 33-35, 176.
[10]The Book of Mormon, "Preface"; 1 Nephi 1:17; 6:1-6; 9:2-5; 13:23-42; 2 Nephi 5:30-32; Jacob 1:1-6; Moroni 10:1-6.
[11]1 Nephi 11:33.
[12]2 Nephi 26:1, 9.
[13]1 Nephi 12:6-8; 11:7.

Without doubt the most important, dynamic, and choice portion of the Book of Mormon deals with Christ's visit to his other sheep in ancient America, the delineation of his teaching them the gospel—as he had the Jews in Palestine—and the description of the astounding miracles that he performed in this land. That marvelous story is told in 3 Nephi, chapters 8 to 28 inclusive.

TERRIBLE DESTRUCTION IN ANCIENT AMERICA

While Christ's body was hanging on the cross, a terrific storm occurred on the Western Hemisphere, causing an extensive destruction of human life and also of property. Complete cities were destroyed. Only the more righteous of the people were spared.[14]

While this thick and distressing darkness prevailed, ". . . there was a voice heard among all the inhabitants of this land, crying":

Behold, I am Jesus Christ the Son of God. I created the heavens and the earth, and all things that in them are. I was with the Father from the beginning. I am in the Father, and the Father in me; and in me hath the Father glorified his name.

I came unto my own, and my own received me not. And the scriptures concerning my coming are fulfilled.

And as many as have received me, to them have I given to become the sons of God; and even so will I to as many as shall believe on my name, for behold, by me redemption cometh, and in me is the law of Moses fulfilled.

I am the light and the life of the world. I am Alpha and Omega, the beginning and the end.

And ye shall offer up unto me no more the shedding of blood; yea, your sacrifices and your burnt offerings shall be done away, for I will accept none of your sacrifices and your burnt offerings.

And ye shall offer for a sacrifice unto me a broken heart and a contrite spirit. And whoso cometh unto me with a broken heart and a contrite spirit, him will I baptize with fire and with the Holy Ghost, even as the Lamanites, because of their faith in me at the time of their conversion, were baptized with fire and with the Holy Ghost, and they knew it not.

Behold, I have come unto the world to bring redemption unto the world, to save the world from sin.

Therefore, whoso repenteth and cometh unto me as a little child, him will I receive, for of such is the kingdom of God. Behold, for such I have laid down my life, and have taken it up again; therefore repent, and come unto me ye ends of the earth, and be saved.[15]

---

[14]3 Nephi 8:20-21, 23.
[15]*Ibid.*, 9:1, 15-22.

CHRIST VISITED HIS OTHER SHEEP

After the darkness had dispersed, a great multitude of people gathered around the temple in the City of Bountiful to discuss the terrible things which had occurred during the three days of darkness.

And they were also conversing about this Jesus Christ, of whom the sign had been given concerning his death.

. . . while they were thus conversing one with another, they heard a voice as if it came out of heaven; and they cast their eyes round about, for they understood not the voice which they heard; and it was not a harsh voice, neither was it a loud voice; nevertheless, and notwithstanding it being a small voice it did pierce them that did hear to the center, insomuch that there was no part of their frame that it did not cause to quake; yea, it did pierce them to the very soul, and did cause their hearts to burn.[16]

The voice spoke twice more, and the third time they understood

----

[16]*Ibid.*, 11:2-3.

—Courtesy of Betty Gibbs

Fig. 52:   SCENES IN NORTH TEMPLE OF BALL COURT, CHICHEN ITZA

These scenes furnish outstanding examples of the extensive use of quetzal feathers and plumed serpents in religious ceremonies in Meso-America.

what it said unto them. It was the voice of God the Eternal Father introducing the Savior. He said:

Behold my Beloved Son, in whom I am well pleased, in whom I have glorified my name—hear ye him.

And it came to pass, as they understood they cast their eyes up again towards heaven; and behold, *they saw a Man descending out of heaven; and he was clothed in a white robe;* and he came down and stood in the midst of them; and the eyes of the whole multitude were turned upon him, and they durst not open their mouths, even one to another, and wist not what it meant, for they thought that it was an angel that had appeared unto them.

And it came to pass that he stretched forth his hand and spake unto the people, saying: Behold, *I am Jesus Christ, whom the prophets testified shall come into the world.*

And behold, I am the light and the life of the world; and I have drunk out of that bitter cup which the Father hath given me, and have glorified the Father in taking upon me the sins of the world, in the which I have suffered the will of the Father in all things from the beginning.

. . . when Jesus had spoken these words the whole multitude fell to the earth; for they remembered that it had been prophesied among them that Christ should show himself unto them after his ascension into heaven.

. . . the Lord spake unto them saying:

Arise and come forth unto me, that ye may thrust your hands into my side, and also that ye may feel the prints of the nails in my hands and in my feet, that ye may know that I am the God of Israel, and the God of the whole earth, and have been slain for the sins of the world.[17]

After the people had obeyed Jesus' command,

. . . they did cry out with one accord, saying:

Hosanna! Blessed be the name of the Most High God! And they did fall down at the feet of Jesus, and did worship him.[18]

CHRIST'S CHURCH AND GOSPEL

Then Jesus selected twelve men, bestowed upon them the Melchizedek Priesthood, and ordained them to the office of apostles, as he had done with twelve other men prior to his crucifixion in Palestine. Thereafter he spent many days teaching the people the gospel. Numerous mighty miracles were performed, because of the faith and righteousness of the people. Christ established his Church, appointed the twelve disciples as apostles to preside over it, and then ascended into heaven. Soon thereafter the twelve whom he had selected fasted and prayed, and in response to their humble

[17]*Ibid.*, 11:7-14.
[18]*Ibid.*, 11:16-17.

supplications Christ appeared unto them. He asked them what they desired. They answered that they desired to know what name to call the Church which he had established before his ascension into heaven.

And the Lord said unto them: Verily, verily, I say unto you, . . . Have they not read the scriptures, which say ye must take upon you the name of Christ, which is my name? For by this name shall ye be called at the last day;

And whoso taketh upon him my name, and endureth to the end, the same shall be saved at the last day.

Therefore, whatsoever ye shall do, ye shall do it in my name; therefore ye shall call the church in my name; and ye shall call upon the Father in my name that he will bless the church for my sake.

And how be it my church save it be called in my name? For if a church be called in Moses' name then it be Moses' church; or if it be called in the name of a man then it be the church of a man; but *if it be called in my name then it is my church, if it so be that they are built upon my gospel.*[19]

And then Jesus Christ explained the meaning of his gospel which he had taught to the Twelve Apostles and to the other Nephites. Following is part of his explanation:

Behold I have given unto you my gospel, and this is the gospel which I have given unto you—that I came into the world to do the will of my Father, because my Father sent me.

And my Father sent me that I might be lifted up upon the cross; and after that I had been lifted up upon the cross that I might draw all men unto me, that as I have been lifted up by men even so should men be lifted up by the Father, to stand before me, to be judged of their works, whether they be good or whether they be evil— . . .

And it shall come to pass, that whoso repenteth and is baptized in my name shall be filled; and if he endureth to the end, behold, him will I hold guiltless before my Father at that day when I shall stand to judge the world.

And he that endureth not unto the end, the same is he that is also hewn down and cast into the fire, from whence they can no more return, because of the justice of the Father.

And this is the word which he hath given unto the children of men. And for this cause he fulfilleth the words which he hath given, and he lieth not, but fulfilleth all his words.

And no unclean thing can enter into his kingdom; therefore nothing entereth into his rest save it be those who have washed their garments in my blood, because of their faith, and the repentance of all their sins, and their faithfulness unto the end.

Now this is the commandment: Repent, all ye ends of the earth, and come unto me and be baptized in my name, that ye may be sanctified by the reception of the Holy Ghost, that ye may stand spotless before me at the last day.

------

[19]*Ibid.*, 27:4-8. (Italics supplied by the writer.)

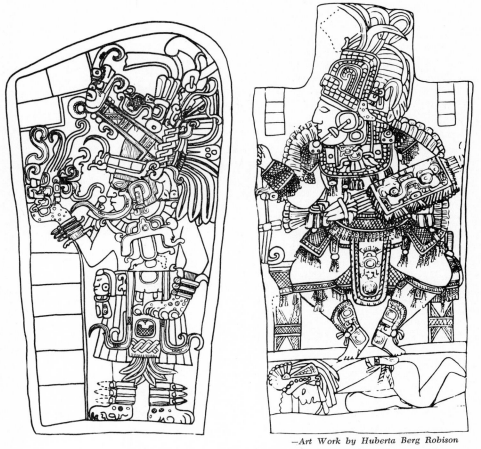

—*Art Work by Huberta Berg Robison*

Fig. 53:   STELA 8, SEIBAL, GUATEMALA

Fig. 54:   STELA 2, CANCUEN, GUATEMALA

These stelae furnish typical examples of elaborate headdresses and precious stones worn by worshipers of the "Fair God" in Middle America.

Verily, verily, I say unto you, this is my gospel; and ye know the things that ye must do in my church; for the works which ye have seen me do that shall ye also do; for that which ye have seen me do even that shall ye do;

Therefore, if ye do these things blessed are ye, for ye shall be lifted up at the last day.[20]

The Prophet Joseph Smith described as follows the marvelous accomplishments of Christ, the resurrected Lord, on the Western Hemisphere, as delineated in the Book of Mormon:

. . . This book also tells us that our Savior made His appearance upon this continent after His resurrection; that He planted the Gospel here in all its fulness, and richness, and power, and blessing: that they had Apostles, Prophets, Pastors, Teachers, and Evangelists; the same order, the same priest-

---

[20]*Ibid.*, 27:13-14, 15-22.

hood, the same ordinances, gifts, powers, and blessings, as were enjoyed on the eastern continent, . . .[21]

FURTHER COMMENT ON OTHER SHEEP

Before Jesus left the Nephites and ascended to his Father in heaven, he told them of the parable of "other sheep I have" which he had related to the Israelites in Jerusalem. The following quotation will give a full explanation:

This much did the Father command me, that I should tell unto them:
That other sheep I have which are not of this fold; them also I must bring, and they shall hear my voice; and there shall be one fold, and one shepherd.
But, verily, I say unto you that the Father hath commanded me, and I tell it unto you, that ye were separated from among them because of their iniquity; therefore it is because of their iniquity that they know not of you. . . .
And verily I say unto you, that ye are they of whom I said: Other sheep I have which are not of this fold; them also I must bring, and they shall hear my voice; and there shall be one fold, and one shepherd.
And they understood me not, for they supposed it had been the Gentiles; for they understood not that the Gentiles should be converted through their preaching. . . .
But behold, ye have both heard my voice, and seen me; and ye are my sheep, and ye are numbered among those whom the Father hath given me.[22]

Christ's explanation to the Nephites shows why the "Fair God" singled out the people of the New World for a visit, and why such an important event was not called more forcibly to the attention of the Israelites in Palestine.

CHRIST THE UNIVERSAL GOOD SHEPHERD

The Book of Mormon serves as the American witness to Jesus Christ, confirming the teachings of the Hebrew prophets and of the Master himself wherein they declared that Christ is the Good Shepherd. This ancient American scripture boldly declares Christ to be the universal Shepherd of all righteous people throughout the earth who will take upon themselves the Master's name and keep his commandments, ". . . For there is one God and one Shepherd over all the earth."[23] Certainly the Good Shepherd has visited his sheep, regardless of the country and age in world's history in which they lived. In fulfilment of prophecies made by holy men of God in

[21]*Documentary History of the Church* (Salt Lake City, 1908), vol. 4, p. 538.
[22]3 Nephi 15:16-17, 19, 21-22, 24.
[23]1 Nephi 13:41; 22:24-26; Alma 5:14-41; Moroni 5:9-24; Helaman 15:13; 3 Nephi 20:22; 21:23-24; Ether 13:3-10.

ancient times, the Good Shepherd visited the Jews in Palestine, the inhabitants of ancient America, the lost tribes of Israel, and Joseph Smith in the latter days. To each of these, he gave the gospel plan of salvation, providing a way whereby those who desired might come into his fold and in due time gain an inheritance in celestial glory with the Good Shepherd.

SUMMARY OF CHRIST'S WORK IN ANCIENT AMERICA

It should be pointed out in summarizing Christ's phenomenal work in ancient America that he, the Only Begotten of the Father,

Fig. 55: SERPENTS' HEADS AT
TENAYUCA, MEXICO

established his Church and kingdom anciently on the Western Hemisphere, and gave its members the Melchizedek Priesthood or *"the Holy Priesthood after the Order of the Son of God."*[24] The Master also gave to the Nephites all of the laws and ordinances of the gospel requisite for the salvation and exaltation of that marvelous race of people. He taught them the numerous details of the true and everlasting gospel. We read in the Book of Mormon:

---

[24]Doctrine and Covenants 107:3.

And he did expound all things, even from the beginning until the time that he should come in his glory—yea, even all things which should come upon the face of the earth, even until the elements should melt with fervent heat, and the earth should be wrapt together as a scroll, and the heavens and the earth should pass away;

And even unto the great and last day, when all people, and all kindreds, and all nations and tongues shall stand before God, to be judged of their works, whether they be good or whether they be evil—

If they be good, to the resurrection of everlasting life; and if they be evil, to the resurrection of damnation; being on a parallel, the one on the one hand and the other on the other hand, according to the mercy, and the justice, and the holiness which is in Christ, who was before the world began.

And now there cannot be written in this book even a hundredth part of the things which Jesus did truly teach unto the people; . . .[25]

After Christ had completed his work with the Nephites in ancient America, he ascended once again into heaven to reign in glory and exaltation with the Eternal Father.

Thus, as Laurette Séjourné has found through her archaeological and historical research, Quetzalcoatl or Jesus Christ played the "essential role as founder of Nahuatl [Nephite] culture," and "the social and religious views that [he inaugurated] dominated Meso-America for over 1500 years" prior to the Spanish conquest. The Savior's memory was ardently worshiped by the Nephites, and later by the American Indians, because he was indeed the Christ, the Savior of the world, the same individual who inaugurated Christianity in Palestine prior to his crucifixion and set in motion the Christian era on the Eastern Hemisphere. Even in ancient America those who took upon themselves the name of Christ were called Christians.[26] His influence was tremendous in both the Old and New worlds, even far beyond my ability to describe; and so the memory of the great works which he performed on both hemispheres will remain in the hearts of mankind forever, because ". . . as the Lord God liveth, there is none other name given under heaven save it be this Jesus Christ . . . whereby man can be saved."[27]

---

[25]3 Nephi 26:3-6.
[26]Alma 46:13-16.
[27]2 Nephi 25:20; Mosiah 3:17; Moses 6:52.

Chapter 5

TEOTIHUACÁN AND THE PLUMED SERPENT

Visiting Teotihuacan—Pyramids of the Sun and Moon

Teotihuacán, situated approximately thirty miles northeast of Mexico City, is perhaps the outstanding tourist attraction in the Valley of Mexico. No one can really claim to have seen our neighboring country to the south if he has not been shown Teotihuacán (Tä'o-tē'wä-kän'); and so—like all other American tourists—I placed that famous archaeological site on my itinerary during my first visit to Mexico in 1941.

When we arrived at Teotihuacán, our Mexican guide—who had resided half of his time in the United States and thereby knew both English and Spanish equally well and also the customs of both peoples—took us first to the Pyramid of the Moon. We were informed that this impressive structure, dating in the B.C. period,[1] rises 115 feet high on a quadrangular base that measures 329 feet by 411 feet.

This pyramid was truncated at the top, where undoubtedly a temple stood. From a spacious court, a broad stairway once led up the south side of the ascending planes, which were broken to provide terraces.[2]

Our guide next took us to the Pyramid of the Sun. It towered majestically above all other structures of that archaeological site, rising to a height of over 200 feet. Its base measured almost 700 feet on each side. The structure was built of adobe bricks and was solid throughout. The exterior was faced with volcanic stone covered with "pre-Spanish cement."

Five bodies in form of truncated pyramids, one on top of another and diminishing in size so as to form terraces, make up the pyramid proper. Here, too, on top, was a small temple, dedicated to the cult of Tonacatecutli, God of Sun, of warmth and of abundance. The temple was crowned with a gigantic monolithic statue of the god adorned with a gold breast plate that returned with almost equal brilliance the rays of the sun which struck it. Like so many other fine works of art of the ancient Mexicans, this statue was destroyed by the orders of Fray Juan de Zumarrago, Mexico's first Archbishop, in his zeal to abolish pagan rites.[3]

---

[1]*Archaeology in Mexico* (Mexico City, 1952), p. 14.
[2]*Idem.*
[3]*Ibid.,* p. 15.

Fig. 56:   Pyramid of the Sun, Teotihuacan, Mexico   Fig. 57:   Pyramid of the Mo
Teotihuacan, Mexico

Both pyramids in shape, size, and purposes of construction had certain resemblances to ancient pyramids, or temple-towers, of Egypt,[4] Assyria, and Babylon, which is a significant fact, since the Book of Mormon claims that the Jaredites came from the great Tower of Babel[5] in Babylon and that the Nephites brought with them a considerable amount of Egyptian culture.[6]

We followed southward along a road called "Road of the Dead,"[7] because of numerous human skeletons discovered by the early Spanish settlers along its length, and came to the Temple of Quetzalcoatl.

QUADRANGLE AND TEMPLE OF QUETZALCOATL

Few times in my visiting of numerous archaeological sites have I been as deeply impressed as I was at my first visit at the quadrangle and Temple of Quetzalcoatl. In order to become introduced to this important archaeological site, we shall quote from the writings of Laurette Séjourné:

---

[4]Milton R. Hunter and Thomas Stuart Ferguson, *Ancient America and the Book of Mormon* (Oakland, 1950), pp. 264-273.
[5]Ether 1:1-16, 32-43.
[6]1 Nephi 1:2; Mosiah 1:4; Mormon 9:32-33.
[7]*Archaeology in Mexico Today, op. cit.*, p. 15.

The quadrangle of Quetzalcoatl is surrounded by platforms six metres high, supported by the pedestals of sanctuaries that split up the whole surface into rhythmic parts.

The rear section of the quadrangle is a pyramid-shaped building completely covered with plumed serpents. The ramps of the stairway leading to the sanctuary which once crowned it are studded with great serpent heads. The plane surfaces above the sloping walls have, superimposed over relief carvings of the symbolic reptile, a series of heads of Quetzalcoatl and of Tlaloc, the rain god, alternating one with another. These two heads are different symbolic expressions of one and the same basic concept of the Nahuatl religion: the vital impulse arising from the unification of opposing elements. Later we shall see that, like Quetzalcoatl, Tlaloc is the bearer of the luminous seed which converts matter—in this case the earth—into creative energy[8]

Our guide remarked:

"This is the famous Temple of Quetzalcoatl. It was built by an ancient people called by some writers the Teotihuacáns and by others the Toltecs. This temple was erected during the early Christian centuries, perhaps as early as the seventh century A.D."

Dr. George C. Vaillant, director of the University of Pennsylvania Museum, gives the date for the beginning of the temple as 666 A.D.

SYMBOLS OF QUETZALCOATL

Dr. Vaillant points out that "The Feathered Serpent is the dominant decorative motive, and the great heads carved in rugged simplicity project from the balustrade and from the facades."[9] These serpent heads, as can be seen from the accompanying photograph (Fig. 58), are surrounded with a motif representing quetzal feathers. Both the serpent heads and quetzal feathers are symbols of Quetzalcoatl, the "White Bearded God."

We soon learned that

Quetzalcoatl, the Plumed Serpent, most revered god, was more frequently represented on pottery and in decoration [at Teotihuacán] than any other subject.[10]

Speaking of the Temple of Quetzalcoatl, archaeologists declare that

---

[8]Laurette Séjourné, *Burning Water—Thought and Religion in Ancient Mexico* (New York, 1956), pp. 86-87.
[9]George C. Vaillant, *The Aztecs of Mexico* (New York, 1950), pp. 71, 79.
[10]*Archaeology in Mexico Today, op. cit.*, p. 13.

Fig. 58: Temple of Quetzalcoatl, Teotihuacan, Mexico

This is a representation of Quetzalcoatl. . . . As proof that this temple was erected in honor of the Feathered Serpent, we see on the wall an enormous sculptured serpent, of the rattlesnake species, symbol of Quetzalcoatl.[11]

The "enormous sculptured serpent" referred to in the foregoing quotation is carved completely across the lower front of the Temple of Quetzalcoatl, as is seen in the accompanying photograph (Fig. 58) on opposite page.

Efforts to Understand the Symbols of Quetzalcoatl

My first impression of the serpent heads on the Temple of Quetzalcoatl was that they were grotesque, ugly creatures and certainly could not be symbols of Quetzalcoatl. Since I was a member of the Church of Jesus Christ, I was quite familiar with the Book of Mormon account of the appearance of Jesus Christ to the inhabitants of ancient America following his resurrection; and I had also heard that he had been identified with Quetzalcoatl. As I looked at those hideous serpent heads, I thought: "I see nothing here that reminds me of the beautiful account in the Book of Mormon of our Lord and Master, Jesus Christ. These snake heads are pagan representations or idols."

The idea that these venomous serpents were supposed to be symbols of the Savior was repulsive to me.

After returning to Utah from Teotihuacán, having had time to think more carefully, I realized that I had been looking through the eyes of a member of the true Church of Jesus Christ. My religious background had caused me to judge the symbols of Quetzalcoatl by the standard of the marvelous teachings of the Book of Mormon, the great revelations regarding Jesus recorded in the Doctrine and Covenants, and the gospel doctrines contained in the Pearl of Great Price and the Bible.

Since my training had been in the Book of Mormon, and since the concept of the Savior taught therein was so superior to the concept of the serpent and the quetzal symbols shown at Teotihuacán, I was in no position to judge accurately nor intelligently; and so I decided that I must study archaeology and Indian traditions in order that I might more aptly place myself in the position of the pagan worshipers of Quetzalcoatl and thereby understand the significance of serpents and quetzal feathers as symbols of Quetzalcoatl or Jesus

---

[11]*Ibid.*, p. 15.

Christ. I was confronted with the problem of trying to ascertain why the inhabitants of ancient America employed such a noxious creature as the serpent, along with the resplendent quetzal bird, to symbolize the glorious and radiant resurrected Savior—the "White Bearded God"; and so I began the study of archaeology and anthropology. During the period since 1941, I have read whatever I could find concerning ancient America.

Thirteen years elapsed, and I made my second trip to Teotihuacán. This time I was accompanied by President and Sister Claudious Bowman, José Dávila, and Sister Hunter. I also returned there the following year with a touring party, and have been there several times since. On each of these occasions we visited the famous Quetzalcoatl Temple and quadrangle.

I now possessed a background and viewpoint far different from the one I had on my first trip. I saw much more and certainly had a clearer understanding than I had had on my first visit to the Temple of Quetzalcoatl. I felt that now, at least to a certain degree, I was able to think, feel, understand, and appreciate as had the ancient builders of Teotihuacán.

The following discussion will portray my transition of understanding and feelings since my first visit to Teotihuacán, giving the results of my research and my efforts to explain why the ancient Americans used the quetzal bird and the serpent—the rattlesnake species—as symbols of Quetzalcoatl.

Importance of Christ's Appearance to the Ancient Americans

By 400 A.D. the religion of the Nephites and Lamanites had degenerated into pagan practices, and the former people as a nation had been exterminated in a terrible war fought on and near the Hill Cumorah. The survivors of that last war—some of whom were white in color and of Nephite stock and others bronze in color and of Lamanite lineage[12]—held sacred in their memories and traditions the knowledge of the greatest event that ever occurred in ancient America, namely, the visitation of Jesus Christ, the resurrected Lord, to their progenitors in the Book of Mormon days. Although a uni-

---

[12]Milton R. Hunter, "Archaeology and the Book of Mormon," *The Improvement Era* (Salt Lake City, 1955), No. 7, vol. 58, p. 498. See also, Milton R. Hunter, *Archaeology and the Book of Mormon* (Salt Lake City, 1956), vol. 1, for an extensive study of this subject.

versal apostasy prevailed, the teachings received directly from the Master having been adulterated, yet certain momentous events had made an everlasting impression on the inhabitants of ancient America. The greatest of these was the appearance of Jesus Christ to the inhabitants of the Western Hemisphere, as has already been explained.

PRESERVATION AND TRANSMISSION OF INDIAN TRADITIONS

On February 4, 1956, in the city of Totonicapán, Guatemala, I and others had an interview with Jesus Carranza Juarez, a member of the Quiché Maya religion and an expert in Indian traditions, for the purpose of acquiring as much knowledge as possible regarding those people. One of the first things he told us was the fact that since men may be killed in war, the women have been the principal preservers of Quiché traditions from ancient times to the present day. Girls learned thoroughly the most cherished traditions, and

Fig. 59:   AIRPLANE VIEW OF QUADRANGLE AND TEMPLE OF QUETZALCOATL, TEOTIHUACAN, MEXICO

when they grew to womanhood they in turn taught their daughters. Also, according to Quiché custom, certain women—perhaps the most intelligent ones of the tribe—were selected to be especially trained in Indian traditions. One of these, a woman 82 years of age, was brought in to rehearse to us certain of the Quiché Maya traditions.

Mr. Carranza also informed us that certain men were selected to become priests. As part of their training they became thoroughly conversant in Mayan traditions, which knowledge they transmitted

Fig. 60: JESUS CARRANZA JUAREZ AND QUICHE WOMAN

—Photograph by Author

to their successors. Through memory and by word of mouth Indian traditions have been accurately transmitted from generation to generation.

Thus mothers of the apostate descendants of Book of Mormon peoples have helped to keep alive the most cherished traditions by telling them to their children. Also, it would be natural for tribal chiefs to rehearse in their council meetings their distorted accounts of the "White Bearded God"; and perhaps the youth, especially those who were being trained for the priesthood, were quite thoroughly instructed by the Indian priests, since religion was the culture center and dominating force of the Maya, Aztec, Toltec, Zapotec, and other great Indian tribes of Mexico and Central America. In the words of Helen Augur:

The outstanding quality of the Middle America culture is that it was a tremendous religious movement. Every ancient site was a ceremonial city dedicated to the gods; all those beautiful objects we see in museums were visible forms of worship. . . .[13]

Thus the story of the sudden appearance of the "White Bearded God" to the ancestors of the American Indians and his great contributions to their culture had its origin in the marvelous visitations of Jesus Christ, the crucified and resurrected Lord, whose descent from heaven to teach the ancient Americans is so beautifully delineated in the Book of Mormon. Of course the Indians told the story of Christ's ministry on the Western Hemisphere in a variety of distorted forms. In fact, many fables, erroneous conceptions, and false religious practices had crept into the principal body of teachings of the true gospel of Jesus Christ, according to Mormon and Moroni—the two last prophet-historians of the Nephites—even before the close of the Book of Mormon. These writers maintained that their people as a nation were destroyed because of this apostasy and the wicked lives that the people were living.

During the period of more than one thousand years' time that elapsed between the close of Nephite history (A.D. 421) and the discovery of America in 1492, no doubt the polluting of the true gospel continued to increase, resulting in corrupted, apostate, and untrue pagan practices. The worship of numerous gods, with religious beliefs and practices ranging from witchcraft to rather noble and true spiritual expressions, prevailed throughout the Americas. The peculiar thing is that such extremes in religious beliefs and practices could have existed side by side in the religious expressions of the same peoples. Enough perverted truths remained, however, in clearly defined forms to make possible the identification of Quetzalcoatl and his religion as adulterated forms and counterfeits of Christ and the true gospel which he established in ancient America shortly following his resurrection.

IMPORTANCE AND USE OF SYMBOLS IN RELIGION

How were the ancient Americans best to preserve through the generations their glorious traditions which were so dear to their

---

[13]Helen Augur, *Zapotec* (New York, 1954), p. 161.

hearts? They must have symbols. Throughout all of history symbols have been used by human beings, not only to convey to their minds important and great events, teachings, doctrine, and the understanding and remembrance of divine truths, but also to preserve truths from age to age. Since Jesus Christ's mission was to give to the world the gospel and through it and his death and resurrection bring about the atonement, a significant phase of the gospel has been the continuous use of symbols to remind faithful worshipers of the Messiah and his mission. For example, after the expulsion of Adam and Eve from the Garden of Eden, God gave them the law of sacrifice to symbolize the atonement of Jesus Christ, the sacrificial lamb being offered in ". . . similitude of the sacrifice of the Only Begotten of the Father."[14] Also, to symbolize the atoning sacrifice of the Messiah, the Lord commanded Moses to institute the Feast of the Passover. This was done the night prior to the departure of the Israelites from Egyptian bondage. From generation to generation following their exodus from Egypt, these people observed the Feast of the Passover. Perhaps the most important symbol used on these occasions was that of the paschal lamb—"a lamb without spot or blemish"—which symbolized the sacrifice of their long-looked-for Messiah. In the Meridian of Time the Master supplanted the law of sacrifice by sacrament. He gave his followers in Palestine, as well as the inhabitants of ancient America, the commandment to observe the Lord's Supper in memory of his flesh and blood which was shed for mankind.[15] Since that day the Sacrament symbols have been held very sacred by Christians.

We learn from the Pearl of Great Price that through divine sources Enoch was taught the gospel of Jesus Christ. On a certain occasion the voice of the Lord spoke to him and explained the atonement, saying ". . . through the blood of mine Only Begotten, who shall come in the meridian of time"[16] shall the atonement of mankind be consummated; and then the Lord declared:

And behold, all things have their likeness, and all things are created and made to bear record of me [Jesus Christ], both things which are temporal, and things which are spiritual; things which are in the heavens above, and things which are on the earth, and things which are in the earth, and things

14Moses 5:4-8.
15Mark 14:23-24; 3 Nephi 18:2-12.
16Moses 6:62.

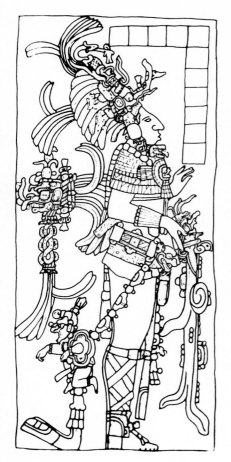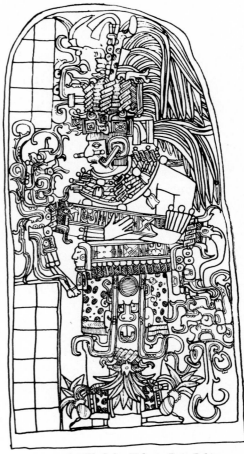

—Art Work by Huberta Berg Robison

Fig. 61:   West Door Panel of Temple of the Cross, Palenque, Mexico

Fig. 62:   Stela 10, Seibal, Guatemala

Observe the elaborate quetzal headdresses, serpents' mouths, jade beads, and other precious stones, all of which are symbols of Quetzalcoatl.

which are under the earth, both above and beneath: *all things bear record of me [Jesus].*[17]

This chapter endeavors to show how even the pagan symbolism of the American Indians bore witness to Jesus Christ.

Christ's Radiance and Splendor as He Appeared to the Nephites

As has already been mentioned, the resurrected Lord appeared to the inhabitants of ancient America. A beautiful account of this visitation is given in the Book of Mormon.[18] The people, vast numbers of whom had assembled in front of the temple at Bountiful,

_____
[17]*Ibid.,* 6:63.
[18]3 Nephi 11:8-14.

saw him ". . . descending out of heaven" as if he were a bird; "And he was clothed in a white robe."[19]

Following these marvelous events, Jesus Christ taught the people the same gospel that he had previously proclaimed in Palestine. He also performed many unusual miracles.

During a period of many days, multitudes of people associated with the resurrected Lord. He was radiant and beautiful with a splendor which surpassed all description. The Nephite historian informs us that his garments and body ". . . did exceed all whiteness, yea, even there could be nothing upon earth so white as the whiteness thereof," and ". . . the light of his countenance did shine upon them."[20] Finally he ascended back into heaven to dwell with God, the Eternal Father.[21]

After the close of the Book of Mormon period, when mothers rehearsed the Indian traditions regarding the "White Bearded God" who had visited their ancestors, when native priests and Indian chiefs explained these astounding events to the young men, young women, and to the warriors, how best could they make their accounts of their traditions vivid and cause those whom they taught to comprehend most completely? The solution was by the employment of symbols.

QUETZAL BIRD A SYMBOL OF THE RESURRECTED SAVIOR

In certain sections of Honduras, Guatemala, and southern Mexico, there has lived since ancient times one of the most gorgeous birds in the world. Some people have called it "the bird of paradise," but "quetzal" is the name by which it is usually known. It has resplendent, long, green tail feathers, certain ones of which measure three and one-half feet in length. A famous Catholic missionary, Father Bernardino de Sahagún, described the quetzal bird as follows:

> There is a bird in this land called Quetzalcoatl; it has very rich and colorful plumage; the bill is sharp and yellow, and the feet are yellow. It has a feather tuft on its head, like a rooster's comb. It is . . . the size of a magpie of Spain. The tail feathers are called Quezalli and they are very green and shiny. They are wide like the leaves of reeds and they bend when the wind

---

[19]*Idem.*
[20]*Ibid.*, 19:25.
[21]*Ibid.*, 18:39.

hits them and they shine very beautifully. These birds have some black feathers in the tail with which it covers these rich [green] ones which are in the midst of the black ones. The black feathers are very black on the outside, and on the inside are the rich dark green feathers, they being not very long nor wide. The tuft this bird has on its head is very beautiful and glossy . . . and the bird has a red and glossy neck. . . . The neck, on the back, and entire back of the bird has resplendent green feathers. Under the tail and between its legs it has a delicate feather of clear green color, soft and resplendent; on the veins or elbows of the wings are green feathers, and black ones under the wings. . . .[22]

Dr. Sylvanus G. Morley, one of the greatest Maya scholars who has ever lived, stated that the

---

[22]Bernardino de Sahagún, *Introduccion al Primer Libro de la Historia*, Libro 11, Cap. 2, Sec. 1.

Fig. 63:
BEAUTIFUL
QUETZAL BIRD

. . . famous quetzal, the national bird of Guatemala, one of the most gorgeous birds in the world, is almost exclusively confined to the highlands of Guatemala and Honduras and the adjacent mountains of Chiapas, [Mexico].[23]

Morley also tells us that

The gorgeous, iridescent, blue-green tail feathers of the quetzal, sometimes three feet long, seem to have been reserved [in pre-Columbian time] for the rulers alone.[24]

He points out that among the Indians of Guatemala today

The royal color is green because green is the color of the highly prized quetzal bird, whose plumage was reserved for the rulers.[25]

As the quetzal bird flew through the air and the brilliant rays of sunlight reflected the resplendent gorgeousness of the colors of its plumage, especially the green, it may have reminded the ancient

---

[23]Sylvanus G. Morley, *The Ancient Maya* (Palo Alto, California, 1947), p. 6.
[24]*Ibid.*, p. 197.
[25]*Ibid.*, p. 409.

Fig. 64:   GUATEMALA FLAG

Quetzal bird is the sacred bird of Guatemala. It is stamped on the country's money.

—Photograph by Author

Americans of the beauty and glory of Jesus Christ who had descended from heaven through the air to visit them and later had returned into heaven in like manner as proclaimed in their traditions of the "White Bearded God." Since Christ did pass through the air in a manner that the people had seen only birds do in their time, what could be more appropriate to the minds of those people in symbolizing the central character in the greatest event that had occurred in the New World than to take as a symbol for him the beautiful quetzal bird? It portrayed all the splendor, the radiance, and the beauty of which the Indians' minds were capable of conceiving.

Perhaps at first when the story of Christ's appearance was told and retold, the "White Bearded God" was said to be as gorgeous, as radiant, as beautiful, and as splendid as the quetzal bird. As time passed, however, his name came to be more or less synonymous with the resplendent bird, the name "quetzal" actually becoming part of the name the Indians applied to the "White Bearded God."

Jesus Christ had informed the ancient Americans that he was the "resurrection and the life"—the "light and the life of the world."[26] Following Book of Mormon days, the American Indians realized that when springtime came the world was filled with new life and growth, the vegetation which clothed mother earth being gorgeously green and beautiful. Since the quetzal bird was primarily green in color, this fact also made it a fitting symbol of Jesus Christ, the giver of light and life to the entire world.

Jade a Symbol of Quetzalcoatl

Jade, being green in color, also was used extensively by the American Indians of Mexico and Central America, especially by the Mayas, as a symbol of Quetzalcoatl. Burial masks, beads, pendants, bracelets, and other ornaments made of jade have been dug up in large quantities in connection with ancient Indian burials. Murals on the walls of Bonampak and other archaeological places supply added evidence that the priests and rulers who were adorned with quetzal feathers were also bedecked elaborately with jade objects, all of which testify that these ancient Americans were worshipers of Quetzalcoatl, the "White Bearded God."

---

[26] 3 Nephi 11:10-11; 9:18; Alma 38:9; Mosiah 16:9.

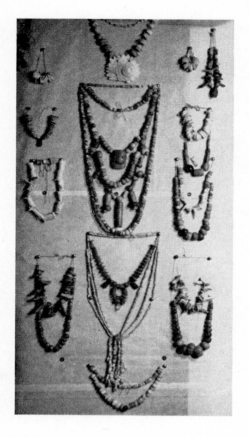

Fig. 65: Jade Beads, Merida

Jade beads in private museum of Alberto G. Marquez, Merida, Yucatán, Mexico. Mr. Marquez obtained these beads from ancient Maya burials.

—Photograph by Author

COATL OR SERPENT A SYMBOL OF QUETZALCOATL

Coatl, the ancient Mexican word for *serpent,*[27] constitutes the latter half of the name *Quetzalcoatl,* the title by which the "White Bearded God" was known by many of the aborigines at the time of the Spanish conquest. This appellation came about as a result of the Indians' extensive use of the serpent as a symbol of Quetzalcoatl, whom we have identified as Jesus Christ. The importance of the serpent-symbol was described by Edward H. Thompson as follows:

. . . The symbol of the Feathered Serpent—the body of the rattlesnake, covered with the plumage of the *quetzal* bird—was to this old civilization what the Cross was to the Christian and the Crescent to the Saracen. Under this symbol the culture hero *Kukul Can*—Feathered Serpent—of Yucatán,

---

[27]Hubert Howe Bancroft, *Native Races* (New York, 1875), vol. 2, p. 511ff.

Quetzalcoatl of the Aztecs and earlier peoples, was first reverenced, then deified and worshipped.[28]

Count Byron Khun de Prorok points out that

The God Quetzalcoatl, a white God, took the name "Feathered Serpent." . . . And there was a singular identification, significant in its completeness, of the sign of the Plumed Serpent with the signs of Egypt and the traditional delineation of the serpent in the Garden of Eden.[29]

Members of the Church of Jesus Christ of Latter-day Saints are informed that in the very beginning of human history the serpent became identified with Satan and in a certain sense became a symbol of the Prince of Darkness; however, peculiar as it may seem and also in spite of the fact that the devil in the form of a serpent had played such a prominent role in the Garden of Eden story, history affirms that *coatl* or serpent in very early times became identified also with the crucifixion and atonement of Jesus of Nazareth and hence it became a symbol of the Son of Man.

The fact that ancient peoples adopted the serpent as a symbol of the Messiah does not necessarily classify them as devil worshipers. It merely indicates that a certain creature or object would be adopted by a people as a symbol of righteousness—even the Messiah—and during another period of human history the same creature or object may serve as a symbol of evil—even the devil.

In this chapter and throughout the book, the serpent will be presented as a symbol of Quetzalcoatl or Jesus Christ and no further reference will be made to its identification with the Prince of Darkness or Lucifer.

SERPENT SYMBOL IN ANCIENT ISRAEL

As far as is known, the *coatl,* or *serpent,* was first used in ancient Israel as a symbol of the crucifixion and atonement of Jesus Christ, "the Anointed One." Since the Son of Man was proclaimed by the prophets to be the giver of resurrection and life to the world and eternal life to those who would keep all of his commandments, the serpent, who played such a prominent part in the Garden of Eden story, became an appropriate symbol of the Master and of his crucifixion and atoning sacrifice.

While traveling through the wilderness on their exodus from

---

[28]Edward H. Thompson, *People of the Serpent* (New York, 1932), p. 196.
[29]Count Byron Khun de Prorok, *In Quest of Lost Worlds* (New York, 1935), pp. 123-124.

Fig. 66:   Serpent's Head, Teotihuacan

This beautiful serpent's head is one of a number such heads which decorate the face of the Temple of Quetzalcoatl at Teotihuacán, Mexico.

Egypt, the Israelites had an experience which became the basis for an added interpretation of the serpent-symbol. Many of the Israelites were bitten by serpents and were thereby poisoned. God commanded Moses as follows:

> Make thee a fiery serpent, and set it upon a pole; and it shall come to pass, that everyone that is bitten, when he looketh upon it, shall live. And Moses made a serpent of brass, and put it upon a pole, and it came to pass, that if a serpent had bitten any man, when he beheld the serpent of brass, he lived.[30]

Prophets later compared the crucifixion and atonement of Christ with the brazen serpent that Moses placed upon the pole. Just as those who were obedient to God's commandment looked upon the serpent with faith and were healed, so are those healed of spiritual defects and eventually given resurrection and eternal life who take upon them the name of Christ and keep his commandments.

Dr. Maurice H. Farbridge, in his book *Studies in Biblical and*

----

[30]Numbers 21:8-9.

Semitic Symbolism, informs us that the serpent was the principal symbol of the hoped-for Messiah from the time of Moses until about 700 B.C. A brass serpent on a pole or beam was maintained as a representation of the Messiah in the chief temple of the Israelite nation during that period of approximately 500 years' time.[31]

Jesus Christ while in mortality clearly identified the serpent symbol with his own crucifixion. We read the following in the New Testament:

And as Moses lifted up the serpent in the wilderness, even so must the Son of Man be lifted up: That whosoever believeth in him should not perish, but have eternal life.[32]

SERPENT SYMBOL AMONG THE NEPHITES

The Nephites, who were of the seed of Israel, migrated from Jerusalem to America about 600 B.C. They brought with them to the New World the concept of the serpent as a symbol of Jesus Christ, his crucifixion, his powers to heal, and to give life, including eternal life. Nephi, the first historian of his people, wrote:

And now, my brethren, I have spoken plainly that ye cannot err. And as the Lord God [Jesus Christ] liveth that brought Isreal up out of the land of Egypt, and gave unto Moses power that he should heal the nations after they had been bitten by the poisonous serpents, if they would cast their eyes unto the serpent which he did raise up before them, . . . there is none other name given under heaven save it be this Jesus Christ, of which I have spoken, whereby man can be saved.[33]

Approximately twenty years before the birth of Jesus Christ, another Nephite prophet, whom we know as Nephi, the son of Helaman, delivered a powerful sermon on the coming of the Messiah. In that sermon he definitely connected the serpent as a symbol of Jesus Christ. To quote:

Yea, did he [Moses] not bear record that the Son of God should come? And as he lifted up the brazen serpent in the wilderness, even so shall he be lifted up who should come.

And as many as should look upon that serpent should live, even so as many as should look upon the Son of God with faith, having a contrite spirit, might live, even unto that life which is eternal.[34]

Alma also taught the Nephites that the serpent was a symbol of Jesus Christ. To quote:

---

[31]Maurice H. Farbridge, *Studies in Biblical and Semitic Symbolism* (New York, 1928), p. 75; H. P. Smith, *Old Testament History* (New York, 1903), p. 240.
[32]John 3:14-15.
[33]2 Nephi 25:20.
[34]Helaman 8:14-15.

Behold, he [the Son of God] was spoken of by Moses; yea, and behold a type was raised up in the wilderness, that whosoever would look upon it might live. And many did look and live.[35]

And then Alma described the atoning powers of Jesus.

From the evidence already presented the fact becomes apparent that the serpent was a Christian symbol, established in ancient Israel at least as early as the days of Moses and carried forward on the Western Hemisphere by the Nephites to the close of the Book of Mormon period. Its purpose was to remind the people of the crucifixion of Jesus Christ and of his great saving powers.

QUETZAL-SERPENT SYMBOLS OF THE INDIANS

It was natural for the descendants of the Nephites and the Lamanites as the years passed to continue with such a symbol, adding adulterated religious practices and altered ideas to the more refined serpent symbol as held in the Book of Mormon days. Thus the Indian descendants of Book of Mormon peoples distorted the serpent symbol into the various pagan forms that were found in Mexico and throughout Central America by European missionaries following the Spanish conquest. Although the quetzal-serpent symbols are degenerated pagan reminders of the "White Bearded God," they also serve as reminders of the true Savior who had once visited ancient America and had given his gospel to its inhabitants.

While visiting thirty-two archaeological sites and museums in Mexico and Central America during the winter of 1954-55, I saw the quetzal-serpent symbolism practically everywhere. Feathered serpents appear on facades of temples and palaces, on ceramics, in stone sculptured works, and in gold representations. Also, according to Lord Kingsborough, "Representations of the lifting up of serpents occur in Mexican paintings,"[36] which show that they used them to symbolize the crucifixion of Quetzalcoatl.

INTERPRETATION OF QUETZAL-SERPENT SYMBOLS AT TEOTIHUACAN AND ELSEWHERE

Bearing all of the foregoing discussion in mind, what did I see on my last trip to Teotihuacán? Instead of repulsive, ugly, grotesque

---

[35]Alma 33:19.

[36]Lord Kingsborough, *Mexican Antiquities,* cited in John Taylor, *Mediation and Atonement* (Salt Lake City, 1882), p. 203.

serpents, I saw on the front of one part of the temple six beautiful serpent heads, each surrounded by quetzal feathers, and six comparable ones on the other side, making twelve. I also observed that there had been twelve serpent heads up the edges of the staircase—six on each side. Each serpent head contained twelve teeth. I saw a repetition of the number twelve in temples, there being four on the north, four on the west, and four on the south side of the Quetzalcoatl quadrangle.

The Temple of Quetzalcoatl now appeared to me to be a beautiful building which had been erected in honor of Jesus Christ by a ". . . people who were skilled in many fields, mainly scientific and artistic. . . ."[37] ". . . Teotihuacán must have exemplified the best work of which a culture was capable."[38] I now observed their objects, which appeared to me to be beautifully carved. I had learned to admire the craftsmanship of the Teotihuacán artisans, and to agree with Vaillant's statement that ". . . the Temple of Quetzalcoatl, Feathered Serpent, the God of Learning, is splendid enough to qualify as the edifice for which Mitl [the builder of Teotihuacán] was renowned."[39]

I had also learned that Teotihuacán means "the place where all go to worship the gods."[40]

As I visited the various archaeological sites and museums, everywhere I looked I saw temples, pyramids, pottery, representations of men, and numerous other things, decorated with feathers of the "sacred quetzal, or bird of paradise," and serpents, as well as serpent heads, all symbolizing Quetzalcoatl or Jesus Christ. These had been made by master artists in murals, stone work, wood carvings, and clay. I marveled to learn that through many pagan generations following the close of the Book of Mormon period to the present time the American Indians had carefully, accurately, and artistically—although in a degenerated and adulterated form—in their quetzal-serpent symbols fulfilled the words of Jesus Christ wherein he declared that ". . . *all things bear record of me.*"

[37]*Archaeology in Mexico, op. cit.,* pp. 12-13.
[38]George C. Vaillant, *The Aztecs of Mexico* (New York, 1950), p. 75.
[39]*Ibid.,* p. 71.
[40]*Archaeology in Mexico Today, op. cit.,* pp. 12-13.

CHAPTER 6

SPIRITUAL SIGNIFICANCE OF QUETZALCOATL SYMBOLS

GOSPEL DOCTRINE OF IMMORTALITY

Perhaps the heart of the gospel of Jesus Christ and the principal motivating force therein is the doctrine of the immortality of man. The Nephite prophets definitely assured the ancient Americans that they were immortal beings, having lived in a celestial world before birth into mortality and, through the atonement, were endowed with the power to rise from the grave and continue to live following death.

The Nephites possessed a sure knowledge regarding a spirit world inhabited by personal beings. Their prophets declared that the gospel plan of salvation was formulated there before the human family was placed upon the earth.[1] The most vital person in this plan was a Savior—a Redeemer of mortals. Jesus Christ was selected to be that Redeemer, according to the Nephite records, ". . . from the foundation of the world."[2]

This divine Messiah was endowed with sufficient power to break the band of death and bring about the resurrection of mankind. Also, he was appointed by the Eternal Father to give a gospel plan of salvation, known as the gospel of Jesus Christ, to mortals; and all who would accept that gospel and render obedience thereto would, following resurrection, be brought back into the presence of the Father and the Son to dwell in celestial glory forever.

The Nephite prophets communed with God and were also visited by holy angels; and through these divine channels they received an extensive knowledge of the plan of salvation, including an assurance of the immortality of man.[3] The following quotation from the Prophet Abinadi illustrates the definiteness of the teachings of the Nephite prophets regarding the immortality of man:

He [Christ] is the light and life of the world; yea, a light that is endless,

---

[1] 2 Nephi 9:18; Mosiah 4:6-10; 15:19-20; Alma 12:30.
[2] Ether 3:14; Mosiah 15:19, Alma 42:26.
[3] Alma 42:7-9; 12:28-30; 2 Nephi 2:5-30.

that can never be darkened; yea, and also a life which is endless, that there can be no more death.

Even this mortal shall put on immortality, and this corruption shall put on incorruption, and shall be brought to stand before the bar of God, to be judged of him according to their works, whether they be good or whether they be evil—

If they be good, to the resurrection of endless life and happiness; and if they be evil, to the resurrection of endless damnation. . . .[4]

—Photograph by Author

Fig. 67:   TEMPLE OF EAGLES, CHICHEN ITZA

Observe also the plumed serpents on the temple.

The Prophet Amulek contributed to the same line of thinking in the following words:

. . . I say unto you that this mortal body is raised to an immortal body, that is from death, even from the first death unto life, that they can die no more; their spirits uniting with their bodies, never to be divided; thus the whole becoming spiritual and immortal, that they can no more see corruption.[5]

If one studies the aggregate information on immortality contained in the Book of Mormon, he may be surprised at the unusual amount of detail contained therein relative to life after death. To the ancient Americans the immortality of the soul was as much a

---

[4]Mosiah 16:9-11.
[5]Alma 11:45

reality as was their mortal existence. This mortal life was regarded as a probationary state in which to prepare for the greater existence beyond the grave.[6] All these eternal truths were revealed to them from the one divine source, Jesus the Christ. Therefore, from the Nephite records we obtain a tremendous advance over the concept of immortality of the other ancient religions of all other countries of the world.[7]

The final climax of all revelation regarding immortality was the appearance of the resurrected Savior to the Nephites. As he had risen from the grave, they were assured that they also would rise, stand before the judgment seat of their Redeemer, and receive rewards according to the lives that they had lived while in mortality.

The inhabitants of the Western Hemisphere drew their knowledge of gospel doctrines, including their immortality concept, from the same "Fountain of Truth"—Jesus Christ—from which all of God's children receive their eternal verities. This "Fountain of Truth"— "the light and life of the world"—is the universal Messiah.

Thus the ancestors of the American Indians, the Nephites and Lamanites during Book of Mormon days, had a positiveness of belief in the eternal nature of man which reached the realm of assured knowledge. This brief statement of the divinely revealed gospel knowledge which the worshiper of Jesus Christ had in ancient America should help us in gaining an understanding of the basic doctrines in the religion of Quetzalcoatl. An analysis of the Quetzalcoatl myths in which the Indians believed at the time of the Spanish conquest—as will be seen as we study those myths—reveals the fact that (although the religious beliefs and practices of the red men were much inferior to the divinely given and highly cherished Christian religion of their ancestors) enough truth had been retained by the American aborigines to make it possible for us to identify the religion of Quetzalcoatl as an adulterated form of the gospel of Jesus Christ.

SYMBOLS OF QUETZALCOATL

By the time of the Spanish conquest the Indians of Mexico had developed an elaborate set of symbols of Quetzalcoatl with equally

---

[6] 2 Nephi 2:19-29.
[7] *Ibid.*, 9:4-19; Mosiah 15:9-12; Alma 12:12-20.

—*Photograph by Author*

Fig. 68:   REPRODUCTION OF MOCTEZUMA'S HEADDRESS

This reproduction of the original headdress, which is in Vienna, is housed in the National Museum of Mexico. It is composed chiefly of gorgeous quetzal feathers.

elaborate forms of worship. The fact has already been mentioned that jade, quetzal feathers (quetzal: bird), and the serpent (coatl: serpent) were perhaps among the most prominently known symbols of the "White and Bearded God." Other precious stones, such as turquoise, had a religious significance also in the ritual of this Indian religion.

A number of the other symbols, such as various other kinds of feathered birds, butterflies, flowers, coyotes, tigers or jaguars, Venus, the dawn, the sun, eagles, fire, the wind, the rain, the harvest, the heart, and time all played a vital part in the religious beliefs and rituals of the Indians of Meso-America.

The Quetzalcoatl myths and the religious rituals connected therewith all centered in a belief in the immortality of man, a belief firmly held by the Aztecs of Mexico and their predecessors. All of the important Indian groups, such as the Zapotecs and Mixtecs of Oaxaca, the Mayas of Yucatán and Central America, the Toltecs or Nahuas of the mesa region of Mexico, the Olmecs of Vera Cruz, and the Totonacs of the Gulf Coast of Mexico, as well as the more advanced native cultures of the Andean region of South America, had religious beliefs which centered in the doctrine of the immortality of man. These various aboriginal peoples maintained that mortal beings before coming to earth lived in a celestial or spiritual world. They also firmly believed that after death they would live forever in a post-mortal realm. They believed that following mortal death each person would go to an eternal reward based upon the type of life that he had lived while in mortality. The most fortunate and favored among them, those who had been initiated into the mysteries of their religion, expected to go to a blessed world beyond the grave—a spiritual, celestial world. Religion existed for the purpose of preparing the devotees for that immortal life beyond the grave; and the symbols in the Quetzalcoatl religion were regarded as spiritual motives.

SYMBOLS OF QUETZAL FEATHERS, SERPENTS, AND JADE

The three symbols of Quetzalcoatl most prominently used by the Indians in the religion of the "Fair God"—quetzal feathers, plumed serpent, and jade—were discussed in the previous chapter. Since they were so vital and highly important in the Indian religions of Middle America, having a spiritual significance, we shall devote more attention to them at this point.

As time passes, scholars of Indian religions are comprehending more fully the deep spiritual meaning attached to these and numerous other religious symbols which were regarded with such reverence by the American aborigines; therefore, the spiritual significance of the Quetzalcoatl symbols is understood more fully and looked upon more sympathetically today than during any period since the Spanish conquest.

QUETZAL FEATHERS, PRECIOUS STONES, AND PRE-MORTAL LIFE

The Nahuatl Indian worshipers of the Valley of Mexico believed in the pre-mortal existence of Quetzalcoatl as well as the pre-mortal life of all human beings. Each person before coming to this earth was thought to have lived in a celestial world which was "surrounded by turquoise and quetzal plumes, precious things symbolizing the soul" or the spirit of men.[8] The sun was regarded as their celestial world. The following Aztec poem clearly shows the existence of spiritual bonds between the individual and the sun:

> I offer, offer flowering cocoa:
> That I may be sent to the House of the Sun!
> Beautiful and very rich is the crown of quetzal plumes:
> May I know the House of the Sun; may I go to that place!
> Oh, no one contains in his soul the lovely inebriate flower:
> Sparse cocoa flowers giving their fragrance in Huexotzinco's water.
> Each time the sun climbs this mountain my heart cries and is sad:
> Would it were the flower of my heart, painted in beautiful colors!
> The King of those who return sings of the flowers!
> There is flowery intoxication; rejoice at the feast, oh ye princes;
> There is beautiful dancing: *This is the House of Our Father the Sun.*
> *We stand on the turquoise wall: the quetzal wood is surrounded;*
> He who dwells in caves is by the water.
> Here may it end at last, the plain of the serpent;
> I carry over my shoulder a turquoise shield,
> Trembling in the wind the red flower of winter.[9]

It seems quite evident that the "House of the Sun" could be none other than the firmament; and it was said to have been surrounded by quetzal plumes and turquoise, sacred symbols of the spirits of men. In the words of Laurette Séjourné:

> The sun is called the *King of those who return*: it would be difficult to find more exact proof of the Nahuatl belief in the heavenly origin of the individual.[10]

The fact that the sky is described in the poem as the house of quetzal plumes, and turquoise (one of the precious symbolic stones) is also mentioned as being there, corroborate a part of Quetzalcoatl myth, wherein this "White and Bearded God" sang: "I shall depart from my house of quetzalli feathers, my house of jade."[11]

Quetzalcoatl continues in lamentation:

> . . . It was an evil thing that one day I left my house. May those who are absent be sad. I took it for hardness and pearl. May he who has a body of earth be glad and sing; I was not reared afflicted with servile labour.[12]

----

[8]Laurette Séjourné, *Burning Waters—Thought and Religion in Ancient Mexico* (London, 1956), p. 62.
[9]Angel Maria Garibay, "Romances de la Muerte," *Las Letras Patrias* (Mexico, 1954), No. 2, p. 18.
[10]Séjourné, *op. cit.*, p. 62.
[11]*Anales de Cuauhtitlan* (*Imprenta Universitaria*, Mexico, 1945), p. 9.
[12]*Ibid.*, pp. 10-11.

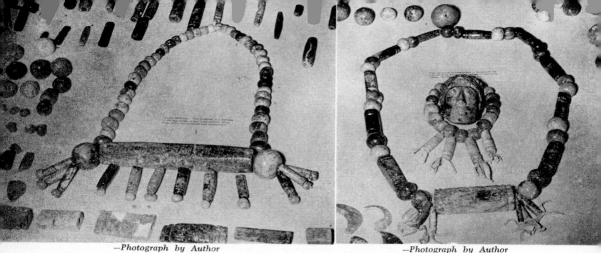

Fig. 69:　Jade Beads from Sacred Well

Fig. 70:　Jade Beads and Other Precious Stones

These jade beads and other sacred stones were dredged from the Sacred Well at Chichén Itzá by Edward Herbert Thompson. His collection is housed in the Peabody Museum, Cambridge, Massachusetts.

It is the opinion of Laurette Séjourné that "The absent ones whose sympathy he asks for can be none other than the inhabitants of the celestial world whence he has suddenly descended."[13] His allusion to those who have "body of earth" must be directed to mortal beings, "to those who have no recollection of their divine origin."

According to a Mexican archaeologist, "Belief in the spiritual principle appears to be the very basis of the Nahuatl religion. All Aztec testimonies clearly show man to be the incarnation of a celestial particle. Here, for example, are the words in which a Tenochtitlán father announces his daughter's pregnancy:[14]

'Know then all of you that our lord has had mercy, for the Lady N., a young maiden recently married, has within her a precious stone and a rich feather, since the young woman is now pregnant. . . .'"

The same religious doctrine is clearly expressed in the midwife's words to a newborn baby:

My well loved and tender son . . . know and understand that thy house is not here. . . . This house wherein thou art born is but a nest, an inn at which thou hast arrived, thy entry into this world! here dost thou bud and flower. . . . Thy true house is another.[16]

These quotations from ancient Aztec documents show that the

[13] Séjourné, *op. cit.*, p. 63.

[14] *Ibid.*, p. 55.

[15] Bernardino de Sahagún, *Historia General de las Cosas de Nueva España* (Editorial Nueva España, S. A., Mexico, 1946), vol. 1, p. 571, cited in Séjourné, p. 55.

[16] Séjourné, *op. cit.*, p. 84.

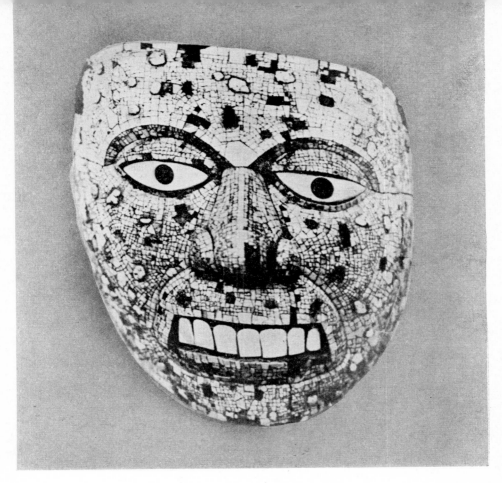

Fig. 71:   MASK OF QUETZALCOATL

Moctzuma presented Hernando Cortes with this " . . . grinning mask of Quetzalcoatl, the
white god and messiah of the Aztecs whose advent Aztec prophecies had long foretold."
The mask was taken to Europe where it has remained until the present time.

Indians of Mexico believed in the divine nature of mortals and that
quetzal feathers and precious stones were symbolic of their spirits;
and so "the plumed serpent is the sign of the revelation of the
heavenly origin of man."[17]

Since the worshipers of Quetzalcoatl believed that the celestial
world was decorated with quetzal feathers, with jade, turquoise,
and other precious stones, each of these became a sacred symbol
not only of the spirit of man, but also of spiritual, celestial life, the
life to which the spirit may attain following mortal death. Since
Quetzalcoatl was regarded by the Indians as the God of the pre-
mortal spirit world, the Creator and Redeemer of man, who now

———————
[17]*Ibid.*, p. 71.

reigns as the Lord of the celestial world, quetzal feathers and precious stones were regarded also as symbols of the "White and Bearded God."

PLUMED HEADDRESSES AND MASKS

Throughout all of Meso-America the various Indian cultures used masks and feathered ornaments very extensively. Because of our religious background and experiences, it is practically impossible for us to place ourselves in their attitude of mind and belief; however, the following may help us partly to understand:

"This aspiration toward the divine throws light on one characteristic of Meso-American culture: the importance of masks and feathered ornaments. It is understandable that once certain high degrees of consciousness are reached, one would wish to clothe the human figure in holy dignity. We may even wonder whether the headdresses which give expression to the dramatic metamorphosis of the serpent of the earth into the plumed serpent are not part of an attempt to convert the body into a hieroglyph for the mystic formula: only thus uplifted does the heart attain to its true centre."[18]

We learn from a short passage from the *Annals of Cuauhtitlan* the origin in the Nahuatl religion of the symbolism of these adornments. According to the Quetzalcoatl myth, when this god received a body he looked in a mirror and was terrified, declaring that he would never consent to show himself to his subjects in such a form. Coyotlinahuatl (the double coyote) stated that he would change this condition. He suggested:

Son of mine, I say that thou shouldst go out so that thy vassals might see thee; and I shall adorn thee that they may see thee. . . .[19]

Coyotlinahuatl immediately set to work and made for Quetzalcoatl

. . . first a dress of quetzal feathers that crossed him from the shoulder to the waist. Then he made him his turquoise mask, and took red dye, with which he reddened his lips, took yellow dye, with which he made little squares on his forehead, then he drew in his teeth as if they were serpent's, and made his wig and his beard of blue feathers and of red guacamaya feathers, and arranged them very well, letting them fall down the back: and when all that finery was made, he gave Quetzalcoatl the mirror. When he looked at him-

[18]*Ibid.*, pp. 130-131.
[19]*Anales de Cuauhtitlan, op. cit.*, p. 9.

—*Art Work by Huberta Berg Robison*

Fig. 72:   LINTEL 9, YAXCHILAN, MEXICO

Fig. 73:   LINTEL 54, YAXCHILAN, MEXICO

Some of the most beautiful and elaborate stone carvings found anywhere in ancient America were made by the Maya craftsmen at Yaxchilan. Since the center of Maya life was religion, it was natural for those ancient artists to portray their priests and rulers wearing beautiful plumed headdresses, jade ornament of various kinds, and the serpent symbol.

self, he saw he was very beautiful, and it was then that Quetzalcoatl at once left his retreat where he had been at watch and prayer. . . .[20]

Laurette Séjourné reached the following conclusions:

"Evidently these ornaments, that had the power of ridding him of the horror his body inspired, symbolized a superhuman state. That is why they appear in Teotihuacán images, and it is worth noting how closely the latter, wig and all, correspond to the mythical description. . . . The feathers that cover him [Quetzalcoatl] mark his entry into the light of the spiritual world."[21] Just prior to his death, it is claimed that Quetzalcoatl ". . . put on his insignia of feathers and green mask."[22]

PLUMED SERPENT AND OTHER AZTEC GODS

Since the principal symbol of Quetzalcoatl was the "plumed

[20]Angel Maria Garibay, *Historia de la Literatura Nahuatl, op. cit.,* vol. 1, p. 311.
[21]Séjourné, *op. cit.,* p. 132.
[22]*Anales de Cuauhtitlan, op. cit.,* p. 9.

serpent," and Quetzalcoatl was the principal god in the Nahuatl religion, it was natural for the Aztec Indians to connect serpents and feathers with several of their other gods and goddesses. For example, we read the following about Huitzilopochtli, the war god, ". . . [he] hurls upon men the fiery serpent [symbol of purifying penitence], the fiery auger [instrument that makes flame rise from a solid body], that is to say, war, devastating torrent, consuming fire" [devourer of darkness and heaviness].[23]

Huitzilopochtli, it was claimed, was born of the goddess Coatlicue. According to the Aztec documents, her conception took place as follows:

. . . it is said that one day while she was sweeping, a feathery ball descended upon her like a lump of thread, and she took it and put it in her bosom close to her belly, beneath her petticoats, and after having swept she wished to take hold of it and could not find it, from which they say she became pregnant. . . .[24]

According to Laurette Séjourné, "As Coatlicue is the Earth Goddess, it is clear that the feathers that allow her to give birth to an immortal symbolize the principle that saves matter from the law of destruction."[25] Another name for this goddess was Quazolotl, which identifies her as "she of the two heads, she of the divided head." She was decapitated, and two snake heads emerged from her mutilated neck. These two serpents were covered with precious jewels, a sign of divinity.[26]

FATHER AND MOTHER IN HEAVEN

Father Bernardino de Sahagún and other early Catholic writers, who received their information directly from the Indians during the early days of the Spanish conquest, recorded some pertinent information which indicates that the Indians not only believed in a premortal existence of man but also claimed that human beings had a father and mother in heaven.[27] They believed that men and women are actually the offspring of divine beings. Father Sahagún recorded the following Nahuatl belief which was reported to him by the Aztecs:

------

[23]Sahagún, cited in Séjourné, *op. cit.*, p. 158.
[24]*Ibid.*, p. 159.
[25]*Ibid.*, p. 157.
[26]*Ibid.*, pp. 160-161.
[27]Laurette Séjourné, *op. cit.*, p. 78, states: "The Nahuatl word for the place where the heavenly pair abide, *Tlacapillachiualoya*, means place where the 'children of men are made.'"

Oh, precious stone, oh, rich feather . . . thou wert made in the place where are the great *God and Goddess* which are above the heavens [in the celestial world]! . . . *Thy mother and thy father, celestial woman and celestial man, made and reared thee.* . . . Thou hast come to this world from afar, poor and weary. . . . Our Lord Quetzalcoatl, who *is the Creator*, has put into this dust a precious stone and a rich feather.[28]

Since precious stones and rich feathers were Aztec symbols of the spirits of men and women, we learn in the foregoing statement that the Indians of Meso-America believed that they have been born to heavenly parents in a celestial world prior to their coming into

Fig. 74: JADE BEADS IN MERIDA
MUSEUM

—Photograph by Author

mortality. They believed, therefore, that mortal beings are of a divine origin, actually the offspring of a *"great God and Goddess . . . father and mother, celestial woman and celestial man, . . ."*

In another Aztec poem we read: "Oh, my friends, would that we were immortal. Oh, friends, where is the land in which we do not die? Shall it be that I go? Does my [heavenly] *mother live there?* Does my [heavenly] *father live there?*"[29]

The Quiché Mayas of Guatemala also believed that mortals

---

[28]Sahagún, *op. cit.*, vol. 1, p. 608.
[29]Angel Maria Garibay, *Las Letras Patrias* (Mexico, 1954), No. 2, p. 12.

were the offspring of heavenly parents. We read in the *Popol Vuh,
The Sacred Book of the Ancient Quiché Maya*:

> And here we shall set forth the revelation, the declaration, the narration
> of all that was hidden, the revelation by Tzacol, Bitol, Alom, Qaholom, . . .[30]

The translators of this Indian book explain this statement as
follows:

> These are the names of the divinity, arranged in pairs of creators in accord
> with the dual conception of the Quiché: *Tzacol* and *Bitol, Creator* and *Maker.
> Alom,* the *mother god,* she who conceived the sons, from *al,* "son," *alán,* "to
> give birth." *Qaholom,* the *father god* who begat the sons, from *Qahol,* "Son
> of the Father," *qaholah,* "to beget." Father Francisco Ximénez [Hē-may'-nes]
> [the first padre to translate the *Popol Vuh* from Quiché into Spanish] calls
> them *Mother* and *Father;* they are the *Great Father* and the *Great Mother,* so
> called by the Indians; and, according to Las Casas, *they are in heaven.*[31]

GOSPEL DOCTRINE OF DIVINE ORIGIN OF MAN

These Indian beliefs of the divine origin of man—the fact that
they believed that mortals were actually and literally born into the
spirit world, a celestial realm, to heavenly parents; that they had a
father and a mother there—are very astounding in the light of the
fact that before the restoration of the gospel of Jesus Christ to the
Prophet Joseph Smith the Christian world had lost the knowledge
of this very important phase of man's existence. No Christian de-
nomination in 1830 actually believed and taught that mortal beings
were actually and literally the children of a Father and Mother in
heaven—divine Parents having begotten spirit offspring or children;
in fact, few churches have accepted that belief even down to the
present time.

Where did the American Indians get such a belief? That concept is taught clearly in the holy scriptures, although most Christian
denominations cannot understand such a sublime doctrine and
therefore reject it. It should be remembered that the ancestors of
the Indians had a copy of the Old Testament written on plates
of brass and that Christ visited the ancient Americans following his
resurrection. From these sources the true doctrine of the literal
Fatherhood of God and of a Mother in heaven had filtered down
to the time of the Spanish conquest in the Indians' traditions. In

---

[30]*Popol Vuh, The Sacred Book of the Ancient Quiché Maya* (Tr. into English by Delia
Goetz and Sylvanus G. Morley, 1950, Norman, Oklahoma), p. 78.
[31]*Ibid.,* footnote no. 3.

this and many other respects, the aborigines were nearer to the divine gospel truths than were their European conquerors.

OLD TESTAMENT TEACHINGS—MEN THE OFFSPRING OF DEITY

The prophets of ancient Israel thoroughly understood that all people of the earth are literally the sons and daughters of God the Eternal Father, claiming that he begat their spirit bodies. For example, we read the following in the Hebrew scriptures: "Let the Lord, the God of the spirits of all flesh, set a man over the congregation."[32] "And they fell upon their faces, and said, 'Oh, God, the God of the spirits of all flesh, shall one man sin, and wilt thou be wroth with all the congregation?' "[33] And again we read in the Old Testament: "I said, ye are gods, and *all of you sons of the Most High.*"[34] The author of Ecclesiastes pointed out this divine truth:

[32]Numbers 27:16.
[33]*Ibid.*, 16:22.
[34]Psalm 82:6.

Fig. 75: PLUMED SERPENT, CHICHEN ITZA

"Then shall the dust return to the earth as it was, and the spirit shall return unto God who gave it,"[35] reminding us of the Aztecs' statement of returning to the home of their immortal Father and immortal Mother "where one does not die!"

TEACHINGS OF JESUS AND HIS APOSTLES

Throughout the entire mortal ministry of the Man of Galilee, he continuously reminded human beings that they were actually and literally children of God. He did not refer to God our Father in a figurative sense. For example, the Master taught the apostles to pray as follows: "Our Father which art in heaven"; and this was the pattern for all the children of men to follow. Shortly following his resurrection, the Master said unto Mary Magdalene: ". . . Touch me not; for I am not yet ascended to my Father: but go to my brethren, and say unto them, *I ascend unto my Father, and your Father;* and to my God, and your God."[36]

Jesus taught the doctrine of the Fatherhood of God so thoroughly while in Palestine that his apostles later made such pertinent statements as the following:

Furthermore we have had fathers of our flesh which corrected us, and we gave them reverence: shall we not much rather be in subjection unto the Father of spirits, and live?[37]

The Spirit itself beareth witness with our spirit, that we are the children of God:

And if children, then heirs; heirs of God, and joint-heirs with Christ; if so be that we suffer with him, that we may be also glorified together.[38]

NEPHITES' KNOWLEDGE OF GOD THE FATHER

Christ not only proclaimed the divine truth to the Nephites that he was the Only Begotten Son of the Eternal Father, but he also declared that all men and women were Elohim's offspring. Also, this was the message of the Nephite prophets, as well as that of their predecessors, the Jaredites.

Thus the ancient Americans of Book of Mormon days worshiped God the Father, regarding him literally as their personal

[35]Ecclesiastes 12:7.
[36]John 20:17.
[37]Hebrews 12:9.
[38]Romans 8:16-17.

Father. He was reverently spoken of as the "Eternal Father," "the very Eternal Father," "the Father of the Only Begotten Son," and other similar titles. For example, numerous lofty expressions which give adoration to the Eternal Father, such as the following one proclaimed by Christ to Nephi, appear in the Book of Mormon:

. . . the Spirit [the spirit personage of Christ] cried with a loud voice, saying: Hosanna to the Lord, the most high God; for he is God over all the earth, yea, even above all. And blessed art thou, Nephi, because thou believest in the Son of the most high God; wherefore, thou shalt behold the things which thou hast desired.

. . . thou shalt also behold a man descending out of heaven, and him shall ye witness; and after ye have witnessed him ye shall bear record that it is the Son of God.[39]

We also quote from a glorious vision given to Father Lehi:

. . . And being thus overcome with the Spirit, he was carried away in a vision, even that he saw . . . God sitting upon his throne, surrounded with numberless concourses of angels in the attitude of singing and praising their God. . . .

. . . he [Lehi] did exclaim many things unto the Lord; such as: Great and marvelous are thy works, O Lord God Almighty! Thy throne is high in the heavens, and thy power, and goodness, and mercy are over all the inhabitants of the earth; and, because thou art merciful, thou wilt not suffer those who come unto thee that they shall perish![40]

Numerous declarations are recorded in the Book of Mormon which show that the prophets had a thorough and comprehensive understanding that the Eternal Father and the Son are two separate personages. A few examples from the Nephite scriptures will illustrate this point. To quote:

. . . Behold the Lamb of God, yea, even the Son of the Eternal Father! . . .[41]

[Again we read] . . . the Lamb of God is the Son of the Eternal Father, and the Savior of the world; and that all men must come unto him, or they cannot be saved.[42]

. . . I know that Jesus Christ shall come, yea, the Son, the Only Begotten of the Father, full of grace, and mercy, and truth. . . .[43]

The Eternal Father and the Only Begotten Son each testified of the existence of the other, as is learned from the Book of Mormon. For example, the Eternal Father spoke from heaven to the Nephites

---

[39]1 Nephi 11:6-7.
[40]*Ibid.*, 1:8, 14.
[41]*Ibid.*, 11:21.
[42]*Ibid.*, 13:40.
[43]Alma 5:48; 9:26; 13:9.

and introduced the Son at the time Christ appeared to the ancient Americans.[44] The resurrected Lord told the Nephites: "Behold, I am Jesus Christ, whom the prophets testified shall come into the world."[45] "I was with the Father from the beginning."[46] ". . . I came into the world to do the will of my Father, because my Father sent me."[47]

The Eternal Father was spoken of as being not only the Father of Jesus Christ, but also the Father of the entire human family; he was the Supreme Being unto whom all intelligent beings turn for inspiration, help, and guidance. Under his direction all things pertaining to the administration of the affairs of the universe were accomplished. Christ taught the Nephites regarding the Fatherhood of God as follows: "For, if ye forgive men their trespasses your heavenly Father will forgive also you; . . ."[48]

The prophets of the Book of Mormon instructed the people to "pray unto the Father in the name of Christ," and he would hear and answer their prayers.[49] Jesus was very definite on that subject in his teachings to the Nephites when he appeared to them following his resurrection. He said: ". . . ye shall call upon the Father in my name. . . ."[50] "After this manner therefore pray ye: Our Father who art in heaven, . . ."[51] "And now I go unto the Father. . . ."[52] One is not surprised, therefore, in the closing chapter of the Book of Mormon to read the words of Moroni, wherein he said: "And when ye shall receive these things, I would exhort you that you would ask God, the Eternal Father, in the name of Christ, if these things are not true; . . ."[53]

Thus the idea of the Fatherhood of God is inherent in the Book of Mormon. It radiates from it as light from the sun. It is rich in expression of the intimacy of the relations between the Father and his earth-children.

This concept of the Fatherhood of God in ancient America was retained from generation to generation, even though the moral conduct of the people lapsed from time to time. The Nephites prayed to and worshiped the Father in the name of Christ, and remembered

---

[44]3 Nephi 11:3-10.
[45]*Ibid.*, 11:10.
[46]*Ibid.*, 9:15.
[47]*Ibid.*, 27:13; 24:1; 26:51.
[48]*Ibid.*, 13:14.

[49]2 Nephi 32:9; 33:12; Mormon 9:21; Moroni 4:2.
[50]3 Nephi 27:7.
[51]*Ibid.*, 13:9.
[52]*Ibid.*, 27:28.
[53]Moroni 10:4.

that upon completion of his ministry among them, Jesus ascended unto the Father—his Father and theirs—the universal Father. Following the destruction of the Nephite nation, the doctrine of Heavenly Parents was retained down to the coming of the Spaniards.

Since Christ and all the Book of Mormon prophets taught the ancient Americans that they were the offspring of Divine Beings, it

—Photograph by Author

Fig. 76:   Quetzalcoatl Serpents

Plumed serpents housed in the National Mexican Museum, Mexico City.

appears to the writer that the Indians could have obtained their belief of a Heavenly Father and Heavenly Mother from no other place than from their ancestors, the Nephites.

Latter-day Saint Concept of Heavenly Parents

When the fulness of the gospel broke forth from heaven in revelation to the Prophet Joseph Smith in the latter days, a very comprehensive understanding of man and his personal relationships to Deity was received. The stupendous truth of the existence of a Heavenly Mother, as well as of a Heavenly Father, was revealed to the Prophet Joseph Smith. A complete realization that we are the offspring of Heavenly Parents—that we were begotten and born into the spirit world, a celestial realm, and grew to maturity there —became an integral part of latter-day gospel knowledge. These verities are basic in the plan of eternal progression.

The prophets of our dispensation have clearly explained the doctrine of heavenly parenthood. In the words of President Joseph F. Smith, and his counselors, John R. Winder and Anthon H. Lund:

"Man, as a spirit, was begotten and born of Heavenly Parents, and reared to maturity in the eternal mansions of the Father prior to coming upon the earth in a temporal body to undergo an experience in mortality."[54]

In her famous poem "O, My Father," Eliza R. Snow expressed beautifully the sublime doctrine of a Father and Mother in heaven. Her poem shows as deep an understanding of pertinent truths regarding pre-mortal life, and as convincing an assurance of immortality and future union with Heavenly Parents as can be found in literature. Let us compare a few lines from her classic presentation of these eternal truths with the Nahuatl's poem reported by Father Sahagún.

L.D.S. Poem: O My Father

O my Father, Thou that dwellest
  In the high and glorious place!
When shall I regain thy presence,
  And again behold thy face?
In thy holy habitation,
  Did my spirit once reside;
In my first primeval childhood,
  Was I nurtured near thy side?

❈ ❈ ❈

I had learned to call thee Father,
  Through thy Spirit from on high;
But until the key of knowledge
  Was restored, I knew not why.
In the heav'ns are parents single?
  No; the thought makes reason stare!
Truth is reason, truth eternal,
  Tells me I've a Mother there.

When I leave this frail existence,
  When I lay this mortal by,
Father, Mother, may I meet you
  In your royal courts on high?
Then at length, when I've completed
  All you sent me forth to do,
With your mutual approbation
  Let me come and dwell with you.[55]

Extracts from Nahuatl Poems:

Where are the great God and Goddess
Which are above the heavens?

❈ ❈ ❈

Thy mother and thy father,
Celestial woman and celestial man,
made and reared thee.[56]

———

Here on earth our hearts say:
"Oh, my friends, would that we were
  immortal,
Oh, friends, where is the land
in which one does not die?

Shall it be that I go?
Does my mother live there?
Does my father live there?"[57]

---

[54]Joseph F. Smith, *Improvement Era*, vol. 13, p. 80.
[55]*Hymns of the Church of Jesus Christ of Latter-day Saints* (Salt Lake City, 1950), p. 270.
[56]Sahagún, *op. cit.*, vol. 1, p. 608.
[57]Garibay, *op. cit.*, p. 12.

Fig. 77:   Altar at Mayapan, Yucatan

Observe the beautiful workmanship displayed in plumes and plumed serpents, symbols of the Mayas' God.

Quetzalcoatl the Redeemer

Since the religion of Quetzalcoatl maintained that mortals were children of heavenly parents, it was of importance for that religion to provide a way whereby believers could eventually join their Heavenly Father and Mother; and so the principal purpose of the worship of Quetzalcoatl, like that of other vital religions, was to prepare its devotees for life beyond the grave.   Thus the aborigines had an unusually forceful doctrine regarding the immortality of man, with a Savior playing a leading role in bringing about that immortality and in offering rewards beyond the grave.

Many examples could be given which would indicate that the Indians regarded Quetzalcoatl as their redeemer. He was claimed to be the power responsible for movement within the World of the Dead, being the spiritual force which made it possible for the deceased to proceed from that world into the kingdom of the spirits; and so the soul through Quetzalcoatl's power as redeemer emerged from the World of the Dead into immortal life.

Quetzalcoatl is represented on the Codex Borgia "holding a skeleton into which he is breathing life,[58] which illustrates his power to bring the dead to life.

It is even claimed that he shed his own blood for the cleansing of mortals, thereby bringing about their redemption.

---

[58]Séjourné, *op. cit.*, p. 136-137.

According to Aztec belief, he rescued the souls of the deceased from the World of the Dead. At the time of Quetzalcoatl's resurrection, it was claimed ". . . that all the rare birds appeared . . . for which reason they [the Aztecs] called him Lord of Dawn."[59] They believed that perhaps the most desirable status to attain was to become a colorful bird, and so the souls of warriors ". . . became various kinds of feathered birds, rich and colourful";[60] and it was also claimed that in this form they went to meet the newborn sun and escort him to the zenith. Human spirits or souls were symbolized by birds, butterflies, and flowers. In a ". . . discourse announcing to the dead man his entry into the other world, the butterfly is mentioned as being among the inhabitants of heaven."[61]

The Indians regarded Quetzalcoatl as the one who redeemed physical matter. For example, they claimed that he breathed divine breath into the Fifth Sun, moving it from its condition of death or inertia.[62] Laurette Séjourné interprets the foregoing information. given by Father Sahagún, as follows:

> . . . if we remember that the newly-born Fifth Sun was launched upon the heavens by the wind, we can understand how such wind must be the spiritual breath that allows of interior birth. The god symbolic of winds brings in his train the laws that subdue matter: he it is who draws opposites together and reconciles them; he converts death into true life, and causes a marvellous reality to flower out of the dark realm of every-day. It is just because he possesses these powers that Quetzalcoatl is considered the supreme magician— he who holds the secret of all enchantments. That is why the day of the week ruled over by this god is dedicated to necromancers and sorcerers of all kinds.[63]

It was through Quetzalcoatl's redeeming power, therefore, that the Fifth Sun, according to Nahuatl belief, was brought to life and became the celestial world, or the highest heaven, of the deceased.

Laurette Séjourné informs us that ". . . in earlier centres . . . we find symbols of resurrection, a fact which should not surprise us, since Quetzalcoatl's transcendence is due precisely to his role as Redeemer. This role, confirmed by all documents, is expressed in

[59]*Anales de Cuauhtitlán* (Codice Chimalpopoca, Imprenta Universitaria, Mexico, 1945), p. 9.
[60]Séjourné, *op. cit.*, p. 144.
[61]*Idem.*
[62]Sahagún, *op. cit.*, vol. 2, pp. 15-16.
[63]Séjourné, *op. cit.*, p. 136.

images of surprisingly suggestive power in the story of his visit to the land of the dead."[64] The *Anales of Cuauhtitlán* states that:

> . . . They say that when he [Quetzalcoatl] died dawn did not appear for four days, because he had gone to dwell among the dead; and that in four days he provided himself with arrows; for which reason in eight days there appeared the great star called Quetzalcoatl. And they add that he was enthroned as Lord.[65]

Venus, "great star of Quetzalcoatl," first shines as the evening star and later as the morning star. "After first appearing in the western sky, Venus disappears 'underground' and remains hidden for several days, reappearing, brighter than ever, in the eastern sky when she reunites with the sun."[66] Thus Quetzalcoatl, believed by

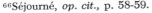

[64]*Ibid.*, p. 69.
[65]*Anales de Cuauhtitlán, op. cit.*, p. 9.
[66]Séjourné, *op. cit.*, p. 58-59.

Fig. 78:   QUETZALCOATL, THE PLUMED SERPENT

Fig. 79:   QUETZALCOATL, THE SKY SERPENT

the worshipers first to have been a celestial man, came to earth as a mortal, died, visited the World of the Dead, arose from that world, glorious and radiant, and then ascended to heaven, marking the path to be followed by man. The Quetzalcoatl religion maintained that "The soul follows the same route: she descends from her celestial home and enters the darkness of matter, only to rise again, glorious."[67] ". . . The Meso-American peoples thought of Quetzalcoatl as a man made god. . . . By saving himself, man—of whom Quetzalcoatl is the archetype—saves Creation. This is why Quetzalcoatl is above all the Redeemer."[68]

A Nahuatl manuscript, written shortly after the discovery of America and published in Spanish under the title *Legendas de Los Soles* (Legend of the Sun), gives a much more detailed account of the myth of Quetzalcoatl's visit to the World of the Dead than does the *Anales de Cuauhtitlán*, previously quoted. It states:

Then the gods took counsel and said, "Who shall dwell here? The sky is fixed; and the Lady Earth, who shall dwell therein, oh gods?" They were all troubled.

But there went Quetzalcoatl; he came to the Kingdom of the Dead, to the Lord and Lady of the Kingdom of the Dead. Thereupon he said: "Behold why I have come. Thou art concealing precious bones. I have come to fetch them."

But the King of the Dead told him: "What wilt thou do, Quetzalcoatl?"

And he answered again, "The gods are troubled about who shall inhabit the earth."

The Lord of the Kingdom of the Dead said, "It is well. Sound my snail trumpet, and four times bear it about the circle of my emerald throne."

But as the snail had no gimlet he called the worms. They made holes through which the wasps and night bees entered at once.

Again said the Lord of the Kingdom of the Dead: "It is well, take the bones!"

But he told his vassals the dead: "Yet tell him, oh gods, that he must leave them behind!"

But Quetzalcoatl answered: "No, I shall take them for ever."

But his double said to him, "Tell them I shall come to take them!" With this he was able to return upward, and he took the precious bones. In one place were the bones of a man, in another of a woman. He gathered them up, he made a bundle, and he took them with him.

But again the Lord of the Dead said to his vassals: "Gods, verily he has taken them, the precious bones. Come and dig him a hole."

They came and did so: he fell into the hole, churning the earth; the quail

---

[67]*Ibid.*, p. 59.
[68]*Ibid.*, pp. 66, 71.

frightened him; he fell like one dead; and so he scattered the precious bones on the ground, and the quail pecked and ate them.

But Quetzalcoatl soon revived, wept over what had happened, and said to his double: "My double, how shall this thing be?"

And he said, "How shall it be? It is true you have lost them. So be it!"

Then he gathered them up, picking them one by one, and made of them a bundle and took them to Tamoanohan.

And when he reached Tamoanohan, Quilaztli ground them down again; he threw the ground bones into a precious earthen pot, and upon them Quetzalcoatl threw his blood, taken from a living member, and then all the gods did penance, for which reason they said: "Those worthy of the gods are born, since for us they did deserving penance."[69]

Certain points of significance should be noted in the foregoing Quetzalcoatl myth. First, immediately following his death and prior to his resurrection, the "White and Bearded God" went to the World of the Dead and stayed a certain length of time. Second, the purpose of his going was to bring from that realm those who were there. This fact is indicated in Quetzalcoatl's efforts to obtain "precious bones" of a man and a woman and bring them from that world. Third, the final deliverance of those bones from the World of the Dead and bringing them to life—in other words, bringing about the resurrection—was achieved when Quetzalcoatl threw his blood upon the bones. They became "living members," "born of the gods."

CHRIST THE REDEEMER

It is a fact of much importance that the Indians at the time of the Spanish conquest still retained a concept that their Redeemer's (Quetzalcoatl's) blood had something to do with their resurrection and redemption.

Book of Mormon students know the source of this Indian belief. They immediately recall the fact that the prophets in ancient America taught the doctrine that Christ's blood was shed for the sins of the world. He was claimed to be the Lamb of God whose blood atoned for the death of man; and the people were taught that the righteous saints would be "cleansed by the blood of the Lamb."[70] Thus the Quetzalcoatl myth indicates that the doctrine of the atonement of Jesus Christ, proclaimed by the ancestors of the American Indians, was handed down—however, in a paganized, polluted form—

----

[69]*Legendas de Los Soles* (tr. from Nahuatl by Angel Maria Garibay and quoted in his *Historia de la Literatura Nahual*. Editorial Porrua, Mexico, 1953), pp. 255-256.
[70]Mormon 9:6; 1 Nephi 12:11; Ether 13:10-11; 13:11; 34:36.

from age to age by the aborigines until the coming of the Spaniards. Sufficient truth, however, remained in the Quetzalcoatl myth for us to recognize that it stems back into the original gospel revelations.

The Indians' traditions of Quetzalcoatl's visit to the World of the Dead supply additional evidence on this point. Let us recall briefly the teachings of the scriptures regarding Christ's visit to the Spirit World, since the Indians' traditions have their roots in the gospel teachings of their ancestors, the Nephites and Lamanites. Of course, the scriptures give us the exact mission that the Master performed in the Spirit World and not merely a mythical account, as is found in the Quetzalcoatl religion. The Indians' traditions, however, show that they retained a partial knowledge of the true event. In referring to the scriptural account, let us quote from Peter:

> For Christ also hath once suffered for sins, the just for the unjust, that he might bring us to God, being put to death in the flesh, but quickened by the Spirit:
>
> By which also he went and preached unto the spirits in prison;
>
> Which sometimes were disobedient, when once the longsuffering of God waited in the days of Noah, while the ark was a preparing, wherein few, that is, eight souls were saved by water.[71]

Paul informed the Ephesian saints that the Messiah ". . . descended first into the lower parts of the earth. He that descended is the same also that ascended up far above all heavens, that he might fill all things."[72]

Several Book of Mormon prophets, ancestors of the American Indians, predicted that Christ would be in the tomb three days between death and resurrection, although they did not explain the details of his activities while there. For example, King Benjamin informed the Nephites that Jesus Christ would be crucified by the Jews, and that ". . . he shall rise the third day from the dead."[73] Nephi wrote: ". . . the Only Begotten of the Father . . . shall manifest himself unto them in the flesh, . . . Behold, they will crucify him; and after he is laid in the sepulchre for the space of three days he shall rise from the dead, with healing in his wings."[74] Samuel the Lamanite pre-

---

[71]1 Peter 3:18-20.
[72]Ephesians 4:9-10.
[73]Mosiah 3:10.
[74]2 Nephi 25:12-13.

—Art Work by Huberta Berg Robison

Fig. 80:   Lintel 52, Yaxchilan, Mexico

Fig. 81:   Stela 5, Yaxchilan, Mexico

Observe the extensive amount of jade and other precious stones worn by these Maya priests.

dicted that ". . . there shall be no light upon the face of the land, even from the time that he [Christ] shall suffer death, for the space of three days, to the time that he shall rise again from the dead."[75]

The Book of Mormon writers claimed that the Messiah would be resurrected and break the bands of death, bringing about a universal resurrection of the inhabitants of the entire world. The central theme of the Nephite record is Jesus Christ—his gospel and his accomplishments as the Redeemer of mankind. In order to call to the readers' memory some of the important Book of Mormon teachings on the atonement, we shall give a few quotations. For example, the Prophet Amulek stated:

Now, there is a death which is called a temporal death; and the death of Christ shall loose the bands of this temporal death, that all shall be raised from this temporal death.

[75]Helaman 14:20; 3 Nephi 10:9.

The spirit and the body shall be reunited again in its perfect form; both limb and joint shall be restored to its proper frame, even as we now are at this time; and we shall be brought to stand before God, knowing even as we know now, and have a bright recollection of all our guilt.

Now, this restoration shall come to all, both old and young, both bond and free, both male and female, both the wicked and the righteous; and even there shall not so much as a hair of their heads be lost; but every thing shall be restored to its perfect frame, as it is now, or in the body, and shall be brought and be arraigned before the bar of Christ the Son, and God the Father, and the Holy Spirit, which is one Eternal God, to be judged according to their works, whether they be good or whether they be evil.

Now, behold, I have spoken unto you concerning the death of the mortal body, and also concerning the resurrection of the mortal body. I say unto you that this mortal body is raised to an immortal body, that is from death, even from the first death unto life, that they can die no more; their spirits uniting with their bodies, never to be divided; thus the whole becoming spiritual and immortal, that they can no more see corruption.[76]

—*Photograph by Otto Done*

Fig. 82:   JADE BEADS, KAMINALJUYU

These jade beads were taken from a tomb in the archaeological site of Kaminaljuyu, situated in the outskirts of Guatemala City. It is claimed by archaeologists that this site dates back into the early Christian period (about A.D. 320), and so its beginning was contemporaneous with the latter portion of the Book of Mormon.

Abinadi taught the following: "But behold, the bands of death shall be broken, and the Son reigneth, and hath power over the dead; therefore he bringeth to pass the resurrection of the dead.

----

[76]Alma 11:42-45.

. . ."[77] Mormon wrote to his son Moroni: ". . . Behold I say unto you that ye shall have hope through the atonement of Christ and the power of the resurrection, to be raised to life eternal, . . ."[78] When he visited the New World following his resurrection, Jesus instructed the Nephites: "Behold, I am the law, and the light. Look unto me, and endure to the end, and ye shall live; for unto him that endureth to the end will I give eternal life."[79]

Conclusion

Since the forefathers of the American Indians told the Nephites about Christ's visit to the World of the Dead while his body lay in the tomb and since that information was had by the aborigines at the time of the discovery of the New World, such traditions furnish irrefutable evidence that the ancestors of the Indians had had the true gospel of Jesus Christ, as is claimed in the Book of Mormon, and that portions of that gospel in a polluted form survived among the aborigines to the days of the Spanish conquest.

The same holds true in regards to Christ's breaking the bands of death and bringing about the immortality and eternal life of man.

Many of the beliefs of the Indian worshipers of Quetzalcoatl presented in this chapter resemble Christian doctrines sufficiently to make it possible for us to recognize that they had a common origin. Certainly Jesus Christ is the Redeemer of the human family, and his plan of salvation is presented beautifully in the Book of Mormon. He climaxed all the teachings therein by personally visiting the ancient Americans and establishing his Church among them. One readily recognizes in the Quetzalcoatl religion many teachings basically akin to Christian doctrines.

------

[77]Mosiah 15:20.
[78]Moroni 7:41.
[79]3 Nephi 15:9.

CHAPTER 7

TEOTIHUACAN – CITY OF THE GODS

ANCIENT TOLLAN OR TULA

Ixtlilxochitl and other learned Indians who transmitted their knowledge either in writing or by personally informing the Spanish chroniclers claimed that the founders of their ancient civilization built a city called Tollan or Tula. In the Nahuatl language, the word Tollan means "Great city or metropolis."[1] The most reliable archaeological and historical evidences indicate that the builders of Tollan were called Nahuas or Toltecs. The *Works of Ixtlilxochitl,* the writing of the scholarly Catholic padre, Sahagún, and other similar authoritative sources maintain that the city was built for the religious capital of the Toltecs. It was also claimed that Quetzalcoatl originated his religion at that place.

ORIGIN OF THE TOLTEC CULTURE

Father Bernardino de Sahagún stated that the Nahuatl religion had its beginning prior to B.C. 500. To quote:

As to the antiquity of this people, it is proven that for more than 2,000 years they have lived in this land now called New Spain, because through their ancient pictures there is evidence that the famous city called Tollan was destroyed a thousand years ago or very nearly . . . and as to the time it took to build it and the time it prospered before it was destroyed, it is consonant with truth that over 1,000 years passed, from which it follows that this land was populated at least 500 years before the Incarnation of our Redeemer. This famous and great city of Tollan, very rich and well-ordered, very wise and powerful, suffered the adverse fortune of Troy.[2]

One who is acquainted with the Book of Mormon knows that the founders of the Nephite (Nahuatl) culture left Jerusalem 600 years B.C. and that by 570 they were building a city in America which they named the City of Nephi after their prophet-leader. It is a marvel that Sahagún could have received from the Indians a date which corresponds so nearly with the time the Nephites arrived in the New World. The Toltecs or Nahuas, as described by Ixtlil-

---

[1]Laurette Séjourné, *Thought and Religion in Ancient Mexico,* p. 82.
[2]Fr. Bernardino de Sahagún, *Historia General de Las Casas de Nueva España,* (Editoria Nueva España, S. A. Mexico, 1946), vol. 1, p. 12.

xochitl, fit all the conditions corresponding to the Nephites as told about in the Book of Mormon.

The early writers say that Tollan was the ancient capital of the Nahuas. If it were founded as early as B.C. 500, as Father Sahagún

—Photograph by Author

Fig. 83: TEMPLE OF QUETZALCOATL, TEOTIHUACAN, MEXICO

claims, it could have been a Nephite city. Modern historians and archaeologists have searched diligently to identify this particular city. Since all of the capital cities of the plateau region of Mexico bore the name of Tollan, it has been impossible to identify definitely any of those cities as being the earliest capital of the Toltecs.

In 1941 a convention of American historians was held in Mexico City. One of the main topics for discussion was the identification of the ancient capital of Quetzalcoatl. The conclusion was drawn that the most favorable candidate for that city was the archaeological ruin of Tollan Xicotitlan (Tula, Hidalgo), situated 125 miles north of Mexico City. Laurette Séjourné vigorously opposes such a conclusion, claiming that Tula "dates back only to the tenth century, that is, to a moment when Meso-America suffered the brutal shock of mass invasion from nomad hunters and had strayed far from the mysticism of earlier epochs."[3] She is of the opinion that such a decision which declares Tula, Hidalgo, to be the ancient Nahuatl religious capital cannot be sustained either by documentary or archaeological evidences. She presents the argument that archaeologists have been working at that site for ten seasons, and with the exception of a few remarkable sculptures, have not unearthed any significant things to indicate that it was a first-rate city. She also maintains that these were imported motifs, and that this city cannot be considered as the site of the cradle of a glorious ancient culture. "The origins of this high culture [meaning apparently the culture that Book of Mormon students identify as Nephite] are a complete mystery," she says.[4] The Nephite culture was the forerunner of the Nahuatl culture, which developed the elaborate, paganized religion of Quetzalcoatl. This religion became filled with numerous symbols, many of which were undreamed of in Nephite days. Séjourné continues:

. . . Because of the appearance of certain tropical motifs, such as serpents, quetzal birds, tropical sea-shells and turtles, it has been thought to have come from the south; but though they may originally have emanated from other zones, these motifs are so strongly integrated into the spiritual unity of Teotihuacán that it is impossible to suppose they could have been transplanted there already converted into symbols. Of course the species represented must have been familiar to the Teotihuatecáns, but archaeology has shown that the peoples of these regions used to travel extensively. We cannot, however, just for this reason pre-suppose that elaborate cultural forms were transferred from one region to another, especially since the characteristic Nahuatl symbolism is not known to have existed anywhere else at this period. Yet it existed in Teotihuacán in exactly the same form in which the Aztecs revived it centuries later.[5]

[3]Séjourné, *op. cit.*, p. 83.
[4]*Ibid.*, p. 81.
[5]*Idem.*

Laurette Séjourné also maintains that the seeds of an earlier culture were transplanted to Teotihuacán, ". . . took roots in the new soil, and blossomed luxuriantly into the Nahuatl religion in all its richness. While artists were painting and carving the religious symbolic language in this huge sacred metropolis, the whole body of knowledge which characterizes Meso-American civilization developed into its final form. . . . The facts, moreover, agree with what the chroniclers always affirm: that the king of Tollan was Quetzalcoatl, Creator of all human wisdom."[6] Quetzalcoatl, she further states, was the one who established the "Parent Culture" in the New World about the time that the Man of Galilee established Christianity in the Holy Land.

In chapter three the writer identified the person who established this "Parent Culture" as the resurrected Messiah, who appeared to the Nephites in the City of Bountiful. It was also pointed out that Tula means "bountiful"; and so the ancient Nephites records, Indian traditions, and modern scholars all agree that the "White and Bearded God" appeared to the ancient Americans in the City of Tula or Bountiful and gave them their religion and culture.

The exact location of the City of Bountiful—or any other Book of Mormon city—is not known and will not be known until definite archaeological evidence or revelation from God gives us that information. Various people, however, make claims regarding the location of Zarahemla, Bountiful, the City of Nephi, and other Book of Mormon places. These claims cannot be sustained with the information and evidence available today.

Laurette Séjourné is of the opinion that Teotihuacán is the ancient Tula or Tollan where the "Fair God" appeared and established the religion of Quetzalcoatl. In presenting her viewpoint, it is not to be regarded that I accept her opinion as the correct one. It could be true that the religion of Quetzalcoatl could have developed at Teotihuacán, but that religion is merely a paganized form of the true gospel of Jesus Christ. It is not the original revelation of eternal verities from the mouth of the Master to the Nephites, who were perhaps the progenitors of the people at Teotihuacán.

According to Séjourné, a few centuries after the time of the Master, "Teotihuacán was already rising firm upon its foundation

---

[6]*Ibid.*, pp. 81, 83.

Fig. 84: PLUMED SERPENTS' HEADS, TEOTIHUACAN

Observe serpents' bodies running along the face of the Temple of Quetzalcoatl. Representations of quetzal feathers surround the serpents' heads.

and had developed the religion, arts, and sciences that were to prevail for more than fifteen centuries. . . . By the fourth century [A.D.] Teotihuacán already possessed great buildings ornamented with plumed serpents, . . ."[7]

NEPHITE RELIGION AND APOSTASY

At the time Christ appeared to the ancient Americans, the Nephites and Lamanites became one people. For approximately 200 years following that appearance, the people lived almost perfect lives, abiding continuously in harmony with the true gospel that the Master had given them.

During the third century A.D., numerous apostate ideas and practices appeared in their religious worship. Many churches arose. The people divided once again into Nephites and Lamanites. By A.D. 325 the major portion of the people—both Nephites and Lamanites—had dropped into a state of gross wickedness. A complete

[7]*Ibid.*, pp. 81-83.

apostasy from the true gospel of the Messiah had occurred. A devastating war broke out between the Nephites and Lamanites, which ended about A.D. 400 in the extermination of the Nephite nation.

It was during this period and following that the cult of Quetzalcoatl was profusely ornamenting the buildings at Teotihuacán with plumed serpents and the rain god symbols, according to Laurette Séjourné.

The hatred toward Jesus Christ was very intense during this period. Sometime between 400 and 421 A.D.—possibly toward the latter date—Moroni informed us in the Nephite records that he was hiding in a cave so he would not be apprehended by the Lamanites and apostate Nephites who had dissented and joined the darker race.[8] He wrote:

> . . . I make myself not known to the Lamanites lest they should destroy me.
> . . . Because of their hatred they put to death every Nephite that will not deny the Christ.
> And I, Moroni, will not deny the Christ; wherefore, I wander whithersoever I can for the safety of mine own life.[9]

During this period of gross apostasy, wickedness, war, and a determined effort to stamp out the gospel of Jesus Christ—even to obliterate his name—the name of Quetzalcoatl was substituted for Jesus Christ, and the symbols of the bird, the plumed serpent, Venus and numerous other symbols became prominent factors in the Toltec's religion. Thus the true gospel of Jesus Christ was completely adulterated from that which the resurrected Messiah nearly four centuries earlier had given to their ancestors.

Perhaps these reasons help to explain why the name of Quetzalcoatl was substituted for the true Messiah.

SPIRITUAL FORCE OF QUETZALCOATL RELIGION

It should be remembered, however, that there remained sufficient of the basic teachings of the Messiah in the Indian religions of Middle America to make it possible for us to identify those people with their predecessors of Book of Mormon days. Although the name of the Lord was changed from Christ to Quetzalcoatl and the religion of the Master corrupted, yet the memory of the "White and

---

[8]Moroni 9:24.
[9]*Ibid.*, 1:1-3.

Bearded God" could not be completely erased from the minds of the common people. Christ continued to live as Quetzalcoatl.

Thus the builders of Teotihuacán carried the embers of their ancient Nephite culture and religion into their new religious capital and fanned those embers into a flame of an adulterated and apostate form of Christianity. The religion of Quetzalcoatl, however, retained a part of the spiritual force that had characterized Christianity during the "Golden Age" of Nephite history. To quote:

> . . . Everything points to the plumed serpent being a symbol whose meaning penetrates far deeper than the representation of some object in nature.
> Quetzalcoatl taught that human greatness grows out of the awareness of a spiritual order; his image must therefore be the symbol of this truth. The serpent plumes must be speaking to us of the spirit which makes it possible for man—even while his body, like the reptile's, is dragged in that dust—to know the superhuman joy of creation. They are thus, as it were, a song to the most exalted inner freedom. This hypothesis is confirmed by the Nahuatl symbolism where the serpent represents matter—being always associated with terrestrial gods—and the bird heaven. The plumed serpent is thus the sign of the revelation of the heavenly origin of man.[10]

CITY OF THE GODS

Since most archaeologists and historians have not read the marvelous Book of Mormon account of Christ's appearance to the inhabitants of ancient America and become acquainted with the spiritual gospel message that he gave them, and also since most students are unfamiliar with the cultural traits of that superb civilization, these scholars are amazed at what seems to them to be a sudden emergence and spiritual force of the Quetzalcoatl religion at Teotihuacán. In the words of Laurette Séjourné:

> It seems, because of its sudden emergence and creative vigour, that Teotihuacán must have been fashioned in the full glare of this revelation. It is like a vast poem, every detail an integral part of a highly inspired whole.[11]

The writer is of the opinion that Teotihuacán—with its numerous Quetzalcoatl symbols and elaborate forms of worship—was fashioned after the full glare of the gospel of Christ—with its superb revelations of truth—had waned. Only the embers of eternal verities, the "seeds of the earlier Nephite culture," remained at Teotihuacán, and there—adulterated and paganized—formed the Quetzalcoatl religion.

---

[10]Séjourné, op. cit., p. 84.
[11]Ibid.

It seems to the writer that the Mexican archaeologist, Laurette Séjourné, may have received a glimmer of light regarding what actually occurred in ancient America; but not having heard of Christ's appearance to the Nephites, she was unable to formulate in her thinking the true basis of the original revelation which finally resulted in the Quetzalcoatl religion; however, it is surprising to observe how near she came to ascertaining the truth through human reason, as will be shown by the following statement:

> Surprisingly, no earlier examples of its [Quetzalcoatl's] principal motifs have been discovered, and its standards remain essentially unchanged until the time of the Spanish conquest. But if it is hard to believe that some of its cultural characteristics—such as its architectural style, the orientation of its buildings, and details of sculptures and painting—can have assumed their final shape right from the start, it is still more difficult to imagine how the system of thought upon which it is based could have appeared suddenly in a state of perfect development. There is no single trace to show how this prodigious work was elaborated. Was it a collective task, or that of one single man? The unchallenged position held by Quetzalcoatl seems to suggest the second hypothesis. However this may be, and in spite of the fact that Teotihuacán has its roots deep in the archaic world, it is clear that only a vision of the vastness of the human spirit—of the divine spark uniting and harmonizing—could possibly have given birth to the dynamic power that must have presided over the founding of a city such as this, built to the glory of the plumed serpent—that is, to conscious men.[12]

It is a significant fact that the meaning of the Nahuatl word—Teotihuacán—is "City of the Gods."

MEN BECOMING GODS

Bernardino Sahagún gives us the following pertinent information regarding the City of Teotihuacán:

> . . . The Lords therein buried, after their deaths were cannonized as gods, and it was said that they did not die, but wakened out of a dream they had lived; this is the reason why the ancients say that when men died they did not perish but began to live again, waking almost out of a dream, and that they turned into spirits or gods . . . and so they said to the dead: "Lord or Lady, wake, for it begins to dawn, now comes the daylight for the yellow-feathered birds begin to sing, and the many coloured butterflies go flying"; and when anyone died, they used to say of him that he was now *teotl,* meaning to say he had died in order to become spirit or god.[13]

Laurette Séjourné is of the opinion that, ". . . far from implying any gross, polytheistic belief, the term Teotihuacán evokes the idea

---

[12]*Ibid.,* p. 85.
[13]Sahagún, *op. cit.,* vol. 2, p. 309.

Fig. 85: TEMPLE OF THE EAGLES AND TIGERS AT MALINALCO, MEXICO

of human divinity and shows that the City of the Gods was the very place where the serpent learned miraculously to fly; that is, where the individual, through inner growth, attained to the category of a celestial being."[14]

The worshipers of Quetzalcoatl believed that mortal life was a school, a preparation, for death, which represented true birth— birth into a spirit world where one was free from finite, mortal existence. The newborn child represented the tomb of the spirit, a tomb opened only by death; and so Sahagún wrote, ". . . the hour of parturition . . . is called the hour of death."[15] Wise Aztec teachers declared:

> . . . that they did not die but woke from a dream they had lived . . . and became once more *spirits or gods*. . . . They said, too, that some were transformed into the sun, others into the moon, and others into various planets. . . .[16]

---

[14]Séjourné, *op. cit.*, p. 85-86.
[15]Sahagún, *op. cit.*, vol. 1, p. 318.
[16]*Ibid.*, vol. 2, p. 309.

According to the religion of Quetzalcoatl, not all men received this glorious birth into the celestial realm. Father Sahagún states that it was the princes and high dignitaries who were changed into spirits or gods. This transformation was made possible for them only by their being initiated into the highest level of the Quetzalcoatl Mysteries. These initiations were rigorously controlled by the religious leaders.

In ancient Mexico the most important religious order was that of the Knights of the Eagle and Tiger. During the Aztec period, however, these Knights had assumed a predominantly warlike character, changing vastly from the original purpose. Muñoz Camargo gathered data about the initiatory rite of the Knights of the Eagle and Tiger as it existed in some of the Nahuatl cities prior to its being greatly altered by the Aztecs.

. . . This ceremony of knighting the natives of Mexico and Tlaxcala and other provinces of the Mexican tongue, is worthy of note. . . . They knighted men with great ceremony, for first of all they were locked for forty or seventy days in a temple of their idols; and they fasted all that time and communicated with none but those who served them; at the end of that time they were taken

Fig. 86:   Interior of the Temple of Eagles and Tigers at Malinalco

to the Great Temple and were there given important doctrines of life which they must keep and guard; and before all this they taunted them with many insulting and satirical words, and struck them, even in the face, with many reprimands. . . . Throughout their fast they did not wash. Before this they were all smeared and painted black, and with signs of deep humiliation that they should conceive and reach so great mercy and reward, watching over their arms throughout their fasting according to the ordinances, uses and customs so well kept among them. They were also in the habit of keeping the doors where they were fasting closed with branches of laurel, a tree much valued among the natives.[17]

The various tests in this initiation show that the devotees believed in subjecting the flesh by fasting and humiliating it in order that the spirit might develop. This detachment from the physical is part of the doctrine of Quetzalcoatl; however, it was a paganized ceremony not practised in Book of Mormon days.

Sahagún informs us that spirits of those initiated went "into the sky where the sun lives. Those who go to heaven are those killed in wars and prisoners who have died in their enemies' power."[18]

He also wrote:

. . . Another place where they said the souls of the dead went, the earthly paradise name Tlalocan, in which it was said there was much rejoicing and comfort, and no sorrow whatever. . . . They go there who are killed by thunderbolts, drowned in water, those suffering from leprosy, sores, scabs, gout, hydropsy, those dying of contagious diseases; they do not burn, but bury the bodies of these sick people.[19]

QUETZALCOATL MYSTERIES

It is claimed that Teotihuacán, the "City of the Gods," was constructed as a religious center for the purpose of initiating Nahuatl worshipers into the higher Quetzalcoatl Mysteries with the belief that the devotees would eventually become gods.

This ritual center was divided into two principal sections, perhaps symbolizing heaven and the earth, joined by a vast ascending avenue. At the highest extremity of this avenue were situated the pyramids of the Sun and Moon. The larger of the two, the Pyramid of the Sun, seems to pierce the heavens. The quadrangle of Quetzalcoatl stands at the lower end of the avenue. Toward the end of this quadrangle is located the famous building known as the Temple of

---

[17]Diago Muñez Cumargo, *Historia de Tlaxcala* (Mexico, 1948), pp. 56-58.
[18]Sahagún, *op. cit.*, vol. 1, p. 318.
[19]*Ibid.*

Quetzalcoatl. Long undulating serpents are carved along the front of the temple. Its front is also studded with heads of the serpent surrounded by quetzal feathers, representations of the plumed serpent. These are alternated with heads of Tlaloc, the rain God, who, according to the Nahuatl belief, worked closely with Quetzalcoatl in giving life to the human family. Serpent heads also appear at certain places on the ramps of the staircase. Another motif of Quetzalcoatl, the seashell, said to be a symbol of revelation, is also found on the temple.

All of these religious motifs denote that Quetzalcoatl was the giver of light, life, and substance to the human family; also, that he was responsible for the immortality of all people, and for making some of them into gods.

It is claimed by certain archaeologists that the initiation requisite for becoming gods in the Quetzalcoatl Mysteries began at the Temple of Quetzalcoatl. Mexican literature speaks of a place called *Calmecac*, "the house where the body buds and flowers," as the Aztecs called the religious college where the nobility was educated. Some writers are of the opinion that the Temple of Quetzalcoatl was that place. Evidence that this was the case lies in the fact that *Calmecac* in Tenochtitlan was under Quetzalcoatl's patronage. In regards to the latter place, in Book Two, pages 36-37, *General History of the Things of New Spain* (Aztec version translated into English by Charles E. Dibble and Arthur J. O. Anderson in 1951), Sahagún stated:

In the sign named *ce acatl*, in the first house, the lords and the leading men celebrated a great festival to Quetzalcoatl, god of the winds. This feast they observed in the house called *calmecac*, which was the house where dwelt the priests of the idols, and where were trained the boys. In this house, which was a monastery, was the image of Quetzalcoatl. On this day they adorned it with rich ornaments and placed before it offerings of perfumes and food. They said this was the sign of Quetzalcoatl.

Although very little is known about the details of the initiation, it is believed by some archaeologists that after performing some initiatory rites in front of the Temple of Quetzalcoatl, the neophites and the priests went out of the quadrangle of Quetzalcoatl and along the ascending avenue, known as the "pathway of the dead," towards the Pyramid of the Sun. It is believed that at various places along the "pathway of the dead" perhaps additional important ini-

—Photograph by Author

Fig. 87:   Aztec Codex

tiatory rites were performed. Finally the procession reached the
superimposed narrow steps which lead to the top of the Pyramid
of the Sun. These they climbed. In front of a gorgeous representation of the sun made of gold, which radiated the sun's rays brilliantly
in various directions, the concluding ceremony in the initiation was
performed. Here the devotees received the final initiatory rites
which were requisite to their becoming gods. Now they were no
more to be mortals, but potentially gods. Thus the final act was
completed which assured them that following death they would
go on in immortality as divine beings and would be assured of the
highest rewards in the world to come known in the pagan rites of
the religion of Quetzalcoatl. For these reasons Teotihuacán received
its name—"the City of the Gods."

In accord with Nahuatl cosmology, all of the ritual buildings
at Teotihuacán were constructed in relation to the sun. The east-
west axis which runs through the Pyramid of the Sun lies seventeen
degrees north of the true line. Through investigation modern schol-

ars have ". . . discovered that the cause of the displacement arises because the pyramid points toward the spot where the sun falls below the horizon on the day of its passage through the sky's zenith."[20] Since the highest point that the sun reaches in its travels represented the center of the firmament, "the sun when it reaches this point becomes the heart of the universe, and this is an attribute belonging to Quetzalcoatl's Sun. That is to say, the pyramid is dedicated to the Fifth Sun, which was expressly created in Teotihuacán. The seventeen-degree shift to the north has thus so fundamental a meaning that this orientation was used until Aztec times."[21]

MEN MAY BECOME GODS

The crowning doctrine of the gospel of Jesus Christ relates to the principle of men becoming gods. It is marvelous that such a doctrine, although in a polluted form, should have been retained by Indian pagans from the time of the close of the Book of Mormon to the coming of the Spaniards.

Through modern revelation received by the Prophet Joseph Smith and his successors, the members of the Church of Jesus Christ of Latter-day Saints not only know that they are spirit children of a Heavenly Father and a Heavenly Mother, but they also know that there is a possibility for some of them ultimately to become exalted to Godhood.

As early as February 16, 1832, Jesus Christ revealed to the Prophet Joseph Smith the sublime truth that *"men may become gods."* Joseph Smith and Sidney Rigdon were shown in vision the three degrees of glory. In speaking of some of those who would inhabit celestial glory, the Master told them:

> They are they who are of the church of the Firstborn [Church of Jesus Christ]. They . . . are priests of the Most High after the order of Melchizedek, . . . which was after the order of the Only Begotten Son.
> Wherefore, as it is written, *they are gods, even the sons of God—* . . .
> These shall dwell in the presence of God and his Christ for ever and ever.[22]

---

[20]*Ibid.*, p. 86.
[21]*Ibid.* Note: "It is interesting to note that until the very end Nahuatl civilization preserved the custom of surrounding its temples with representations of serpents. Among the few remains found at the Pyramid of the Sun, there are two fragments of reptiles from a base molding. This leaves no doubt that the pyramid conforms to this rule."
[22]D. & C. 76:54-62.

President Joseph F. Smith beautifully expressed the doctrine as follows:

Man is a child of God, formed in a divine image and endowed with divine attributes and even as the infant son of earthly father and mother is capable in due time of becoming a man, so the undeveloped offspring of celestial parentage is capable by experience through ages of aeons of evolving to God.[23]

President Lorenzo Snow stated that ". . . *as God is, man may become.*"[24] President Charles W. Penrose wrote: "Mormonism does not tend to debase God to the level of man, but exalts man to the perfection of God."[25]

The principal purpose of the gospel of Jesus Christ and the ultimate goal of eternal progression is to receive eternal life, i.e., to become as God is. It is thoroughly understood, however, that a vast majority of the human family will never become gods, because to do so they must accept the true gospel, receive all of the ordinances —including celestial marriage—and obey all of God's commandments faithfully to the end.

CONCLUSION

If Joseph Smith, Lorenzo Snow, and the other latter-day prophets had lived at the days of the Spanish conquest and the gospel had been restored at that time, the Indians of Meso-America would have understood on the subject of men becoming gods what they were talking about. These aborigines had lost the true pattern which must be followed by our Heavenly Father's children to become gods, and yet they had retained the heart of the doctrine which had been lost by Christendom in the Old World.

It is a remarkable and a pertinent thing that not only a spark of divine truth but even the heart of the gospel of Jesus Christ persisted among the American Indians in the doctrines that mortals are children of God and that men may become gods. Since these sublime truths are so important in the plan of salvation, certainly Christ would have revealed them to the Nephites, and thereafter the doctrines filtered down among the aborigines to the time of the discovery of America.

------

[23]Joseph F. Smith, *Improvement Era* (Salt Lake City, 1908-1909) vol. 12, p. 81.
[24]Lorenzo Snow, *Millennial Star* (Liverpool, England), vol. 54, p. 404.
[25]Charles W. Penrose, *Millennial Star* (Liverpool, England), vol. 23, pp. 180-181.

CHAPTER 8

QUETZALCOATL THE PLUMED SERPENT

PLUMED SERPENT SYMBOL

Ever since the days of the arrival in the Western Hemisphere of the Catholic fathers, the plumed serpent symbol has encountered more misunderstanding and received more severe attacks than any other ancient American religious symbol. Even today tourists who visit such archaeological sites as Teotihuacán, Mexico, look at the serpent heads with horror and cry, "Devil worship! Devil worship!" Evenly highly educated people who have not studied the religions of the Indians are prone to have a similar reaction. The late Dr. Daniel G. Brinton, who ranked as one of America's outstanding scholars in the field of Indian traditions and religions, made mention of the frequent misunderstanding of this symbol as follows:

> The serpent symbol in America has, however, met with frequent misinterpretation.. It had such an ominous significance in Christian art, and one which chimed so well with the favorite proverb of the early missionaries —"The gods of the heathens are devils"—that wherever they saw a carving or picture of a serpent they at once recognized the sign manual of the Prince of Darkness, and inscribed the fact in their notebooks as proof of their cherished theory.[1]

Dr. Brinton then pointed out that after he had studied and investigated extensively he was convinced that none of the tribes of the red race attached such a meaning to the serpent, but that the native Americans employed this symbol ". . . to express atmospheric phenomena and the recognition of divinity in natural occurrences."[2] He claimed that practically always the Indians used the serpent symbol to typify something "favorable and agreeable." Where then should we look for the origin of such a symbol of ancient America's Messiah? In the previous chapter we pointed out that the origin lay in the true gospel of Jesus Christ as proclaimed both in the Old and New worlds; however, the fact should be kept in mind that following the close of Book of Mormon history the true

---

[1]Daniel G. Brinton, *The Myths of the New World* (Philadelphia 1905), p. 143.
[2]*Ibid.*

gospel was badly corrupted. With the loss of the ancient American prophets who communed directly with God, the Indian descendants of the Nephites and Lamanites were forced to rely upon traditions. As time passed it was natural for numerous changes to creep into their religious thinking and practices, making their forms of worship more pagan continuously. However, as has been mentioned, divine sparks of truth persisted—leaving the Indians with many religious doctrines which can be identified as having had their origin in the true gospel of Jesus Christ as taught to their ancestors by the resurrected Messiah.

Laurette Séjourné gives her interpretation of the symbolism of Quetzalcoatl—the "plumed serpent"—as follows:

—Photograph by Author

Fig. 88: PLUMED SERPENT ON CHICHEN ITZA MURAL

Reproduction of a mural on the wall of the Temple of the Warriors at Chichén Itzá, Yucatán, Mexico.

Quetzalcoatl's image, the plumed serpent, had for pre-Columbian peoples the same evocative force as has the crucifix for Christianity. . . .[3]

. . . Everything points to the plumed serpent being a symbol whose meaning penetrates far deeper than the representation of some object in nature. . . . The plumed serpent is thus a sign of the revelation of the heavenly origin of man.[4]

Quetzalcoatl the Sky Serpent or Rain God

Writers for many years have recognized the fact that the Indians of Mexico and Central America at the time of the coming of the Spaniards were worshiping Quetzalcoatl as the sky serpent. The serpent was identified with the Milky Way. The late Dr. Sylvanus G. Morley described an art object of the ancient Mayas as follows:

Across the sky stretches a serpent-like creature with symbols of constellations presented on its side and signs for solar and lunar eclipses hanging from its belly. From widely opened jaws, as well as from the two eclipse signs, pours a flood of water, falling straight earthward below the heavenly serpent; the old woman goddess with long talon-like fingernails, patroness of death and destruction, a withering serpent on her head and crossbones decorations on her skirt, holds an inverted bowl from which also gushes a destroying flood.[5]

The foregoing is in an agreement with the description of the sky serpent given by Dr. Daniel G. Brinton:

As an emblem of the fertilizing summer showers, the lightning serpent [Quetzalcoatl] was the God of fruitfulness. Born in the atmospheric waters, it was an appropriate attribute of the ruler of the winds.
. . . the winds were often spoken of as great birds. Hence the union of these two emblems in such names as Quetzalcoatl, Gucumatz, Kukulcan, all titles of the god of the air in the language of Central America, all signifying the "Bird-serpent."
The "masters" in native magic craft explained to the bishop Nuez de la Vaga that this compound symbolism was to represent "the snake with feathers, which moves in waters," that is, the heavenly waters, the clouds and rain.[6]

Quetzalcoatl, the sky serpent, was identified with lightning. The Indians regarded the flashes of lightning through the cloudy heavens as a symbol of their benevolent God Quetzalcoatl. Not only did the lightning remind them of the movements of a serpent, but

---

[3]Laurette Séjourné, *Burning Waters—Thought and Religion in Ancient Mexico* (London, 1956), p. 25.
[4]*Ibid.*, p. 84.
[5]Sylvanus G. Morley, *The Ancient Maya* (Palo Alto, 1946), p. 214.
[6]Daniel G. Brinton, *The Myths of the New World* (Philadelphia, 1905), p. 140.

they thought that it played a major part in making possible rain showers to water their thirsty crop. In the words of Dr. Brinton:

Quetzalcoatl the "Bird-serpent" was also said to be the god of riches and patron consequently of merchants. For with the summer lightning come the harvest and ripening fruits, come riches and traffic. Moreover "the golden color of the liquid fire," . . . naturally led where this metal was known, to its being deemed the product of lightning. . . .

Quetzalcoatl, called also Yolcuat the rattlesnake, was no less intimately associated with serpents than with birds. The entrance to his temple in Mexico represented the jaws of one of these reptiles, and he finally disap-

Fig. 89: SERPENT'S HEAD ON TEMPLE OF QUETZAL-COATL, TEOTIHUACAN

—*Photograph by Author*

peared in the province of Coatzacoalco, the hiding place of the serpents, sailing towards the east in a bark of serpents' skins. All this refers to his power over the lightning serpent, and over that which it typified. . . .

Because the rattlesnake, the lightning serpent, is thus connected with the food of man, and itself seems never to die but annually to renew its youth, the Algonquins called it "grandfather" and "king of snakes"; they feared to injure it; they believed it could grant prosperous breezes, or raise disastrous tempests; crowned with the lunar crescent it was the constant symbol of life in their picture writing; . . .[7]

---

[7] *Ibid.*, pp. 141-143.

The dew from heaven, or rain, came from the sky river. Itzamna, the Messiah of the Itzá-Mayas of Yucatán, means "the dew from heaven." One of his most prominently known symbols, as for Quetzalcoatl, was the serpent, the emblem of Israel raised on a pole by Moses approximately B.C. 1200.

Ixtlilxochitl, the famous sixteenth century Indian historian, even called Quetzalcoatl the ". . . God of Rain."[8]

The Tlalocs were the principal rain gods of the Toltecs and Aztecs, while the Chacs or Chacmools served in a similar capacity for the Maya Indians of Yucatán.[9] The worshipers of Quetzalcoatl in the Valley of Mexico, as well as the devotees of Kukulcan in Yucatán, depicted the "White and Bearded God" in Indian art and sculpture as working closely with these rain gods. At times the same symbols were used for each.[10] In his Aztec version of the *General History of the Things of New Spain* (the book recently quoted), the Catholic padre Sahagún clearly shows this to be the case. To quote:

. . . On the first day of this month [February], they celebrated a feast in honor—according to some—of the Tlaloc gods, whom they held to be gods of rain; [or]—according to others—of their sister,, the goddess of water, Chalchiuhtli icue; [or]—according to [still] others—in honor of the great priest or god of the winds, Quetzalcoatl. And we may say that [they celebrated the feast] in honor of all these. . . .

On the Temple of Quetzalcoatl at Teotihuacán, the representations of the plumed serpent are interspersed with those of Tlalocs, the rain gods.

Désiré Charney described the plumed serpent as the "god of rain, the fertilizing element. The cross is the symbol of four winds: the bird and serpent, the rebus of the air god (Quetzalcoatl)—their ruler. This god was intimately connected with Tlaloc and his sister or mate Chalchintlicue, and that is why the three deities are often found side by side, sometimes mixed or confused. . . . The cult of Quetzalcoatl and Tlaloc was spread . . ."[11] throughout Middle America.

---

[8]*Works of Ixtlilxochitl*, cited in Hunter and Ferguson, *Ancient America and the Book of Mormon* (Oakland, 1905) pp. 203, 211.
[9]J. Eric S. Thompson, *The Rise and Fall of Maya Civilization* (Norman, Oklahoma, 1954), pp. 103, 114, 190ff., 227ff.
[10]Séjourné, *op. cit.*, p. 101.
[11]Désiré Charney, *The Ancient Cities of the New World* (New York, 1887) p. 454.

QUETZALCOATL THE WIND GOD

The sky serpent or Quetzalcoatl not only symbolized the lightning, accompanied by clouds and rain, resulting in abundant harvests, but also was regarded as the wind god.

Juan de Torquemada shows in his writings the close relationship between Quetzalcoatl and Tlalocs or Chacs (rain gods) in the religion of the Indians. He wrote: "They also said that this Quetzalcoatl swept the roads so that Tlaloc gods would come to rain. . . ."[12]

Ixtlilxochitl, the reliable Indian prince, clearly states that the plumed serpent or sky serpent was the god of the air. To quote his exact words:

[Quetzalcoatl was the] god of wind. . . . there was destroyed that memorable and sumptuous building and tower in the city of Cholula, . . . it being destroyed by the wind. And later those who escaped the extermination. . . . built a temple on its ruins to Quetzalcoatl, whom they placed as god of wind, because the wind was the cause of the destruction, they understanding that this destruction was sent by his hand.[13]

A statement made by Torquemada adds a significant thought to the testimony of the other sixteenth century writers. To quote:

Among these Indians was *Quetzalcoatl. He was—as they say—God of the winds, for they attribute to him the power to command the winds to blow or to stop blowing.*[14]

The scholarly Catholic padre, Father Bernardino Sahagún, in his history of New Spain—written in the Aztec language—stated:

Fifth chapter, which telleth of the god named Plumed Serpent (Quetzalcoatl).

[Quetzalcoatl was the] god of wind. . . . there was destroyed that memorable and sumptuous building and tower in the city of Cholula, . . . it being destroyed by the wind. And later those who escaped the extermination . . . built a temple on its ruins to Quetzalcoatl, whom they placed as god of wind, because the wind was the cause of the destruction, they undered; then it was said: "[Quetzalcoatl] is wrathful."[15]

Father Sahagún also wrote:

. . . He who was man, they took for a god, and said that he used to sweep the path of the gods of water, and they predicted this event, for before

---

[12]Juan de Torquemada, *Monarquia Indiana*, Tome I., p. 205.
[13]*Works of Ixtlilxochitl, op. cit.*, pp. 190-191.
[14]Torquemada, *op. cit.*
[15]Bernardino de Sahagún, *General History of the Things of New Spain* (Florentine Codex, tr. from Aztec by Arthur J. O. Anderson and Charles E. Dibble, Santa Fe, 1950). pp. 2-3.

Fig. 90: TLALOC AND QUETZALCOATL SYMBOLS

Symbols of Quetzalcoatl and Tlaloc alternated on front of Temple of Quetzalcoatl at Teotihuacan, Mexico. Observe the beautifully carved serpent's body running along the lower part of the temple.

the waters [rainstorms] began there are great winds and dust, and so they used to say that Quetzalcoatl, god of winds, swept the paths for the rain gods, so that they might come and rain.[16]

After quoting their statement, Laurette Séjourné concluded:

At first sight such a task seems too menial for the Creator of the universe of man, but if we remember that the newly-born Fifth Sun [in the Quetzalcoatl myth] was launched upon the heavens by the wind, we can understand how such wind must be the spiritual breath that allows of interior birth. The god symbolic of wind brings in his train the laws that subdue matter: . . . he converts death unto true life, and causes a marvelous reality to flower out of the dark realm of every-day. It is just because he possesses these powers that Quetzalcoatl is considered the supreme magician—he who holds the secrets of all enchantments. That is why the day of the week ruled over by this god is dedicated to necromancers and sorcerers of all kinds.[17]

CELESTIAL SUN AND THE GOD OF WIND

The Quetzalcoatl myth proclaims that when the Fifth Sun was placed in the heavens, it did not move. Since it was motionless, its viewers considered that it was dead. It lacked the spirituality necessary to be a proper home for Quetzalcoatl and those who, through proper initiation, became spiritually capable of dwelling there. Since Quetzalcoatl was regarded as a Creator, he is proclaimed to

[16]Bernardino de Sahagún, *Historia General de Las Cosas de Nueva España* (Mexico, 1946), vol. 1, p. 23.
[17]Séjourné, *op. cit.*, p. 136.

have been the power, or the wind, which set the Fifth Sun in motion and thereby into life and spirituality. We read ". . . then the wind began to blow with a strong blast and made the sun move on its course. . . ."[18] We also read: "Only the sacrifice of the gods—that is, of men capable of sacrifice—and the breath of Quetzalcoatl—manage to stir the sun; this makes one think that without such intervention the Fifth Sun would have been no more capable of life than the previous ones that had been annihilated."[19] Thus the Sun—the celestial world—was made to live, and prepared as the home of the celestial beings following death and resurrection.

CHRIST'S POWER OVER NATURE

When one reads these startling beliefs regarding Quetzalcoatl and the conclusion made by the Mexican archaeologist, Laurette Séjourné, one's mind immediately recalls the story of Jesus of Nazareth stilling the waves of the Sea of Galilee. In the gospel of Matthew, we read:

> And, behold, there arose a great tempest in the sea, insomuch that the ship was covered with the waves: But he [Jesus] was asleep. . . .
> . . . Then he arose, and rebuked the winds and the sea; and there was a great calm.
> But the men [the apostles] marveled, saying, What manner of man is this, that even the winds and the sea obey him![20]

Both the Jaredites and the Nephites claimed that Christ controlled the winds and sent the rains to water the parched earth. The Book of Mormon contains numerous statements maintaining that bounteous crops, increase in flocks and herds, and prosperity in general, come to men as blessings from Jehovah or Jesus. A few quotations from the records of the ancient Americans will suffice to show that Christ the Messiah controlled the forces of nature. He told the Jaredites that ". . . the winds have gone forth out of my mouth and also the rains and the floods have I sent."[21]

The writer of the Jaredite record described Christ's control over the wind, as the small colony crossed the ocean to America—their promised land. To quote:

> And it came to pass that the *Lord God* [Christ] *caused that there should be a furious wind blow upon the face of the waters, towards the promised*

---

[18]Sahagún, *op. cit.*, vol. 2, p. 16.
[19]Séjourné, *op. cit.*, p. 77.
[20]Matthew 8:24-27; Luke 8:22-25.
[21]Ether 2:24.

—*Photograph by Author*

Fig. 91: PLUMED SERPENT'S HEAD ON HIGH PRIEST'S TOMB IN CHICHEN ITZA

Observe the masterful workmanship required to produce this beautiful head. The Temple of Kukulcan is in the background.

land; and thus they were tossed upon the waves of the sea before the wind. . . .
And it came to pass that the wind did never cease to blow towards the promised land while they were upon the waters; and thus they were driven forth before the wind.[22]

We also read in the book of Ether the following: ". . . when they had humbled themselves sufficiently before the Lord he did send rain upon the face of the earth."[23]

The Nephite historians testified also that Christ was the God who controlled the laws and forces of nature—the winds, the clouds and the rains. While the families of Lehi and Ishmael were crossing the ocean, a "terrible tempest" arose. It seemed as if the ship would sink and those aboard would be drowned in the sea. We read in the Book of Mormon: ". . . I, Nephi prayed unto the Lord; and after I prayed the winds did cease, and there was a great calm."[24]

---

[22]*Ibid.,* 6:5-12.
[23]*Ibid.,* 9:28-30, 35.
[24]1 Nephi 18:9-22.

Fig. 92: Carved Stone
Pillar on Front of
Temple of the Cross
(East Doorway),
Palenque, Mexico

Regarding this carved pillar,
Désiré Charnay wrote: "The
. . . slab represents an old man
clothed in a tiger skin, blowing
out air, with a serpent round his
waist, whose tail coils up behind and coils in front, the
well-ascertained attributes of
Quetzalcoatl, god of wisdom."

—Art Work by Huberta Berg Robison

The word of Jehovah, as recorded in the Book of Mormon, wherein he declared, "I will command the clouds that they rain no rain upon"[25] the earth, clearly demonstrates that Christ is the God who controls the winds and clouds and sends the rains.

From the Nephite records, let us present one of the classic examples of Christ's control over the laws of nature, his power to send rain. Approximately twenty years before the birth of the Messiah, a prophet named Nephi (Nephi II) prayed diligently unto the Lord as follows:

O Lord, behold this people repenteth; . . . Now, O Lord, because of this their humility wilt thou . . . cause that this famine may cease in this land.

O Lord wilt thou harken unto me, and cause that it may be done according to my words, and send forth rain upon the face of the earth, that she may bring forth her fruit, and her grain in the season of grain.

[In response to this prayer, Christ] . . . caused rain to fall upon the earth, insomuch that it did bring forth fruit in the season of her fruit. And it came to pass that it did bring forth her grain in the season of her grain. . . . [and] the people of Nephi began to prosper again in the land.[26]

The most forceful and explicit account of Jesus as the God who controls the wind, rain, hurricanes, and earthquakes—the God of natural phenomena—in any scripture or book in the world is found in chapters 8 and 9 of 3 Nephi. Therein the historian vividly describes the storm and destruction on the Western Hemisphere at the time of Christ's crucifixion.

Then the inhabitants of the entire country heard the voice of Jesus Christ declaring that the destruction had been brought about because of the gross wickedness of the people. He declared: "Behold I am Jesus Christ the Son of God. I created the heavens and the earth, and all things that in them are. . . . I am the light and the life of the world, I am Alpha and Omega, the beginning and the end."[27]

After having experienced such terrific convulsions of nature, no wonder the inhabitants of ancient America always remembered that Christ was the God who controls the winds, rains, earthquakes, and all natural phenomena of the universe. The deep impression made in the minds of the Nephites and Lamanites was handed down in tradition for 1500 years, even to the time of the coming of the

---

[25]2 Nephi 15:6.
[26]Helaman 11:10-20.
[27]3 Nephi 8:15-18.

Spaniards; and so the inhabitants of the New World were sure that
Christ or Quetzalcoatl controlled the forces of nature.

SERPENT THE SYMBOL OF WISDOM

Various people have identified the serpent as a symbol of wisdom. Christ admonished his apostles: ". . . be ye therefore as wise
as serpents, and harmless as doves."[28] It was natural, then, that the
plumed serpent be regarded: ". . . As the God of wisdom, the titular
deity of mankind."[29]

Désiré Charney described a stela at Palenque as follows: "The
other slab represents an old man clothed in a tiger's skin, blowing
out air, with a serpent round his waist, whose tail curls up behind
and coils in front, the well-ascertained attributes of *Quetzalcoatl,
god of wisdom.*"[30] (See Fig. 92.)

Ixtlilxochitl stated that "Quetzalcoatl through literal interpretation means serpent of precious plumage; in an allegorical sense it
means *very wise man.*"[31]

A sixteenth century Maya document, *The Book of Chilam Balam
of Chumayel,* photographed in Merida, Yucatán, in 1910 by G. B.
Gordon of the University of Pennsylvania, gives an account in its
first sixteen pages of "the first settlers of Yucatán, called *Ah-Canuil,*
meaning the people of the serpent or those who venerated the
serpent for its wisdom and knowledge."[32] The God of these Itzá
Mayas was called Itzamna. In the words of T. A. Willard:

> Itzamna or the Master, who, according to the devout priest and historian
> Lizana, raised the dead, healed the sick, and was deified as the Son of Hunab-
> Ku the great and only God of the Itzás, presents a startling comparison of
> his position with those ancient people, to Jesus, the Christ and Master in our
> Christian religion.[33]

All of these symbols apply aptly to Jesus Christ—he who visited
the ancient Americans following his resurrection.

---

[28]Matthew 10:16.
[29]Charney, *op. cit.,* p. 460.
[30]*Ibid.,* p. 217.
[31]*Works of Ixtlilxochitl,* cited in Hunter and Ferguson, *Ancient America and the Book
of Mormon* (Oakland, 1950), p. 203.
[32]T. A. Willard, *Kukulcan the Bearded Conqueror* (Hollywood, California, 1941),
p. 99.
[33]*Ibid.,* p. 69.

Gucumatz, the Green-Feathered Serpent

The *Popol Vuh*, a record of the Quiché Maya of Guatemala, was written by a Quiché Indian shortly after the Spanish conquest. ". . . it contains the cosmogonical concepts and ancient traditions cf this aboriginal American people, the history of their origin, and the chronology of their kings down to the year 1550."[34]

This record described Gucumatz as the principal God who created the world and the human family. He was a God who lived with other divine beings in the sky before life was placed on the earth. The *Popol Vuh* states that the sky deities "were in the water surrounded with light. They were hidden under green and blue feathers, and were called Gucumatz. By nature they were great sages and great thinkers. In this manner the sky existed and also the Heart of Heaven, which is the name of God and thus He is called."[35] A footnote explains the foregoing statement:

They were in the water because the Quiché associated the name Gucumatz with the liquid element. Bishop Nuñez de la Vaga says that Gucumatz is a serpent with feathers which moves in the water. . . .[36]

Gucumatz, *a serpent covered with green feathers*, from the Quiché word *guc* (*kuk* in Maya), "green feathers," particularly those of the Quetzal, and *cumatz*, serpent; it is the Quiché version of Kukulcán, the Maya name for Quetzalcoatl, . . . or God . . .[37]

Throughout the *Popol Vuh* the Quiché Maya worshiped this Creator God. Finally in Part III Gucumatz "took the bodily form of Tohil . . . [and was] specifically identified with Quetzalcoatl."

Father Francisco Ximénez (Hee-mā'-nes) obtained the manuscript of the *Popol Vuh* from the Indian writer. In the Santo Tomás church at Chichicastenango, Guatemala, Ximénez translated the document from Quiché into Spanish.

The book states that Tohil became the principal God of the Quiché Mayas. According to Father Ximénez, Tohil got his name from *toh*, "rain." "Farther on, the author writes that Tohil and Quetzalcoatl were the same being. . . . The name *Tohil*, is, in effect, associated with the idea of rain and thunder."[38]

---

[34]*Popol Vuh—The Sacred Book of the Ancient Quiché Maya* (English tr. 1950 by Delia Goetz and Sylvanus G. Morley, Norman, Oklahoma), p. 5.

[35]*Ibid.*, pp. 81-82.

[36]*Ibid.*, p. 81.

[37]*Ibid.*, p. 78.

[38]*Ibid.*, p. 175.

Fig. 93: JADE PLAQUES WITH HUMAN AND ANIMAL DESIGNS

Fig. 94: JADE SERPENTS' HEADS

These jade plaques were dredged from the Sacred Well at Chichén Itzá, Yucatán, by Edward Herbert Thompson. They are housed in Peabody Museum at Cambridge, Mass.

On page 189 of the *Popol Vuh*, we read: "Because, in truth, the so-called Tohil is the same god of the Yaqui, the one called Yolcuat-Quitzalcuat"; and then the translators of the Quiché book explain further:

The great civilizer was worshiped as a divinity by the ancient Mexicans, who gave him different names. They called him Ehecatl, or God of the Wind; Yolcuat, or the Rattle Snake; Quetzalcoatl, or serpent covered with green feathers. The last meaning corresponds also to the Maya name Kukulcán, and to the Quiché, Gucumatz. Here the text shows that the Quiché also identified Quetzalcoatl with their own god Tohil. Both were actually rain gods.[39]

A little later in the *Popol Vuh*, the god Tohil is described as a handsome youth in human form.[40] Also, in certain of the Mexican myths, Quetzalcoatl was regarded as a young man.

The material that we have given from the *Popol Vuh* regarding Gucumatz or Tohil, the Quiché Maya rain god, gives the significant identification of this god as "a serpent covered with green feathers." Green is the color in which nature is clothed in the springtime. In the fall all vegetation seems to die; however, the rain god, also known as the sky serpent or "green feathered serpent," sends the showers

---

[39]*Ibid.*, p. 189.
[40]*Ibid.*, pp. 195-199.

Fig. 95: ROYAL TOMB, PALENQUE, MEXICO

Reproduction of the burial in the Royal Tomb, Temple of Inscriptions, Palenque, made by Dr. Alberto Ruz. The reconstructed man's body is wearing the jade mask, beads, bracelets, etc., which were taken by Dr. Ruz from the tomb. A photograph of the figurine of the bearded man made of jade, which lies toward the bottom of the coffin, is reproduced elsewhere in the book.

from the sky upon the earth in the springtime. The light and the heat from the sun, or sun god, warm the earth as it receives the heavenly showers, resulting in a rebirth of all life in nature. Leaves burst forth on the trees. Flowers bloom. Grass, corn, and various plants come through the ground. All nature has been resurrected —she is alive and green once again.

Thus the Indians very appropriately gave to their greatest divinity—the "White and Bearded God"—the numerous symbols which we have discussed. To the American aborigines, these were significant spiritual symbols of the marvelous workings of the divine, universal Creator-God, the giver of all blessings and good gifts, the Messiah.

GREEN CORN GOD

Maize was of vital importance in the religious as well as the economic life of the Mayas. Their civilization was built upon this plant. Maize was the focal point of Maya worship. Every Maya who worked the soil built a shrine in his own heart to corn and the maize god.

The *Book of Chilam Balam of Chumayel* gives a legend of maize in allegorical language. To quote: "Three, seven, eight thousand was the creation of the world, when he who was hidden within the stone, hidden within the night was born, [and] occurred the birth of the first precious stone of grace. The first infinite grace. . . . Not yet had he received his divine rank. Then he remained alone within the grace. Then it was pulverized. There were his long locks of hair . . . his divinity was assumed when he came forth."[41]

An outstanding scholar of Maya culture, Dr. J. Eric S. Thompson, explained this parable as follows:

The precious stone of grace is jade, which in Mexican allegorical writing is the ear of corn before it ripens. The passage states that green corn, like precious jade, is hidden within the rock. Then the rock is smashed asunder, and the maize is born and becomes divine. The maize god always has long hair, perhaps derived from the beard of the maize in husk. Hence the reference to the long locks. The full passage is of some length and is replete with allegory and mysticism *(in one paragraph Christian ideas have led to the identification of Jesus, as the Bread of life, with the maize God).*[42]

---

[41]*Book of Chilam Balam,* cited in J. Eric S. Thompson, *The Rise and Fall of Maya Civilization* (Norman, Oklahoma, 1954), p. 237.
[42]*Ibid.*

PRIESTHOOD AND PRIESTS OF QUETZALCOATL

The priests of Quetzalcoatl, many of whom were regarded as reincarnations of the "Fair God," were also called Quetzalcoatl or "successors to Quetzalcoatl."[43]

> . . . In Tenochtitlan [the Aztec capital city] the high-ranking priests all took the title of Quetzalcoatl, and naturally this name, so constantly perpetuated through the centuries, was not the only factor uniting them [the Aztecs] with the founder of the Nahuatl religion. Until the close of the Empire of Meso-american prince-priests, thought to be reincarnations of Quetzalcoatl, performed rituals in which important moments from his mythical life were recalled.[44]

It seems quite certain from a study of the Book of Mormon that the practice of regarding the priests of Quetzalcoatl as successors of the "Fair God"—or even as reincarnations of Quetzalcoatl—could have had its origin at the time that Christ bestowed the priesthood on his American disciples and established his Church among the Nephites. The resurrected Messiah ordained twelve apostles to preside over his Church.[45] The Nephite record states: "and . . . the Lord God ordained priests, after his holy order, which was after the order of the Son, . . ."[46] Thus they received "the *Holy Priesthood, after the Order of the Son of God.*"[47] Those who through "faith, with broken hearts and contrite spirits, having witnessed unto the Church that they truly repented of all their sins," received baptism and took upon themselves the name of Christ.[48] Also, the Church was called the Church of Christ.[49] Since the ancient American followers of the resurrected Lord were known by his name and the priesthood called after him, what would have been more natural when the name of Quetzalcoatl was substituted for Christ than to substitute also the name of "priests after the Holy Order of the Son" to "priests of Quetzalcoatl or successors of Quetzalcoatl"? It was only one step further to regard these priests as reincarnations of Quetzalcoatl; and this occurred as man-made doctrines crept into the religion, corrupting the true gospel of Christ and bringing about the religion of Quetzalcoatl.

---

[43]Séjourné, *op. cit.*, pp. 25-27, 30.
[44]*Ibid.*, pp. 64-65.
[45]Nephi 11:19-22.
[46]Alma 13:1.
[47]D. & C. 107:3.
[48]Moroni 6:1-3.
[49]*Ibid.*, 6:4; 3 Nephi 27:1-10.

The priests of Quetzalcoatl were adorned with quetzal feathers and precious stones in commemoration of their god Quetzalcoatl. The rulers, also regarded as divine, wore headdresses of quetzal plumes and precious stones.

Father Sahagún informs us regarding the worshipers of Quetzalcoatl that ". . . they say that when the Lords and Nobles died they placed a green stone in their mouths . . . and they say this was the dead man's heart. . . ."[50]

Precious stones, usually green in color, were regarded as spiritual symbols of life in nature and symbols of man's spirit. The heart was regarded by the Aztecs as the center of man's life and they believed it must be saved from destruction in order that the deceased person might go forward into immortality following death. For this reason precious stones were placed "in the mouths of the dead, to represent the heart emerging, brilliant and pure, from the fire consuming the body."[51]

When Maya and Aztec priests and rulers were buried, their faces were covered with jade masks and their bodies were adorned with turquoise and jade beads. Bracelets were placed around their wrists and ankles. Other sacred objects made of precious stones were also put in their tombs. These bracelets, masks, and various objects of precious stone—usually jade and green in color—were buried with the dead as symbols of spiritual life.

Since the sun was regarded as the celestial world, the most frequent sign symbolizing it in Meso-American hieroglyphics was a precious stone.

Figure 95 is an excellent example of a jade mask, beads, and other precious stones taken from a Maya burial by Dr. Alberto Ruz Lhullier on June 15, 1953. This Maya burial has become known as the Royal Tomb. It is in the Temple of the Inscriptions at Palenque, Mexico. The dates of A.D. 603 and A.D. 633, according to the Goodwin-Martinez-Thompson correlation, are carved on the tomb. Spinden and Makemson's dating are 260 years earlier, which would give dates of A.D. 343 and A.D. 373. Dr. Alberto Ruz states

---

[50]Séjourné, *op. cit.*, p. 73.
[51]Sahagún, *op. cit.*, vol. 1, p. 317.

that ". . . a recent carbon 14 reading lends support to the Spinden and Makemson solutions."[52]

Otto Done, José Dávila, and I were at Mérida, Yucatán, Mexico, at the time Dr. Ruz was completing the representation of the ancient Maya priest or king and placing on it the sacred relics from the tomb. He graciously permitted us to photograph it claiming that

Fig. 96: MASK FROM BURIAL IN ROYAL TOMB, PALENQUE

—*Photograph by Author*

our photographs were the first ones ever taken of these things, since he was just completing their reconstruction. He had photographed the sacred objects in the coffin, however, at the time of first raising the lid following their discovery.

Figure 82, page 152, shows the jade relics taken some years ago from a burial in the archaeological site of Kaminaljuyu, situated in the outskirts of Guatemala City.

---

[52]Alberto Ruz Lhullier, "The Mystery of the Temple of the Inscriptions, Palenque," *Archaeology* (Spring, 1953), vol. 6, No. 1, pp. 3-11.

CONCLUSION

In conclusion it is suggested that we should fully understand that to the American aborigines the plumed serpent symbolized the power back of rains, winds, storms, all life, new birth or resurrection in nature, bounteous crops, and all the blessings that come as a result of heavenly showers and warm sun rays reacting on the earth to bring about abundant harvests and the numerous comforts of life. Thus the plumed serpent as a symbol of Quetzalcoatl connoted only that which was favorable and agreeable, being a spiritual symbol of the divine Creator, the light and life of the world.[53]

[53]3 Nephi 11:14.

Fig. 96a: GOLD DISK FROM SACRED WELL, CHICHEN, ITZA

One of the most beautiful sacred objects that Edward Herbert Thompson dredged from the Sacred Well.

CHAPTER 9

VIRACOCHA — THE "WHITE AND BEARDED GOD" OR JESUS CHRIST

SPANIARDS' ARRIVAL IN PERU

In 1527, when the Spanish conquistadores sailed into one of the harbors on the west coast of South America, Pedro de Candia, a lieutenant in the freebooter armada of the mighty Pizarro, stepped from the boat, helmet and breastplate freshly burnished and glistening, his gun over his shoulder, and a huge double-handed sword in his sword-belt. His gigantic stature, his mighty shoulders, and his complete attire made of him an impressive figure. He was followed by others from the ship.

As Pedro walked forward, a crowd of dark-skinned natives dropped to their knees and groveled in the dust as though they were paying obeisance before a god come down from heaven. Pedro was puzzled, embarrassed, perplexed.

With head erect and shoulders straight, he walked between a lane of beardless, bowed figures whose foreheads were pressed to the dust on either side of his path. All around him rose the whisper —"*Viracocha, Viracocha*" (vē' rä kō' chä).

Pedro de Candia had no idea what the natives meant. He felt ill at ease, flustered, and even somewhat irritated. Impulsively and suddenly he lifted his gun from his shoulder and fired a shot into the air.

The natives became terrified and, cringing, they whispered "*Illa Tiki, Illa Tiki!*" This appelation meant "The god of lightning."[1]

Pedro grew more confused. He had no idea that the beardless, brown-skinned natives actually took him for the "White and Bearded God," Viracocha or Con (Kon) Tiki, who had been so thoroughly known and so highly reverenced by the Indians' Andean ancestors. Nor did he know that Huayne Capac the Great, the last Inca to

---

[1]Paul Herrmann, *Conquest by Man* (New York, 1954), p. 182.

reign prior to the Spanish invasion, had predicted that white bearded men, similar in appearance to the ancient Peruvian settlers, would soon come and conquer the land. As Huayne Capac, the great Inca ruler, lay on his deathbed, he had called to him the chiefs of the Ayllus, the leading clans of the kingdom, and among the things he told them is the following:

> Many years ago it was revealed to me by our father, the Sun, that after the rule of twelve of his children, an alien people would come which had never been seen before in these regions and would conquer and subdue this kingdom and many others as well. I am inclined to suppose that this refers to the people recently sighted off our shores. They are said to be a powerful race, superior to us in everything. Now we know that with me the number of twelve Incas has been reached. Therefore, I predict to you that a few more years after I have gone to my ancestors, that strong people will appear and bring fulfillment of the prophecy of my father, the Sun; they will conquer our kingdom and rule over us. I command you to obey and serve them, for they are superior to us in everything, because their laws are better than ours, their weapons more powerful and invincible.
>
> Peace be with you—I go now to my father, the Sun, who has called me. . . .[2]

This could all sound like myth if it were not for the fact that the Aztec Indians of the Valley of Mexico, as well as the Maya Indians of Yucatán, cherished similar prophecies regarding their great empires.[3] Those predictions were primarily responsible for the fact that the Inca, Aztec, and Maya rulers all capitulated after offering relatively little resistance; and their empires, composed of millions of inhabitants, came under the control of a mere handful of Spanish conquistadores.

INDIANS' TRADITIONS OF WHITE BEARDED MEN ANCIENTLY

Furthermore, the Spanish soldiers and Catholic padres who first visited Mexico, Central America, and also South America were apprised by the Indians that back in the distant past the Americas were inhabited by ". . . a race described as *white and with beards*— . . ."[4] At that time a "Fair God" had visited the ancient white peoples —ancestors of the American Indians—and had given them their religion and culture.

---

[2] Cited in Herrmann, *ibid.*, pp. 183-184.
[3] *Idem*, pp. 165-172; A. Hyatt Verrill, *America's Ancient Civilizations* (New York, 1953), pp. 58-59.
[4] Thor Heyerdahl, *American Indians in the Pacific* (Stockholm, Sweden, 1952), pp. 229-345; *Works of Ixtlilxochitl*, cited in Milton R. Hunter and Thomas Stuart Ferguson, *Ancient America and the Book of Mormon* (Oakland, 1950), pp. 24-25; 2 Nephi 5:20-24.

Also, when the Spaniards entered Peru in 1527, they were greeted by the Peruvian Indians, with frightened awe, as "Viracocha!" A German scholar, Paul Herrmann, recently concluded:

[The foregoing facts,] . . . as Siegfried Huber has pointed out in his book *In the Kingdom of the Incas*, would be "utterly inexplicable in the absence of some pre-existent tradition, that is, unless white, bearded men had been known in olden times and their return in later ages expected." It is therefore certain that the Viracocha myth is not an invention of either Indian or Spanish priests; . . . [5]

Faithful members of the Church of Jesus Christ read statements made by great scholars, such as the foregoing one made by Paul Herrmann and Siegfried Huber, and with joy in their hearts meditate on the marvelous story so beautifully delineated in the Book of Mormon.

Indians' Traditions of a "Fair God"

As explained in the preceding chapters, the peoples of practically all the countries of Mexico and Central America had their traditions of a "Fair God" who had given them their culture.[6] The same fact holds true with the countries of South America. This chapter will be confined to the Indian traditions of the Andean region of that country. Dr. Daniel G. Brinton, one of the most reliable research scholars of the past century in the field of American Indian traditions, described this "White and Bearded God" of South America as follows:

His hair was abundant, his beard fell to his waist, and he dressed in long and flowing robes. He went among the nations of the plateau, addressing each in its own dialect, taught them to live in villages and to observe just laws . . . and then he departed . . . *he rose up to heaven*.[7]

Meaning of Viracocha

Viracocha! More than four hundred years have passed since the Spanish conquests, and today the word *Viracocha* is the form of address meaning simply "lord" in Peru, Bolivia, and Ecuador. Also, in practice it is identical with "white man," for today white

---

[5]Herrmann, *op. cit.*, p. 183.
[6]Milton R. Hunter, "Quetzalcoatl—the White Bearded God or Jesus Christ," *Improvement Era* (Salt Lake City, 1956), Jan. vol. 59, p. 26ff.; Feb. vol. 59, p. 82ff.
[7]Daniel G. Brinton, *American Hero-Myths* (Philadelphia, 1882), p. 220. Italics supplied by writer.

Fig. 99   Fig. 100

—Courtesy of publishers of Heyerdahl, *American Indians in the Pacific*

Fig. 97:   BEARDED MAN FROM CHIMU CULTURE, PERU

Fig. 98:   POTTERY BEARDED MAN, PERU

Fig. 99:   BEARDED WHITE MAN, PERU

Fig. 100:   BEARDED MAN LATE CHIMU PERIOD

These four bearded men supply evidence which conforms to Indian traditions of a white and bearded race which established the early culture at Tiahuanaco and other Andean sites. The first three were modelled during the Early Chimu period, in the first half millennium A.D. or earlier. Fig. 100 is from the subsequent Late Chimu period.

people are still considered to be the sons and people of Viracocha the Almighty

Who then, and what, is Viracocha?

In brief, according to Peruvian traditions, he was the God who created the heavens and the earth, placed the human family on the earth, gave them their religion and culture, suddenly came to the ancient Peruvians and lived among them for some time, performed many miraculous deeds, and then disappeared just as suddenly as he had arrived.

PERUVIAN NAMES FOR THE "WHITE BEARDED GOD"

Fortunately, the early Catholic padres and Spanish *conquistadores of the Andean* countries carefully recorded many of the traditions of the Indians. Their accounts give us much information regarding the "White Bearded God," under the various names applied to him by different Indian tribes. This God constituted the central figure of the Indian traditions of the several Andean countries of South America.

According to the information recorded by the early Spanish chroniclers, the ancient Peruvians who pre-dated the Incas made common use of the name of Con Tici, (Con Ticci or Kon Tiki), while the Incas preferred the name of Viracocha for their "Fair God." Dr. Philip Ainsworth Means, an outstanding scholar in the field of Andean traditions, described the "Fair God" of Peru as follows:

> The Creator-god most celebrated in the Chronicles of Peru is known under various names. . . . He has generally been referred to as Viracocha or as Pacha-Camac, the former designation being used in the highlands, the latter on the coast. Both of them, however, are Quechua and, consequently, more or less late in date. It seems clear enough that pre-Incaic names for the Creator-god were *Con, Con-Tici, Illa-Tici,* and sundry approximations thereto, sometimes prefixed to the name Viracocha in later times. . . .[8]

Thor Heyerdahl, author of the famous *Kon Tiki,* adds the following information to that given by Means:

> . . . With the prefix *Illa* meaning "light," and *Con,* being an alternative name for the creator, we know that the early Peruvian culture-hero *Con-Tici* or *Illa-Tici* was venerated as Tici-the-Creator and Tici-the-Light.

---

[8]P. A. Means, *Ancient Civilization of the Andes* (New York, 1931), p. 422.

Tici is a word of ancient origin, adopted in Quechua mythology from an earlier language, distinct from their own. It is preserved as a live word in Quechua dialects either as *tecsi* or *ticsi*, meaning "origin." Thus Markham says, in referring to Blas Valera, the best-informed mestizo chronicler of the sixteenth century, whose major works are unfortunately lost: "The names given for God by Valera, as used by the ancient Peruvians, are also given by some others of the best authorities. They are Illa Tici Uira Cocha. The first word means light. Tici is the foundation of things, or beginning."[9]

TRADITION OF VIRACOCHA AND HIS WHITE FOLLOWERS BUILDING TIAHUANACO

In the words of Heyerdahl:

There is within the borders of the former Inca Empire no prehistoric site with monuments and other architecture of more impressive dimensions, and with evidence of a higher cultural level, than the ancient megalithic ruins of Tiahuanaco in the Bolivian highland plains south of Lake Titicaca.[10]

When the Incas first immigrated into Peru and Bolivia, so they reported to the Spanish conquistadores, they obtained traditions from their predecessors that in ancient times a "White Bearded God" had visited a superior white race of people in the Andean region and had assisted them in establishing an unusually high culture and superb civilization.[11] This "Fair God" was also accredited with having assisted that bearded race of white people in the construction of the massive archaeological structures of the Andean region, such as those at Tiahuanaco.

The Incas adopted the traditions of the people whom they supplanted and carried those traditions on to the time of the Spanish conquest. Regarding this fact, Paul Herrmann wrote:

. . . It is certain, however, that when the Incas discovered the giant city Tiahuanaco on Lake Titicaca, allegedly built by Viracocha and his followers, and even more when they came upon the grandiose divine city Pachacamac, south of Lima, they invoked this strange god by the name of Con Tiki, the Eternal, and that they called him Pachayachachi, Creator and Ruler of the World.[12]

---

[9]Heyerdahl, *op. cit.*, p. 239.
[10]*Ibid.*, p. 228.
[11]*Ibid.*, p. 229ff. Note: Recall the Book of Mormon account of Jesus Christ visiting the Nephites.
[12]Herrmann, *op. cit.*, pp. 282-283.

—Courtesy of publishers of Heyerdahl, *American Indians in the Pacific*

Fig. 101: BEARDED MAN (VIRACOCHA) FROM NORTH PERU

The feline emblem and puma teeth symbolize divinity, and so this bearded man is regarded by archaeologists as a representation of Viracocha.

INDIANS' TRADITIONS OF VIRACOCHA

Thor Heyerdahl has made an extensive study of the traditions of the Indians of the Andean countries and the archaeology of that region. He published his findings in an 800 page volume entitled *American Indians in the Pacific*. Heyerdahl maintains that:

The memory of the hero-god Viracocha was vividly preserved among aborigines in wide regions of the former Inca Empire, even through the last century.[13]

And then, speaking from personal experiences, he states that "in many places Viracocha stories still survive to-day among the elder natives."

Daniel G. Brinton, in his book *American Hero-Myths*, quoted Zegarra, a leading Peruvian scholar of the past century, as having

[13]Heyerdahl, *op. cit.*, p. 233.

described the "White Bearded God" who visited the people in the Andean region in ancient times as follows:

"The tradition was that Viracocha's face was extremely white and bearded." [Brinton then adds]: There is, indeed, a singular uniformity of statement in the myths. Viracocha, under any and all his surnames, is always described as white and bearded, dressed in flowing robes and of imposing mien.[14]

Pascual de Andagoya (1541-1546), the Spaniard whose explorations from Panama led to Pizarro's discovery of Peru, wrote:

The first lord, of whom there was any recollection in Cuzco, was the Inca Viracocha. This was a man who came to that land alone; but there is no record of whence he came, except that Viracocha, in the language of the people, means "Foam of the sea." He was a white and bearded man, like a Spaniard. The natives of Cuzco, seeing his great valour, took it for something divine, and received him as their chief. He ordained many excellent laws and regulations for the government of the land; . . .[15]

Pachacuti-Yanqui Salcamayhua (1620), himself a beardless Quechua Indian writer, in his book, An Account of the Antiquities of Peru, specifically pointed out that

. . . an immigrant creator with a *beard* had been active among his forefathers before the advent of the Spaniards. He relates that at a very remote period shortly after Peru had been populated, there came from Titicaca Island to the tribes of the mainland an old man with a beard, dressed in a long robe. He went about in the highlands preaching his religious beliefs to the Indians.[16]

Another early Spanish conquistador, Cieza de Leon (1553-1560), collected the Peruvian traditions which affirmed that long before the reign of the first Inca, men, "white and bearded like the Spaniards," had lived in Vinaque and on Titicaca Island. Cieza was also highly impressed by the Incas' memory of Viracocha, who they reported had visited these ancient Peruvians and accomplished mighty works among them. To quote:

The natives had heard from their forefathers that Viracocha was much beloved, because he was humane and benevolent to all, and because he cured sick people, . . .[17]

Another Indian account states that the "White Bearded God"

. . . healed the sick and restored sight to the blind. Everywhere, at his approach, the demons took to flight.[18]

---

[14]Brinton, *op. cit.*, p. 192.

[15]Pascual de Andagoya, *Narrative of the Proceedings of Pedrarios Davila . . .* (Hakluyt Soc., London, 1865), vol. 34, ch. 97.

[16]Pachacuti–Yanqui Salcamayhua, cited in Heyerdahl, *op. cit.*, p. 250.

[17]Cieza de Leon, cited in *idem*, p. 253.

[18]Adolf Bastian, *Die Culturlander des Alten Amerika* (Berlin, 1878), p. 56, cited in De Roo, *op. cit.*, p. 218.

Cieza de Leon also recorded in his journal that

. . . before the rule of the Incas in these realms, and even before they were known, these Indians relate other things much older than all that has been told. . . .

. . . they tell that from the south [of Cuzco] there came and stayed a white man of tall stature, who, in his appearance and person showed great authority and veneration, and that as they saw he had great power, turning hills into plains and plains into hills, making fountains in the solid rocks, they recognized such power in him that they called him Creator of all made

Fig. 102: Statue of Viracocha

A photograph of a statue of Viracocha hangs on the wall of the office of Dr. George C. Muelle, director of the National Archaeological Museum at Lima. He graciously permitted me to photograph it and publish it in this book.

things, Beginning thereof, Father of the Sun, because, besides this they say that he made greater things, as he is said to have given men and animals their existence, and finally that wonderful benefits came from his hands.

And the Indians who told me this had heard from their forebears, who had also heard it from the songs which these had had since very ancient times, that he went off northwards along the Sierras while accomplishing these wonders, and that they never saw him again.

In many places they tell how he gave rules to men how they should live, and that he spoke lovingly to them with much kindness, admonishing them they should be good to each other and not do any harm or injury, but that instead they should love each other and show charity.

In most places they generally call him Ticci Viracocha, . . .

In many parts temples were built to him, in which they placed stone statues in his likeness, in front of which they made sacrifices. The large stone statues which are at the site of Tiahuanaco must be from those times. And although they relate of his former fame this which I tell of Ticci Viracocha, they cannot tell more of him, neither that he returned to any part of his kingdom.[19]

STONE STATUES OF VIRACOCHA

When the early Spaniards first arrived at the site of Tiahuanaco, they found a considerable number of anthropomorphic monoliths, or stone statues of men, which had been carved at an early date. Many of these were bearded figures representing the "Fair God." One in particular was a stone statue erected south of Cuzco, on the main Inca road from Titicaca, by the Indians of Cacha. According to Garcilisso de la Vega (1609), it had been erected in honor of Tici Viracocha. He informs us that this statue was placed on the great pedestal inside an Inca temple built of cut stone. To quote Garcilisso:

The image represented a man of good stature, with a long beard measuring more than a palmo [one palmo is about nine inches], in a wide loose robe like a cassock, reaching to the feet.[20]

The early Spaniards marveled at the close resemblance of this image, found among beardless Indians, to their Old World saints and apostles. According to Cieza de Leon (1553-60), several of the early Spanish writers came to the conclusion that the Viracocha statue represented not a heathen god but one of the apostles who must have come to Peru before the days of Columbus.[21]

---

[19]Pedro de Cieza de Leon, *Parte primera de la Cronica del Peru* (Sevilla, Spain, 1553), cited in Heyerdahl, *idem*, p. 253.

[20]Inca Garcilisso de la Vega, *Primera Parte de los Comentarios Reals, que tratan del origin de los Incas* (Madrid, 1722), p. 71.

[21]Leon, cited in Heyerdahl, *op. cit.*, pp. 302-303.

In order to protect the statue of Viracocha, some of the Indians hid it near Cuzco; but, according to R. Karsten, it was re-discovered by a pious Spaniard and destroyed.[22]

Daniel G. Brinton, quoting from *Religion Anonyma,* written in 1615, described a marble statue of Illa Tici Viracocha which stood in the great Cuzco Temple. This statue was claimed to have been ". . . both as to hair, complexion, features, raiment and sandals, just as paintings represent the apostle, St. Bartholomew. . . ."[23] This statue was destroyed, as was the other one of Viracocha.

Thor Heyerdahl quotes Francisco de Avila (1608) as stating that

> . . . in Peru an idol called Coniraya Viracocha was invoked and worshipped almost down to the coming of the Spaniards. . . . "This invocation and custom of calling the idol by the name of Viracocha certainly prevailed long before there were any tidings of Spaniards in the country."[24]

Fortunately some of these statues of Viracocha, the "White Bearded God," survived to the present time. A photo of one of them is reproduced in this book. (See Fig. 105, page 205.)

BETANZOS' ACCOUNT OF VIRACOCHA

When the Inca Empire was first discovered and conquered, Juan de Betanzos came from Spain to Peru, married an Indian girl, and lived among the natives the remainder of his life. This gave him an unusually good opportunity to collect and preserve the aboriginal Peruvian beliefs and traditions. Like nearly all early chroniclers, he paid much attention to Peruvian accounts of the pre-Inca "White Bearded God," Viracocha, or Con Tici Viracocha. Betanzos wrote his account in 1551, and it was published in Madrid in 1881 under the title, *Suma y narracion de los Incas.* Since this book is not available to me, I shall have to depend on the information presented by Thor Heyerdahl.

Betanzos claimed that the Indians had told him that Con Tici or Viracocha

> . . . made the sun and day, and ordered the sun to move in the course it now moves and afterwards, they say, he made the stars and the moon.[25]

---

[22]R. Karsten, *The Civilization of the South American Indians* (London, 1938), p. 200.
[23]Brinton, *op. cit.,* p. 148.
[24]Francisco de Avila, cited in Heyerdahl, *op. cit.,* p. 254.
[25]Juan de Betanzos, *Suma y narracion de los Incas* (Madrid, Spain, 1881), cited in Heyerdahl, *op. cit.,* p. 235.

Then Betanzos gives an elaborate story of God's coming down to earth and creating the human family on the shores of Lake Titicaca. As part of that story, he explained the Indian tradition of the origin of the massive buildings and the huge stone statues of human beings found there by the Spaniards, the credit for their construction being given to Viracocha. After the work of creating the human family was completed, this "Fair God" left the earth but returned many, many years later to live among the people a certain length of time. Regarding this event, Thor Heyerdahl makes the following significant comment:

> . . . We learn through Betanzos that Viracocha only "returned" to earth when he moved with his followers from the shores of Titicaca to the nearby site of Tiahuanaco. Long before this appearance he had, according to Betanzos' informants, created heaven and earth and the original population of the country who dwelt in darkness until he came and established himself in human shape at Tiahuanaco.[26]

Betanzos gave the following interesting description of the "Fair God" of Peru:

> . . . when I asked the Indians what shape this Viracocha had when their ancestors had thus seen him, they said that according to the information they possessed, he was a tall man with a white vestment that reached to his feet, and that this vestment had a girdle; . . . and that he carried in his hands a certain thing which today seems to remind them of the breviary [book] that the priests carry in their hands. . . . And when I asked them what this person called himself . . . they told me that his name was Con Tici Viracocha Pachayachachic, which in their language means God, Maker of the World.[27]

SARMIENTO'S ACCOUNT OF VIRACOCHA

Sarmiento de Gamboa (1572), another Spanish chronicler of the colonial period, recorded the traditions of the ancient Peruvians of pre-Incan times. His account confirms Betanzos'. Sarmiento informs us that the Incas believed that after the creation ". . . Ticci Viracocha sent a great flood to punish the sins of the first men, but the ancestors of the Cuzcos . . . were saved and so left some descendants."[28] Later ". . . Viracocha suddenly appeared on the Titicaca plateau with his servants, to help restore mankind and give them light."[29]

---

[26]*Idem.*
[27]Betanzos, cited in *idem.*
[28]Sarmiento de Gamboa, *History of the Incas,* cited in *idem,* pp. 247-248.
[29]*Idem,* p. 247.

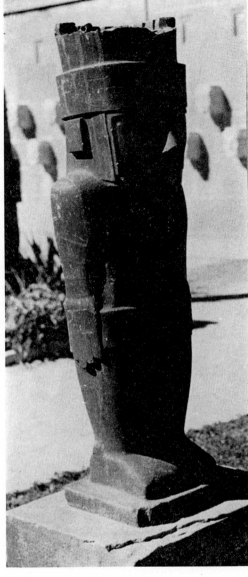

Fig. 103: TIAHUANACO STONE
STATUE

This stone statue of a man has been
moved from Tiahuanaco to LaPaz,
Bolivia.

—Photograph by Author

Sarmiento's description of Viracocha, as he appeared at the
time of his preaching among the ancestors of the Peruvian Indians,
is much the same as was Betanzos'. Referring to the Indians from
whom he had received reports, Sarmiento wrote:

> . . . all agree that Viracocha was the creator of these people. They have
> the tradition that he was a man of medium height, white and dressed in a
> white robe like an alb secured around the waist, and that he carried a staff
> and *a book* in his hands.[30]

Viracocha ordered these people that they should live without quarreling,
and that they should know and serve him. He gave them a certain precept

------
[30]*Idem.*

which they were to observe on pain of being confounded if they should
break it. . . .[31]

In regards to the compiling of his history, Sarmiento wrote:

I have collected the information with much diligence so that this history
can rest on attested proofs from the general testimony of the whole kingdom,
old and young, Incas and tributary Indians.[32]

MILES POINDEXTER'S STATEMENT REGARDING VIRACOCHA

Miles Poindexter, in his book *The Ayar-Incas,* wrote:

There was a universal Inca tradition reported by Cieza de Leon, Sarmiento, and Salcamayhua of a white teacher who had appeared in the highlands in the very earliest times and given the people their civilization. . . .
Cieza de Leon relates that this legendary leader was first seen coming from
the south. . . .[33]

Sarmiento said that this teacher ". . . preached to the people *with loving words. . . . He worked miracles and punished the wicked.*"[34] It is claimed that Viracocha had such power and authority that he commanded the forces of nature, and they obeyed.

BOCHICA, THE VIRACOCHA OF THE CHIBCHAS

The peaceful and highly cultured Nuyscas or Chibchas, who
lived in the lofty plateau of the northern Andes at the time of the
arrival of the Spaniards, had a sufficiently high cultural level and
social standing to place them with the Mayas, the Aztecs, and the
Incas, among the most outstanding nations of aboriginal America.
They, like most other highly cultured Indian groups, attributed their
ancestors' culture to a foreign teacher generally referred to as Bochica. He is also known by the names of Nemterequetaba and Xue.
According to native tradition it was claimed that he had come from
the East and entered the territory of Bogotá at Pasca on its southern
border. The following is quoted from W. B. Stevenson:

North of Peru, the Nuysca Indians of the plain of Cundinamarca in Colombia had a legend of one called Bochica, a white man with a beard, who
appeared suddenly amongst them, while savages, and taught them how to
build and sow, and formed them into communities, settling their government.[35]

---

[31]Pedro Sarmiento de Gamboa, *History of the Incas* (1572, in Works issued by the
Hakluyt Society, Series No. XXII, Cambridge, 1907), p. 28.
[32]Ibid., p. 29.
[33]Miles Poindexter, *The Ayar-Incas* (Rahway, N. J., 1930), vol. 2, p. 86.
[34]Sarmiento, cited in *ibid.*, p. 87.
[35]W. B. Stevenson, *A History and Descriptive Narrative of Twenty Years' Residence
in South America* (London, 1825), vol. 1, p. 398.

Fig. 104: Tiahuanaco Statue of Man

This stone statue now stands in a plaza in the center of LaPaz, Bolivia, with numerous other statues and carved stones.

—Photograph by Author

Dr. Daniel G. Brinton, in his book *American Hero-Myths*, quotes Lucas Fernandez Piedrahita, an author, who wrote A.D. 1688, as follows:

The knowledge of these various arts they attributed to the instructions of a wise stranger who dwelt among them many cycles before the arrival of the Spaniards. He came from the East, and from the llanos of Venezuela or beyond them, . . . His hair was abundant, his beard fell to his waist, and he dressed in long and flowing robes. He went among the people of the plateau, addressing each in his own dialect, taught them to live in villages and to observe just laws. Near the village of Coto was a high hill held in special veneration, for from its prominent summit he was wont to address the people who had gathered around its base. . . . For many years . . . did he rule the people with equity, and then he departed, going back to the East whence he came, said some authorities, but others averred *that he rose up to heaven.* At any rate, before he left he appointed a successor in the sovereignty, and recommended him to pursue the path of justice. . . .[36]

A Catholic padre named Pedro Simon is quoted by Lord Kingsborough as stating:

---

[36]Daniel G. Brinton, *American Hero-Myths* (Philadelphia, 1882), p. 300.

Other names applied to this hero-god were Nemterequeteba, Bochica, and Zuxu or Sua, the last mentioned being also the ordinary word for the Sun. He was reported to have been of light complexion, and when the Spaniards first arrived they were supposed to have been his envoys, and were called *sua* or *gagua,* just as from memory of a similar myth in Peru they were addressed as Viracocha.[37]

Several points in the quotations relative to Bochica definitely connect him with Christ. He, like the Messiah, was white and bearded, appeared suddenly among the people, gave them their religion and culture, was the god of light, and finally ascended to heaven.

TRADITION THAT VIRACOCHA TAUGHT THE INHABITANTS OF ANCIENT AMERICA FROM A BOOK

Several different Catholic padres and Spanish chroniclers of the colonial period reported that Indians of the Andean region had told them that Viracocha, or the "White Bearded God," taught their ancestors from a book. Also, Spanish conquistadores and Catholic priests reported that they had actually seen statues representing the "Fair God" with a book in hand, hands, or under his arm. Most of these statues were destroyed; however, at least one survived, and a photograph of it is reproduced in connection with this chapter. Thor Heyerdahl made a very important observation regarding the representation of the book on this statue. To quote:

. . . Regular books, as known from pre-Columbian Mexico, have never been discovered in Peru, yet an unidentifiable object, the memory of which the sight of a "book" or a "breviary" might well recall to a native mind, appears carved in the hands of the pre-Incan Tiahuanaco stone statue. . . .[38]

JESUS CHRIST TAUGHT THE NEPHITES FROM A BOOK

Members of the Church of Jesus Christ, and others who have studied the history and religion of this people, are cognizant of the fact that the inhabitants of ancient America, particularly the Nephites, possessed many books written on metal plates,[39] and perhaps they used other types of writing materials and were acquainted with methods of writing which would be much more rapid than

---

[37]Pedro Simon, *Noticias Histiales de las Conquistas de Tierra Firma en el Neuvo Reyno de Granada,* Pt. 4, chapters 2, 3, 4, cited in Lord Kingsborough, *Mexican Antiquities,* vol. 8.
[38]Heyerdahl, *op. cit.,* p. 248.
[39]1 Nephi 1:16-17; 6:1-6; 9:1-5; 19:1-6; Helaman 3:13-15; Omni 1:18; 3 Nephi 8-11; Mosiah 21:25-28; 8:6-19.

Fig. 105: STATUE REPRESENTATION OF
VIRACOCHA CARRYING A BOOK

This stone statue still stands at Tiahuanaco, Bolivia.

—Courtesy of the publishers of Heyerdahl,
American Indians in the Pacific

could be applied in engraving on gold plates. To illustrate this point, the readers are referred to King Benjamin's sermon. His congregation was so large that he had a tower erected on which to stand; and even then

> . . . they could not all hear his words because of the greatness of the multitude; therefore he caused that the words which he spake should be written and sent forth among those that were not under the sound of his voice, that they might also receive his words.[40]

Further evidence of books and methods of writing among the Nephites is clearly given in connection with the account of Christ's

_____

[40]Mosiah 2:6-8.

appearance to the people on the Western Hemisphere shortly after his resurrection. He taught them his gospel; and in doing so he read to them from a book. He also made reference to the various books and records which they possessed, giving instructions regarding the continuance of keeping records. The resurrected Lord declared:

> Therefore give heed to my words; write the things which I have told you; and according to the time and the will of the Father they shall come forth to the Gentiles. . . .

> . . . after he [Jesus] had expounded all of the scriptures unto them which they had received, he said unto them: Behold, other scriptures I would that ye shall write, that ye have not.

> And it came to pass that he said unto Nephi: Bring forth the record which ye have kept.

> And when Nephi had brought forth the records, and laid them before him, he cast his eyes upon them and said: . . .

> And it came to pass that Jesus commanded that it [Samuel's prophecy] should be written; therefore it was written according as he commanded.[41]

The principal purpose the Nephite prophets had in writing their records was to preserve all available information and revelations from heaven which maintained that Jesus was the Christ, the Savior of the world, the Only Begotten Son of the Eternal Father in the flesh.[42] One of the Lord's avowed purposes in having these Nephite records preserved was to bring them forth in the latter days ". . . to the convincing of the Jew and Gentile that *Jesus* is the *Christ*, the *Eternal God,* manifesting himself unto all nations."[43]

Since these sacred records were regarded so highly and used so extensively throughout the entire course of Nephite history, and since their contents were taught to the people by the resurrected Christ, who is the central figure in them and the principal purpose for which they were written, is it not possible that such a profound impression would have been made on the inhabitants of ancient America that they would preserve—not only in their traditions but also in stone—a definite remembrance of their "Holy Book" and its connection with the "White and Bearded God"? Indian traditions have supplied an abundance of evidence to the effect that such was the case.

---

[41]3 Nephi 23:4, 6-8, 13.
[42]2 Nephi 26:12; Mormon 5:9-14; Jacob 1:4.
[43]"Preface," Book of Mormon.

Viracocha Identical with Jesus Christ

Perhaps by now the readers have arrived at a conclusion regarding the question asked earlier in the chapter, namely, "Who, then, and what is Viracocha?"

An analysis of the numerous Indian traditions regarding the "White and Bearded God," who played such a prominent role in the traditions of the aborigines of South America, has supplied ample evidence to convince the writer that these traditions are survivals in distorted forms of the true knowledge of Jesus Christ held by the inhabitants of ancient America in Book of Mormon days. In other words, the writer maintains that Viracocha, or the "White and Bearded God" under whatever name he may have been known by any of the Indian tribes, could have been none other than Jesus of Nazareth, the Only Begotten Son, the Savior of mankind, who, after his resurrection, visited the ancestors of the Indians here on the Western Hemisphere, taught them the gospel, and then ascended into heaven to dwell with the Eternal Father.

Students of the religion and history of the Andean peoples recognize the fact that Viracocha is so similar to the God of the ancient Hebrews and of Christianity that he must be accepted as the same Eternal Being; for example, Miles Poindexter wrote:

. . . Viracocha, . . . in all essentials, was the same omnipotent spirit as our own God. All through the chronicles appears the thought, like the imprecations of the Prophets of the Jews, that disaster and death were the penalty of apostasy, blessings and power the reward of fidelity to the true God.[44]

According to the Latter-day Saints' belief, the God of the Old Testament—he who appeared to Abraham, Isaac, Jacob, Moses, and others of the ancient Hebrew prophets—was none other than Jesus of Nazareth; therefore, Jehovah, the God of the Jews, is the same as Christ, the Savior and Redeemer of the Christians. Following his resurrection, the same God who had lived among the Jews and given them the true plan of salvation, did a similar work among the inhabitants of ancient America. Thus the memory of Christ's appearance to the progenitors of the Indians, as well as many of his

---

[44]Miles Poindexter, *The Ayar-Incas* (New York, 1868), vol. 1, p. 235.

Fig. 106: GATEWAY OF THE TEMPLE OF THE SUN AT TIAHUANACO

This gateway at one time was one of the most beautiful of the mammoth-sized stonework objects in ancient America. It is artistically carved.

teachings, although somewhat adulterated, persisted more than fifteen hundred years in the Indians' traditions of the "White Bearded God," he being called Viracocha in Peru, Quetzalcoatl in Mexico, and other names among various other Indian tribes.

INDIAN TRADITIONS OF VIRACOCHA, AND BOOK OF MORMON
QUOTATIONS REGARDING JESUS CHRIST LISTED FOR COMPARISON

To assist in sustaining and clarifying the foregoing conclusion and to provide a basis for comparisons, short quotations from Indian traditions from the preceding material discussed in this chapter are listed in one column and quotations from the Book of Mormon are listed in a parallel column.

Quotations from Indian Traditions regarding Viracocha, the "White Bearded God":	*Quotations from the Book of Mormon regarding Jesus Christ*:
[Viracocha was the] Creator of all things, Beginning thereof, Father . . .	Behold, I am Jesus Christ the Son of God. I created the heavens and the earth, and all things that in the mare. . . .—3 Nephi 9:15.

[He was the] foundation of all things or the beginning . . .

. . . I am Alpha and Omega, the beginning and the end.—*Ibid.,* 9:18.

[Jesus is] . . . the all-powerful Creator of heaven and earth . . . —Jacob 2:5.

[Viracocha] called himself . . . God, Maker of the world.

He made the sun and the day. He made the stars and the moon. . . .

[Jesus is] . . . a God of miracles, . . . that same God who created the heavens and the earth, and all things that in them are. —Mormon 9:11.

[Viracocha] created heaven and earth and the original population . . .

. . . I [Jesus], the Lord your God, have created all men, . . .—2 Nephi 29:7; 1 Nephi 17:36.

. . . man have I [Jesus Christ] created after the body of my spirit; . . . —Ether 3:16.

[He] placed the human family on the earth.

Behold, the Lord hath created the earth that it should be inhabited; and he hath created his children that they should possess it.—1 Nephi 17:36.

[The "White Bearded God"] had great concern over it [the human family].

. . . it behooveth the great Creator that he suffereth himself to become subject unto man in the flesh, and die for all men, . . . —2 Nephi 9:5.

[Viracocha] was venerated as Tici-the-Creator and Tici-the-Light.

Behold I am Jesus Christ, . . .

. . . I am the light and the life of the world; . . . —3 Nephi 11:10-11; 9:18; Alma 38:9.

[He was the] God of Light.

He [Jesus] is the light and the life of the world; yea, a light that is endless, that can never be darkened; . . . —Mosiah 16:9.

[Viracocha controlled the forces of nature, being] the giver of rain.

[Christ declared:] . . . the winds have gone forth out of my mouth, and also the rains and the floods have I sent forth. —Ether 2:24.

[Jesus Christ] . . . the Lord . . . caused that rain should fall upon the earth, . . . —Helaman 11:17.

[Viracocha was the] giver of culture, industries, and religion to mortals.

(The entire Book of Mormon teaches that Jesus Christ was the giver of culture and industries.)

[In ancient times Viracocha] sent a flood to punish the sins of . . . men.

. . . if it were not for the prayers of the righteous, who are now in this land, that ye would even now be visited with utter destruction; yet it would not be by flood, as were the people in the days of Noah, . . . —Alma 10:22.

[Viracocha] suddenly appeared [to the ancient Americans.]

And I saw the heavens open, and the Lamb of God descending out of heaven; and he came down and showed himself unto them.—1 Nephi 12:6.

He came [to earth] . . . in human shape.

He was a tall man with a white vestment . . . [which] had a girdle.

[The "Fair God" wore a] long robe [or was] dressed in a white robe.

. . . they [the ancient Americans] cast their eyes up again towards heaven; and behold, they saw a Man descending out of heaven; and he [Jesus] was clothed in a white robe; and he came down and stood in the midst of them; . . . —3 Nephi 11:8.

[Viracocha] was extremely white, bearded, and beautiful.

[Viracocha's] face was extremely white and bearded.

. . . the light of his [Christ's] countenance did shine upon them, and behold they [the twelve disciples] were white as the countenance and also the garments of Jesus; and behold the whiteness thereof did exceed all the whiteness, yea, even there could be nothing upon earth so white as the whiteness thereof.—Ibid., 19:25.

[Viracocha appeared to a] white race of people.

. . . [Some of the Book of Mormon people] were white, and exceedingly fair and delightsome, . . . —2 Nephi 5:21.

. . . Lamanites who had united with the Nephites were numbered among the Nephites;

. . . and their skin became white like unto the Nephites; . . . —3 Nephi 2:14-15.

[Viracocha possessed] both divine and miraculous powers.

[He] healed the sick and restored sight to the blind. Everywhere, at his approach the demons took to flight.

. . . Viracocha was much beloved, because he was humane and benevolent to all, and because he cured sick people, . . .

[Jesus asked the multitude] Have ye any that are sick among you? Bring them hither. . . . all the multitude, with one accord, did go forth with their sick and their afflicted, and their lame, and with their blind, and with their dumb, and with all them that were afflicted in any manner; and he did heal them every one as they were brought forth unto him.—Ibid., 17:7, 9.

He carried . . . a book in his hands.

[Viracocha] read and taught the people from a book.

[After Jesus] had expounded all the scriptures unto them which they had received, he said unto them: Behold, other scriptures I would that ye should write, that ye have not.—Ibid., 23:6-7, 14.

Fig. 107: Bonampak Mural

Three white men are depicted on this mural which dates approximately A.D. 600. Observe their white robes and elaborate quetzal-feathered headdresses. Perhaps they were the high priests at Bonampak.

[Viracocha taught] his religious beliefs to the Indians.

And he [Jesus] did expound all things, even from the beginning until the time that he should come in his glory— . . .

And now there cannot be written in this book even a hundredth part of the things which Jesus did truly teach unto the people; . . . —*Ibid.*, 26:3, 6.

He taught the people to observe just laws.

Behold, I [Christ] am he that gave the law, and I am he who covenanted with my people Israel; . . . —*Ibid.*, 15:5.

He gave rules telling men how they should live.

Behold, I have given unto you the commandments; therefore keep my commandments. And this is the law and the prophets, for they truly testified of me. —*Ibid.*, 15:5, 9-10.

[Viracocha] taught with love and kindness.

And it came to pass that when Jesus had thus spoken, he cast his eyes round about again on the multitude, and beheld they were in tears, . . .

And he said unto them: Behold, my bowels are filled with compassion towards you.—*Ibid.*, 17:5-6.

He spoke lovingly to them with much kindness, admonishing them that they should be good to each other and not do any harm or injury, but instead they should love each other and show charity.

But behold I [Jesus] say unto you, love your enemies, bless them that curse you, do good to them that hate you, and pray for them who despitefully use you and persecute you; . . . —*Ibid.*, 12:44.

Disappearing suddenly, . . . [the "White Bearded God"] rose up to heaven.

. . . he [Jesus] departed from them, and ascended into heaven. And the disciples saw and did bear record that he ascended again into heaven.—*Ibid.*, 18:39.

A comparison of the foregoing quotations shows that a surprisingly large number of the divine truths contained in the Book of Mormon were preserved in Indian traditions in an adulterated form. Furthermore, it is evident from the quotations that both sources—Indian traditions and the Book of Mormon—sustain each other in bearing witness to the fact that Viracocha—the "White Bearded God" and Jesus Christ are the same individual.

Chapter 10

A VISIT TO PERU AND BOLIVIA

FLIGHT TO LIMA, PERU

The plane to Peru left Miami, Florida, at 4 o'clock in the morning, which was a delightful time and advantageous to the passengers to afford them the opportunity to see the country over which we were flying. While daylight was coming, we flew over the gulf of Mexico and then over Yucatán and Honduras. Our first landing was at Tegucigalpa, Honduras. The next landing was at Managua, Nicaragua. From there we passed above the other Central American countries and on over Colombia and Ecuador in South America.

The entire route to the north border of Peru supplied us with beautiful scenery, the terrain below us being covered with thick vegetation. Since the Central American countries are quite narrow, we could see the blue waters of both the Atlantic and Pacific oceans part of the time.

TOPOGRAPHY OF PERU

When we reached the northern end of Peru, the terrain changed abruptly. The beautiful green foliage of Central America, Colombia, and Ecuador was replaced by a barren, sandy, desert strip, ranging from ten to one hundred miles in width and extending along the western coast of South America for practically 2,000 miles.

As I looked from the plane at the earth below me, I saw only sand hills and sand plains—sand! sand! miles and miles of glistening, white, and glaring sand, as it reflected the sun's rays. Now and then, however, I could see a town or city, surrounded by a green patch made possible through the waters of a stream which was making its way from the high Andes to the Pacific Ocean.

During the following month, I traveled by car and by air along the coastal plain from the north border of Peru to the Chilean border on the south and can verify that the Peruvian coastal plain is a vast, sandy desert, perhaps in many respects like the Sahara Desert in northern Africa.

Fig. 108:   STONE WALL AT CUZCO, PERU

It is claimed that this wall was erected approximately A.D. 1,000. The street is only six feet and two inches wide. Observe the Indian woman walking up the street.

From a geographical and topographical viewpoint, Peru can be divided into three distinct types of country: first, the sandy coastal plain; second, the massive, high, and rugged mountain range, which is scantily covered with low-growing vegetation; and third, the tropical east side of the majestic Andes, which slope rapidly, forming the upper Amazon basin. The vegetation changes completely in this area, soon becoming a dense jungle composed of a profuse growth common to tropical areas.

ARRIVAL AT LIMA

We arrived at Lima, Peru, that evening. Since I was acquainted with very few people there, I was delighted to see Frederick S. Williams and his wife waiting at the airport when I arrived. President Williams had served as the Argentine Mission president and was also the man who opened the Uruguay Mission. Between those missions and up to the present time, he has spent many years in South America and is now in Lima in business. Fortune could not have smiled upon me more favorably than to have a man of his experience and acquaintance with the language and customs of the South American people to meet me at the plane and to be, with his wife, my personal guide and escort during the entire month of July, except while I was in Bolivia. Their kindness and generosity were beyond my words to describe; and so for all they did for me, I express deep appreciation.

President Williams made numerous contacts for me with government officials, with directors of museums—both public and private —and with touring agencies. He and his wife also took me in their automobile to a number of the Peruvian archaeological ruins, a courtesy which was most helpful in furthering the purpose of my trip.

Ancient Cultures of the Andean Region

When the Spaniards conquered the Indians of Peru in 1532, the Inca ruler had an extensive empire over which he and his forefathers had held control for many centuries. Many of the Catholic padres and others of the Spanish colonizers who were interested in the various Indian cultures made extensive inquiries of the aborigines regarding the history of their ancestors. The major portion of the information obtained, however, pertained to the Inca empire and not to the pre-Inca peoples. At the time of the Spanish conquest, the history of the earlier Andean cultures was quite vague in the minds of the Indians. When the Catholic chroniclers asked who built the great ancient City of Tiahuanaco and other similar places, they were merely told that these places were built by white and bearded men long before the time of the rise of the Inca empire.

Archaeologists, through their painstaking research and careful work, however, have shown that numerous important ancient cultures thrived in Bolivia, Peru, Ecuador, and Colombia long before the rise of the Inca empire; in fact, the people of the Andean region were civilized as early as B.C. 1,500. Recent carbon 14 tests show that people were living in Peru as early as B.C. 3,000.[1] In his book *Realm of the Incas*, published in 1957, Dr. Victor W. Von Hagen describes and dates various Peruvian cultures.

The Andean cultures reached unusual heights in several fields of endeavor, particularly in metallurgy, in weaving, in pottery making, in medicine, in dentistry, in agriculture, and in rockwork.

---

[1]Victor W. Von Hagen, *Realm of the Incas* (New York, 1957) pp. 29-30.

The marvelous Tiahuanaco culture, one of the earliest established by white men in the Andean region, is claimed to have reached
a high stage of development in the B.C. period. The Tiahuanacans
lived in Bolivia on the shores of Lake Titicaca in an extensive valley
of the mighty cordillera, which has an altitude of 12,000 feet. The
"White and Bearded God" was regarded as the person responsible
for that ancient culture; and it was he, under the name of Viracocha,
who was devotedly worshiped for many centuries by those ancient
people. After the Tiahuanaco culture had flourished many centuries
near Lake Titicaca, the Tiahuanacans established an extensive empire, controlling the country between the lake and the Pacific Ocean.
This empire is claimed to have flourished from A.D. 1,000 to 1,300.

In addition to the Tiahuanacans, the people of several other
high cultures—such as the Chavín, the Paracas, the Chimú, the
Nasca, the Mochica, and the Inca cultures—played important roles
in Andean history prior to the Spanish conquest. The one best known
of any other of these ancient cultures is that of the Incas with the
capital city named Cuzco, Peru, situated in a valley approximately
11,000 feet in altitude.

According to tradition, the ancestors of the Inca originally lived
on the Isle of the Sun in Lake Titicaca, Bolivia. The "Sun-God," it
was believed, created the first Inca, Manco Capac, and his sister-
wife, instructed them in the arts of civilization, and commanded
them to take their culture to other people. In this way began the
line of Inca, or ruling class of people.

From Lake Titicaca, the first Inca, his wives and associates,
wandered northward, passing between two high ranges of the Andes,
and came to the Valley of Cuzco. Upon their arrival, they established the City of Cuzco, which was the beginning of a mighty
empire. According to archaeologists, as well as Indian tradition,
Manco Capac established Cuzco around A.D. 1,000 to 1,050. He
was a worshiper of Viracocha, or Kon-Tici, the "White and Bearded
God," as were many other peoples of the Andean Region. Dr. Victor
W. Von Hagen quotes from one of the early chroniclers as follows:

"In the year 1,000 A.D.," wrote Pedro de Cieza de Leon, ". . . in the name
of [Kon] *Tici-Viracocha* and the Sun and the rest of his gods, Manco Capac
founded the new city."[2]

---

[2]*Ibid.*, p. 40.

And then Von Hagen states that in 1545 Pedro de Cieza de Leon received from the Indians of Cuzco an account of their history which was "as good and simple a premise as any. The Inca tradition emphasizes the fact that those people developed within the Cuzco Valley, and the excavations of Dr. John Rowe have confirmed this."[3] Dr. Rowe wrote:

> Enough has been done . . . to show that the Inca civilization was a product of long development in the Valley of Cuzco itself and that consequently it is unnecessary to look farther afield for the civilization's cultural origins.[4]

After the founding of Cuzco by Manco Capac, the first Inca or ruler, gradually one after another of the stalwart Inca emperors extended his control over other valleys throughout Peru. The result was that a mighty empire arose which controlled a vast territory from Quito, Ecuador, to Santiago, Chile, by the time of the coming of Pizarro and his Spanish *conquistadores*.

History speaks not only of the line of rulers at Cuzco as the Incas, but also of the rulers and their subjects—the entire population of the empire—as Incas.

PACHACAMAC

Shortly after my arrival in Lima, Frederick S. Williams and his wife took me in their automobile southward approximately twenty miles on the coast highway from Lima to the vast archaeological ruins of Pachacamac. The buildings in this ancient city were composed of sun-dried adobe blocks. Walls of numerous private dwellings, palaces, chiefs' houses, and a citadel join one upon another on a hill near the present-day highway. A central street, intersected and paralleled by many narrow streets, extends through the ancient city. The street is walled by the high sides of the principal houses.

After driving through the center of this ancient city, we turned westward and went through what is termed "the Valley of the Dead," or the old cemetery. Farther to the west overlooking the Pacific Ocean, we came to a large pyramid called the Pyramid of the Sun. The principal god of the ancient Incas and their subjects was the

---

[3]*Idem.*
[4]John Rowe, "Inca Culture at the Time of the Conquest," *Handbook of South American Indians* (Washington, 1946), vol. 3, p. 198.

sun. We climbed the steps, ascending a series of terraces to the top of this pyramid. Red paint, we observed, was still plainly visible on the plastered sides of some of the pyramid. On the summit of the pyramid, facing the Pacific Ocean, stands a row of a dozen tall niches ". . . which are still grim and black with the smoke of torches which centuries ago illuminated sacrificial rites or signaled to passengers upon the sea. What a spectacle from the sea, or from the neighboring islands, must have been this level row of high-flaming

—Photograph by Author

Fig. 109:   BAPTISMAL FONT AT PACHACAMAC, PERU

Frederick S. Williams and his wife are standing in the baptismal font.

chambers on the summit of the great pyramid which crowned the sea-girt hill!"[5]

The views both to the west and to the east from the top of this pyramid are very inspiring. To the west we saw the mighty Pacific with its blue, placid waters. To the east the view of the majestic Andean mountains filled us with awe. As we gazed toward the majestic cordillera, our vista extended in the interminable perspec-

[5]Miles Poindexter, *The Ayar-Incas* (New York, 1930), vol. 1, p. 107.

tive of the mighty canyon of Lurin, which opens into the far heart
of the Andes. We saw peaks lifting themselves higher and higher
on either side of the canyon into what appear to be endless heights
in the dim distance until they finally blended into indistinguishable
shapes in the clouds which hung in dense masses above the higher
summits.

From the top of the Pyramid of the Sun, looking to the northeast, we had a good view of the restored Temple of the Moon. It
stands near the edge of the main part of the ancient city. An old
swimming pool—now restored—used extensively perhaps by the
ancient Peruvians, is situated near the Temple of the Moon.

Baptismal Font

We descended the Pyramid of the Sun and crossed the Valley
of the Dead, where we came upon a very important archaeological
structure. It is a cistern-like structure, rectangular in shape and
about the size of baptismal fonts commonly used by the members
of the Church of Jesus Christ of Latter-day Saints.

Frederick S. Williams remarked: "President Hunter, I am
thoroughly convinced that we are looking at a baptismal font which
was used by the ancient inhabitants of this land for the practice
of baptism by immersion. I have been here with various people on
several occasions and all of them were of the opinion that this
structure could have served for no other purpose than for baptisms."

"It certainly appears to me that it is an ancient baptismal font.
I can think of no other reason for which such a structure could have
been used," I replied.

The font was constructed of hewn rock so closely fitted together
that it would be impossible for water to leak through any cracks.
The rocks were placed together, however, without the use of mortar
or cement. The rockwork was masterfully done. The font is approximately ten feet long and six feet wide. It is about as deep as a tall
man's shoulders, as can be seen in the photograph, with President
and Sister Williams standing in it. Steps lead into it from its northeast corner. Still to be seen is a little rock ditch which carried water
in ancient times and emptied it into the font. On the west wall near

the floor, a square hole, approximately three inches in diameter, constitutes the end of a rock pipe which had served as a drain to empty the water from the baptismal font. This pipe extends underground for perhaps twenty yards and then opens into a rock ditch.

A few feet away from this baptismal font—lying to the south and extending around to the southwest—are the remains of rock foundations for what appear to have been three rooms. President Williams

—Photograph by Paul Cheesman

Fig. 110:   QUEEN'S BATH, PERU

Observe how a person could walk down steps into the bath, sit on a stone seat, and place his feet in the water. Compare the small size of the place where the water runs through the bath with the much larger cistern-like structure, designated as a baptismal font. Also compare these two archaeological structures with the swimming pool shown in the next photograph.

remarked: "These rock foundations are possibly the remains of what were at one time three dressing rooms, which no doubt were used by those preparing for the rite of baptism."

"That could very well be," I replied. "They are certainly suited for such a purpose."

Fig. 111: SWIMMING POOL AT PACHACAMAC, PERU

The swimming pool is situated within the rock walls towards the front and center of the photograph. The Temple of the Moon stands in the background.

Since returning from Peru, I have shown the photograph of the Pachacamac baptismal font to many groups of people. Most of those who have seen it agree that it certainly appears to be an ancient baptismal font. A few of them, however, have asked: "Why could not this structure have served as a bath instead of a baptismal font?"

I have replied to that inquiry: "I saw baths in some of the ancient ruins in Peru, and they differed greatly from this particular structure. This baptismal font is a much larger basin than were the ordinary ancient Peruvian baths." The accompanying photograph (Fig. 110) will show that the baths were quite small. Also, as may be observed in the photograph, the bath provided a rock seat for the person using it, as well as running water in which he could put his feet while taking his bath.

I also saw some ancient swimming pools in connection with the Peruvian archaeological ruins, such as the one situated near the Temple of the Moon shown in Fig. 111. Those ancient swimming pools are quite large, as are swimming pools today. A study and comparison of these various structures indicate that the one that President Williams classified as a baptismal font was not large enough for a swimming pool and was too large for a bath. It seems to me, therefore, that the only logical conclusion is that the one under consideration was a baptismal font used at one time for immersion.

BAPTISM IN NEPHITE DAYS

Certainly to find a baptismal font at Pachacamac, Peru, is not surprising nor out of line with what one could expect to find in American archaeological ruins. As has been pointed out, the inhabitants of the Western Hemisphere in ancient times, the Nephites, had the gospel of Jesus Christ. It is a well-known fact that one of the most important ordinances of that gospel as they practiced it was the rite of baptism by immersion. Nephi and other Book of Mormon prophets taught the people the doctrine of baptism. The ancient record described Alma performing this ordinance in the Waters of Mormon. Furthermore, when Christ appeared to the inhabitants of the New World following his resurrection, he gave the twelve men whom he commissioned to preside over his Church specific instructions regarding how to baptize, and he commanded them to practice the rite after his departure.

BAPTISM PRACTICED BY AMERICAN ABORIGINES

Numerous writers—including Catholic padres, early Spanish chroniclers, and Indian historians—maintain that when the Spaniards first arrived in America the Indians in many parts of the New World were practicing the ordinance of baptism. As had happened in the Old World among the Christians, however, many of the Indian tribes had changed the true order of baptism in various ways, but a resemblance to the ancient ordinance as given by Christ to the Nephites existed.

There is a cistern-like structure at Chichen Itzá which, according to the guides, was used by the Mayas before the discovery of America for baptism by immersion.[6] When I was shown that cistern-

---

[6]Milton R. Hunter, *Archaeology and the Book of Mormon* (Salt Lake City, 1956), vol. 1, pp. 89-92.

like structure and told by the guide that it was a baptismal font, I studied its appearance and structure carefully and concluded that it certainly could have been used for that purpose, and so I published a photograph of it on page 90 of *Archaeology and the Book of Mormon*, Volume I.

VISITING ANDEAN ARCHAEOLOGICAL SITES

My purpose for making this trip to South America was to visit archaeological sites and museums; and so after our trip to Pachacamac, I made arrangements to fly from the coastal city of Lima to the Incan and Tiahuanacan ancient archaeological cities. I wanted to visit Cuzco—the ancient Inca capital; Machu Picchu—the Inca city built on a mountain peak and discovered by Hiram Bingham; Lake Titicaca; the famous ruins of Tiahuanaco in Bolivia, as well as numerous other places of archaeological interest situated high up in the rugged Andes.

While Frederick S. Williams was making arrangements with government officials and museum directors for me to photograph many of the archaeological collections after my return to Lima, Elder Monte B. McLaws, Elder Dee Wilde, and I visited a number of ancient cities of considerable archaeological importance, situated in the high altitudes of the Andes.

We rode in a non-pressurized plane, which went 22,000 feet in the air. The pilot had to attain that altitude, because many of the mountain peaks ranged that high. One passenger lost consciousness because of the great altitude at which we were flying. This was a trip long to be remembered.

The first stop made by the airplane in which we were riding was at the famous city of Cuzco, Peru, the ancient capital of the Inca empire. As the plane landed, we saw painted in large letters on the slope of the mountain the statement *Viva El Peru* (Long Live Peru).

We were taken from the plane to a hotel and advised to go to bed for the remainder of the day while our bodies adjusted to the change of altitude from sea level to 11,000 feet. None of us were inclined, however, to spend precious daylight time in bed; and so

—*Photograph by Paul Cheesman*

Fig. 112:   Terraced Farming, Machu Picchu, Peru

we secured a guide who showed us a number of places of interest in Cuzco, an unusual city nearly 1,000 years old.

Many of the streets are the narrowest I have ever seen. I measured an ancient one and found it to be six feet and two inches wide. It is evident that it was not made for automobiles and other modes of modern-day traffic, but perhaps for llamas and mules, and, of course, for people on foot.

We visited the Temple of the Sun and other ancient Inca historic sites. On some of the buildings I observed carved representations of serpents, the symbol of Quetzalcoatl in Meso-America. I learned that the serpent was also the symbol of Viracocha in the Andean region.

Perhaps the most interesting of all the features shown to us by the guide was the superb stonework in the ancient buildings.

Some of the rocks were six feet wide, equally as high, and perhaps four feet thick. I had read before going to Peru that the rocks were placed together without the use of mortar or cement and that they were fitted so closely that it was impossible to put a knife blade in the crack between two rocks. We decided that most of them were fitted so closely that it would be difficult to put a razor blade in the joints between them.

I was astonished to observe that the ancient stonemasons had cut the mammoth rocks with many angles. We counted twelve angles on one rock—a rock over six feet square. The angles were cut and the rocks placed in such a way that all joints overlapped

Fig. 113:   Stone Wall at Cuzco, Peru

The stone with twelve angles measures six feet in each direction. Observe the numerous angles at which the stones are placed together. No cement or mortar was used between the stones; and they fit together as closely as if they had been made out of wood.

—*Photograph by Paul Cheesman*

each other; in other words, each rock was placed across the joint of the two rocks under it. This intelligent process employed by master workmen of the Andean region perhaps one thousand years ago—and at some of the archaeological sites even earlier—has resulted in the masonry's standing throughout the ages in spite of earthquakes or any other force of nature which would ordinarily destroy a building. We concluded that few if any builders anywhere in the world have surpassed the ancient peoples of the Andean region as efficient rock masons. Elders McLaws, Wilde, and I spent many exciting hours, as we intently examined the workmanship of those master builders who did their work hundreds and hundreds of years ago.

STONEWORK IN THE ANDES

After examining the stonework done by the ancient builders of the Andean region, numerous writers have speculated regarding how such superbly masterful work could have been accomplished and also what types of tools the ancient workman used. Dr. Von Hagen states:

It is now upon us to see how the builders worked.

One of the positions taken by many writers on these problems—and included therein are many archaeologists—is this: that the Cyclopean stone-work that one sees in Cuzco and especially in the fortress of Sucsahuaman (one of the greatest single structures ever reared by ancient man), was pre-Inca, and all this stone-work is attributed to some vague and shadowy anterior civilization called by them the "Megalithic empire." This position has little archaeological support. . . .

And of stone. When the gigantic size of the stones that form these structures is viewed for the first time, the utter enormity of the task of shaping, transporting them, and putting them into place—the edges so chamfered as to join without even a semblance of joining—is such that the viewer refuses to submit to the inescapable conclusion that the stone was quarried, pulled into place without dray animals, fashioned by stone instruments, and raised by crude leverage. Although such monoliths be as much as 20 tons in weight and variously shaped, they were made and fitted easily without cement, seemingly as a Chinese craftsman handles a piece of ivory. Such structures, unless destroyed by man, have resisted the insults of time for hundreds of years.[7]

Then Dr. Von Hagen presents his theory regarding the methods employed by the ancient stonemasons. He maintains that all the

----

[7]Von Hagen, op. cit., pp. 161-163.

work was done with stone tools. He described the quarrying of stone as follows:

Rock was searched for natural faults; after boring, the holes were filled with wooden wedges, swollen with water, and in time this swelling action cracked the huge rock masses. . . .

Transport of stone was by manpower. We know no more of transport techniques than we have from deduction. Although the Indian did not have the wheel, he used wood and stone rollers, and the rock in the rough was pulled by ropes with manpower. They used levers operating on bosses, perhaps sledges for dragging, but had only the most elementary knowledge of dynamics and of methods for handling mass-weight.[8]

And then only two pages later, he states: "How the Inca mason obtained this minute precision in which the enormous stone had to

Fig. 114:   Llamas in Front of the Fortress of Sucsahuaman, Peru

be lifted and set down a hundred times before the massive [stone] fitted perfectly on all sides like a bottle stopper, still cannot be satisfactorily explained."[9] I would agree that if one accepted his theory he would experience difficulty in explaining satisfactorily the processes and tools used by the highly efficient ancient Andean stonemasons.

---

[8] *Ibid.*, p. 164.
[9] *Ibid.*, p. 166.

In direct opposition to Dr. Von Hagen's theory, a number of statements are found in the authoritative history of the ancient Americans—the Book of Mormon—which maintain that the ancient builders possessed iron, steel, and practically all other metals, as well as draft animals, including horses, asses, and elephants—the latter being the most useful of all.[10] They also not only knew the use of the wheel but drove horses on wheeled carriages and perhaps used wheels for other purposes.[11]

Dr. Von Hagen pointed out, "many writers . . . including many archaeologists" maintain that a pre-Inca civilization was responsible for the magnificent stone structures found throughout the Andean region.

WHITE MEN AND STEEL

As was suggested in the previous chapter, the early Spanish chroniclers maintained that in ancient times white settlers arrived in Peru. It is claimed that these men with fair skins were responsible for the construction of the marvelous stoneworks at Cuzco, Machu Picchu, Sucsahuaman, Tiahuanaco, and other famous archaeological sites. Tradition affirms that most of these great structures were made prior to the development of the Inca empire and that the Inca and his subjects merely made additions to those structures. We observed that the top parts of certain buildings were composed of masonry much inferior to the lower parts, and our guides informed us that the inferior masonry was made by the Incas, especially during the later period.

In regards to the archaeological ruins of Tiahuanaco, Von Humboldt, the famous explorer, wrote: ". . . at the arrival of the Spaniards the natives attributed the construction of them [Tiahuanaco buildings] to a race of white and bearded men who inhabited the ridge of the Cordilleras long before the foundation of the empire of the Incas."[12] In 1863 Bollaert wrote in his paper on "The pre-Incarial Ruins of Tiahuanaco": "There are vague traditions that Tiahuanaco was built by white and bearded men."[13] Cieza de Leon

---

[10]1 Nephi 18:25; 2 Nephi 5:15; 20:34; Jarom 1:1-8; 2 Nephi 12:7; Enos 1:21; 3 Nephi 3:22; 4:4; Ether 9:19.
[11]Alma 18:9-12; 26:6.
[12]Von Humboldt, cited in Thor Heyerdahl, *American Indians in the Pacific* (Stockholm, 1952), p. 230.
[13]W. Bollaert, cited in *Ibid.*

Fig. 115: STONE STEPS AT TIAHUANACO, BOLIVIA

These cyclopean steps are carved out of one stone having an estimated weight of approximately 300 tons. Alwina R. Hulme, Monte B. McLaws, and Dee Wild are on the steps.

was one of the first Europeans to view Tiahuanaco (1553-1560). To quote his words: "I asked the natives . . . if these buildings had been constructed in the time of the Incas. They laughed at this question, affirming . . . that they had been made long before they ruled"; and then Cieza informs us that the pre-Inca builders were "white and bearded men."[14]

Miles Poindexter collected much valuable information regarding the traditions of the ancient Peruvians. He published his findings in two large volumes. He wrote:

Nearly everywhere, however, there existed the tradition of a superior white race who had brought an ancient culture and erected the great monuments. The well-preserved Peruvian tradition was that the stone structures . . . had been built by *"bearded white men"* with iron tools.[15]

Again Poindexter writes:

It is not impossible that the ancient builders—whose works would never have been believed possible but that their imperishable solidity and excellence have preserved them as bodily evidence of an achievement which otherwise all the archaeologists would have proved to be preposterous—had steel tools.[16]

And then he discusses some of the traditions regarding the ancient white Peruvians which maintain that these early settlers

---

[14]Cieza de Leon, cited in *Ibid.*, p. 231.
[15]Poindexter, *op. cit.*, vol. 1, p. 232.
[16]*Ibid.*, p. 236.

had *"instruments of iron."* He even cited cases where steel and iron tools have been found in archaeological excavations.[17]

The Peruvian traditions and Poindexter's observations are not only interesting but are also important, since the Book of Mormon writers claim that "a superior white race" migrated to America from western Asia and that this race had iron and steel tools; in fact, the Nephite record claims that the people worked ". . . in all manner of wood, and of iron, and of copper, and of brass, and of steel, and of gold, and of silver, and of precious ores, which were in great abundance."[18]

VIRACOCHA, THE "WHITE AND BEARDED GOD"

As previously mentioned, the Spanish chroniclers and Peruvian Indian writers maintained that Viracocha—the "White and Bearded

------

[17]*Ibid.*, pp. 237-239.
[18]2 Nephi 5:15; 20:34; Jarom 1:8; Mosiah 11:3, 8; Ether 7:9; 10:23.

Fig. 116: MACHU PICCHU, PERU

The ruins of Machu Picchu stand on the heights overlooking the Urubamba River. They are composed of terraces, gabled houses, temples sacred palaces, and a residential section. Its situation on top of a tall mountain supplies a daring example of city planning.

—Photograph by Author

God"—visited the white people in ancient Peru and gave them their religion and culture. I was interested while visiting in South America to learn that the Indians of Peru still retain this tradition. Oscar Nin Echegaray, the guide who took us to several archaeological sites near Cuzco, told us a number of traditions that he had obtained from the Indians relating to Viracocha. He maintained that the tradition was still prevalent among the natives that Viracocha had visited their ancestors, that he was a white and bearded man, and that he had brought the cross to the ancient Peruvians many years before the arrival of the Spaniards. Mr. Echegaray has an excellent command of the *Quechua* language, which was the language of the people of the Incas, and is the language of the Indians of the highlands of Peru at the present time, and so he obtains Indian traditions from them in their own language.

As was the custom of the aborigines of Meso-America in regards to Quetzalcoatl, the Indians of Peru erected temples to Viracocha. Writing in 1548, Cieza de Leon informs us that at Cacha, fifty miles

Fig. 117:   Ancient Water Works at Tambomachay Ruins near Cuzco, Peru

—Photograph by Paul Cheesman

—*Photograph by Author*

Fig. 118:   Sections of Stone Water Ditch at Tiahuanaco

south of Cuzco, stood a great temple of Kon-Tiki Viracocha.[19] The remains of the walls of that temple still stand, the structure being made of worked stone with adobe.

Archaeological Sites near Cuzco

We went to the marvelous and famous fortress called Sucsahuaman, situated near Cuzco. We also went to Pisac, Machu Picchu, and several other archaeological sites in the neighborhood of Cuzco, and at all the places we saw stonework which astounded us.

At this point I would like to draw to the reader's attention the fact that the ancient inhabitants of the Andean region developed irrigation. Aqueducts brought water from adjacent mountains, and the fructifying streams were conveyed from terrace to terrace by conduits so arranged as to prevent the washing of soil.[20] The photograph (Fig. 117) shows some of these ancient waterworks still in use. They date back, according to some authorities, nearly to the time of Christ.

The water in these waterworks was conveyed in pipes made of stone. It has already been mentioned that in the coastal city of Pachacamac we observed ancient rock aqueducts as well as a pipe

[19]Cieza de Leon, cited in Von Hagen, *op. cit.*, p. 116.
[20]Poindexter, *op. cit.*, p. 89.

Fig. 119:   QUECHUA INDIAN OF PERU WITH HIS LLAMAS

running from the baptismal font to such an aqueduct. A few days after seeing these aqueducts in Peru, I saw similar stone aqueducts at Tiahuanaco, Bolivia. The latter ones, however, are not now in use.

During July of 1958, J. David Billeter, Robert Wright, Ellsworth Knudson, my son M. Reed Hunter, and I saw rock aqueducts among the archaeological remains of ancient Corinth, Greece, which are almost duplicates of those I had seen a year earlier in Bolivia and Peru.

FROM CUZCO TO LAPAZ

Elders McLaws, Wilde, and I had a very interesting trip on the train and boat from Cuzco, Peru, to LaPaz, Bolivia. While traveling we were able to observe many things regarding the life and customs of the Indians of the Andean region. We saw group after group of natives with their domesticated llamas, each animal with a pack on its back, while the Indians trudged along on foot. We photographed many groups of Indians with their llamas.

Since our native land is North America, where we see no llamas

—Courtesy of the Deseret News Press

Fig. 120:   THE AUTHOR AND RELICS FROM PERU

A gold idol from an ancient Peruvian tomb and a small replica of one of the cyclopean Tiahuanacan stone statues are held in the author's hands. On the wall hangs an alpaca rug which he purchased near Cuzco, Peru.

except in zoos, these were very interesting to us. These peculiar animals, sometimes referred to as "Andean camels," moved with an aristocratic deliberation. Their ostrich-like heads, which they hold high in the air, their tails jauntily curled, and their straight slender legs give an impression of grace and fastidiousness as they daintily pick their way. We were told that each of the mature animals carries 75 pounds—no more—if the Indian wants his animal to co-operate. We observed that there are many colors of llamas, just as there are many colors of cattle or other animals. To me they were most attractive—in fact, beautiful.

At the various places where the train stopped en route from Cuzco, Peru, to the border of Bolivia, numerous Indians were at the train platform to sell their wares to the tourists. The articles of most attraction to the North Americans were the beautiful rugs, house slippers, and other items made from alpaca skins.

The alpaca is an animal similar to the llama; however, it is a little shorter in height and heavier in build. The principal difference is that it has long, fur-like wool in contrast to the shorter hair of the llama. This is the principal wool-bearing animal of the Andean region, supplying large quantities for the purpose of making cloth, rugs, and other wares appropriate to that region. The alpacas, too, vary in color. The Indians take the fur of several animals, each of a different color, and from them make colorful rugs of various designs. Fgure 120 is a photograph of an alpaca rug that I purchased from the Indians which will serve as an illustration of their rugs.

Lake Titicaca

When we arrived at the border of Bolivia, we came into a large valley in which lies the beautiful Lake Titicaca. This lake is approximately 12,500 feet above sea level. In the distance beyond the lake to the east, serving as a picturesque background, the gigantic Andes rise heavenward. Natives have lived for thousands of years on islands in this lake and in the valley surrounding it; in fact, this is the region which is said to have been the home of the earliest Andean civilizations.

The lake is located entirely in Bolivia; however, its western and northern shores constitute part of the boundary between the countries of Peru and Bolivia. We left the train in Peru at the shore of Lake Titicaca and entered a ship which took us across its beautiful waters. The lake trip was most interesting and unusual. We saw a number of Indians on the lake fishing in their little balsa boats made of reeds. Many of those people, we were told, secure a considerable part of their food from this body of water.

—Photographs by Phoebe Green

Fig. 121: QUECHUA INDIANS IN FISHING BOAT ON LAKE TITICACA

Fig. 122: LAKE TITICACA, BOLIVIA, AND QUECHUA INDIANS

LaPaz, Bolivia

We went by train from Lake Titicaca to LaPaz, the capital of Bolivia. This city is located between 13,000 and 14,000 feet above sea level and in the same extensive valley as the lake. It is surrounded by the high Andes, a number of peaks extending upward to an altitude of over 22,000 feet. They are perpetually snow-capped, constituting a most beautiful mountain range.

We stayed in LaPaz for three or four days as guests of Robert and Alwina Hulme, most hospitable and wonderful people. We appreciate deeply all that they did for us.

While at LaPaz we visited and photographed the artifacts in the Tiahuanacan National Museum and in private museums. A number of gigantic stelae and other archaeological relics have been moved from Tiahuanaco to LaPaz. They now stand in the public plaza. Among the latter are some very tall stelae in human form which, according to the report of the Indians to the early Catholic chroniclers, were made by the white and bearded worshipers of Viracocha.

Fig. 123: Stone Statues from Tiahuanaco, Bolivia

These stone statues have been moved from Tiahuanaco to the city of LaPaz, Bolivia. They stand in a square in the center of town.

TIAHUANACO

While driving to Tiahuanaco, we passed through a number of small Indian villages and encountered several caravans of llamas with packs on their backs. The barefooted Indian women caused us to marvel. They hurried along the graveled road on a little trot, carrying heavy loads on their heads or backs, and never seemed to flinch.

The most exciting experience we had while in Bolivia was to visit Tiahuanaco. This famous archaeological site is situated approximately twenty-five miles north of LaPaz and a few miles south of Lake Titicaca. Mrs. Hulme, one of her friends—an archaeologist—along with Elder McLaws, Elder Wilde, and I went there in a rented car.

The most important archaeological artifacts at Tiahuanaco are the mammoth-sized stones, many of which stand on their ends like

—Photograph by Author

Fig. 124: Monte B. McLaws, Dee Wilde, and Viracocha Statue

This statue is claimed to be a representation of Viracocha, the "Fair God" of the Andean region. Observe the book in its arm. The statue is still at Tiahuanaco, Bolivia.

tall stelae, and the gorgeous gateway of that ancient city. The latter is composed of stones beautifully carved.

We were told that a few of the largest objects made of single rocks at Tiahuanaco weigh 150 to 300 tons. We saw a massive tier of steps carved from one rock which was estimated to weigh nearly 300 tons. "The stonework of Tiahuanaco is some of the best in the Andes. Stones are fitted together with insets and tenons; larger stones are bound with copper clamps. All this architectural megalithic stonework presupposes a social organization, a strong central government which could divert the use of manpower into non-productive channels of so large a scale."[21] Certainly the people must

[21]Von Hagen, op. cit., p. 34.

--*Photographs by Author*

Fig. 125: SIDE VIEW OF STELA COVERED WITH CARVED SERPENTS, TIAHUANACO

Fig. 126: FRONT VIEW OF STELA COVERED WITH CARVED SERPENTS, TIAHUANACO

have had a long technical tradition in order to construct such gigantic and beautifully carved stonework.

Tiahuanaco was a city built for religious purposes—a place to worship the gods. It is claimed that it ". . . must have been the greatest ceremonial center in all the Andes."[22] The most important god worshiped at Tiahuanaco was Viracocha. There is still a large stone representation of that god, holding a book in his arms (Fig. 124) at that place.

We also observed carved serpents on some of the stelae, indicating that in far-off Bolivia the serpent was regarded as one of the symbols of the "White and Bearded God," even as it was a symbol of Quetzalcoatl in Meso-America.

Serpent designs appear many times on pottery of the ancient Peruvians, and they are also found woven into their cloth. Thus these symbols of Viracocha were represented in a variety of ways.

A point of significance and interest is the fact that in faraway Lebanon and Israel even today the natives are still using the serpent as a design on their pottery. Dr. Winslow Whitney Smith, while on a visit to Israel two or three years ago, purchased from roadside merchants some pottery decorated with serpents. He was not seeking such pottery but merely purchased what the people were making and selling. It is quite unusual that two peoples so far apart in distance and time should make pottery so similar in design. The answer could be that the two peoples had a common heritage which caused them to use the same religious symbol.

Since the puma was also a symbol of Viracocha in Peru, the god was ofttimes represented with large puma teeth, as the photograph of a vase shows. A photograph of Viracocha, shown with puma teeth, hangs on the wall of the office of Dr. George C. Muelle, the director of the National Archaeological Museum at Lima. It is reproduced in this book through his courtesy.

In ancient Egypt the falcon was a sacred symbol having a religious significance. Such was also the case in ancient Peru. Observe the falcon on a vase of the Paracus culture. In 1957 this vase was found in a tomb and photographed by Paul Cheesman of Miami, Florida.

---

[22]*Ibid.*, p. 32.

Return to Salt Lake City

The day following our trip to the marvelous archaeological site of Tiahuanaco, I flew from LaPaz—whose airport is 14,404 feet in altitude, the highest one in the world—to Lima, Peru.

I stayed in Lima two more weeks, saw many marvelous things, and took archaeological trips in various directions before I returned to Salt Lake City by way of Miami, Florida.

This visit to Peru and Bolivia constitutes one of the outstanding experiences and archaeological excursions of my life. I am indeed grateful to C. N. Shelton, president of the TAN Airlines, and his brother and vice president, Ralph V. Shelton, for making possible this trip. Ralph Shelton and Paul Cheesman, both of Miami, Florida, are avidly interested in the archaeological evidences of the Book of Mormon. They have outstanding collections of photographs of the South American ruins.

The trip to the Andean region gave me the opportunity to observe numerous evidences indicative of high civilizations in ancient America, including the existence of a white race of people, and numerous archaeological artifacts which are in harmony with the claims made by the Book of Mormon.

CHAPTER 11

VIRACOCHA THE CREATOR

THE CREATOR

All of the early Spanish chroniclers, receiving their information from the Indians shortly after the discovery of the New World, maintained that the "Fair God" was the Creator of man, of the heavens, of the earth, and of all that is in the universe.

The Viceroy Don Francisco de Toledo, who governed Peru from 1569 to 1581, appointed Captain Pedro Sarmiento de Gamboa to collect accurate information from the Indians and write a history to send to Philip II, king of Spain. Sarmiento maintained that he "collected the information with much diligence so that this history can rest on attested proofs."[1] He gathered his material from various classes of Indians, which included both the Incas and tributary nations. His account was written in A.D. 1572. In it he states:

> The natives of this land affirm that in the beginning, and before this world was created, there was a being called Viracocha. He created a dark world without a sun, moon and stars. Owing to this creation he was named Viracocha Pachayachachi, which means "Creator of all things." And when he had created the world he formed a race of giants of disproportioned greatness, painted and sculptured, to see whether it would be well to make man of that size. *He then created men in his own likeness as they are now;* and they lived in darkness.[2]

Sarmiento continued by stating that Viracocha gave the people many good laws, ordering them ". . . that they should live without quarreling, and that they should know and serve him. . . . They kept this precept for some time, . . . But as there arose among them pride and covetousness, they transgressed the precept of Viracocha Pachayachachi and falling, through this sin, under his indignation, he confounded and cursed them."[3]

This sounds exactly like another version of the great role in the human drama played by Jesus Christ as the Creator of the world

---

[1]Pedro Sarmiento de Gamboa, *History of the Incas* (1572). (Hakluyt Society, Second Series No. XXII, Cambridge, 1907), p. 28.
[2]*Idem.*
[3]*Ibid.,* p. 29.

Fig. 127: STONE STATUES FROM TIAHUANACO, BOLIVIA

These statues are in a public square in LaPaz, Bolivia. The taller one appears to be carrying a book.

—Photograph by Author

and man, and of giving the human family the gospel plan of salvation.

DELUGE

Sarmiento's account stated that Viracocha sent a great flood to destroy the human family. To quote:

They say that it rained 60 days and nights, that it drowned all created things, . . .

Some of the nations, besides the Cuzcos, also say that a few were saved from this flood to leave descendants for a future age. Each nation has its

special fable which is told by its people, of how their ancestors were saved
from the waters of the deluge. [And then the writer tells some of these
fables.][4]

Fig. 128:   CLOTH TAKEN FROM A TOMB IN PERU CONTAINING THE SERPENT
AND THE CROSS DESIGNS, SYMBOLS OF THE "FAIR GOD" OF ANCIENT AMERICA

Sarmiento gives a very remarkable account which he claims
differs in details from what the "true Scriptures teach us"; however,
what he accounts is directly in harmony with the story told in the
Book of Mormon. To quote the words of Sarmiento:

> . . . One thing is believed among all the nations of these parts, for they
all speak generally and as well know of the general flood which they call
uñu pachacuti. From this we clearly understand that in these parts they have
a tradition of the great flood, . . .[5]

He then gives a significant account of Indian traditions which
declare that the Andean region was populated from across the
ocean following the flood. Continuing his account, we quote:

> . . . and now the Indies of Castille or America must have begun to receive

----

[4]*Ibid.*, pp. 30-32.
[5]*Ibid.*, p. 32.

population immediately after the flood, although, by their account, the details are different from those which the true Scriptures teach us. This must have been done by divine Providence, . . .[6]

All of this fits in perfectly with the true account of Jehovah's (Jesus') bringing the Jaredites from the Tower of Babel to America following the flood. This story is given in Ether, the next to last book in the Book of Mormon.

Sarmiento stated that the story given by the Incas at Cuzco differed from the account of the flood given by most of the other Indian nations. He wrote:

> . . . But the Incas and most of those at Cuzco, those among them who are believed to know most, do not say that anyone escaped from the flood, but that Viracocha began to create men afresh, as will be seen further on. . . .[7]

[6]*Idem.*
[7]*Ibid.*, p. 31.

Fig. 129:   INDIAN CHILDREN AT SUCSAHUAMAN, PERU
—Photograph by Paul Cheesman

GRAND COUNCIL

Later Sarmiento stated:

It is related that everything was destroyed in the flood called *uñu pacha-cuti*. It must now be known that Viracocha Pachayachachi, when he destroyed the land as has already been recounted, preserved three men, and one of them named Taguapaca, that they might serve and help him in the creation of new people. . . .

Viracocha gave various orders to his servants, but Taguapaca disobeyed the command of Viracocha.[8]

For this disobedience, his hands and feet were tied, and he was launched on a *balsa* raft which was placed on Lake Titicaca. "He was carried by the water down the drain of the lake, and was not seen again for a long time."[9]

Father Abraham, as accounted in the Pearl of Great Price, had a vision regarding a "Grand Council" that was held in heaven by the Gods when they were planning the creating and peopling of this world.[10] The four most important persons at the council were God the Father, Christ the Only Begotten Son, Michael or Father Adam, and Lucifer or Satan. The latter rebelled against the others and, with his followers, was cast out of heaven.[11] The other three worked together as the Gods who created this earth and man.[12] The story of Taguapaca seems to be a distorted account of Satan's rebellion and banishment from the presence of Elohim, Jehovah, and Michael, and the sons and daughters of the Eternal Father who accepted Christ as their Savior.

CREATION ACCOUNT

Sarmiento continued his account of the creation of man as follows:

The flood being passed and the land dry, Viracocha determined to people it a second time; and, to make it more perfect, he decided upon creating luminaries to give light. With this object in mind he went, with his servants [the three men that Viracocha had saved from the flood], to a great lake in

---

[8]*Ibid.*, pp. 32-33.
[9]*Ibid.*, p. 33.
[10]Abraham 3:21-28; 4:1-31.
[11]*Ibid.*, 3:27-28; Moses 4:1-4.
[12]Milton R. Hunter, *Pearl of Great Price Commentary* (Salt Lake City, 1951), pp. 67-73; Milton R. Hunter, *The Gospel through the Ages* (Salt Lake City, 1945), pp. 104-110.

Fig. 130: FALCON VASE

This falcon vase was taken from a tomb in the Paracas district on the southwestern coast of Peru. The Paracas culture dates B.C. 400 to A.D. 400.

the Collao, in which there is an island called Titicaca [Tee-tee-cä'cä], . . . Viracocha went to this island, and presently ordered that the sun, moon, and stars should come forth, and be set in the heavens to give light to the world, and it was so. . . .

Leaving the island, he passed by the lake to the main land, taking with him the two servants who survived. He went to a place now called Tiahuanacu [Tiahuanaco] in the province of Colla-suyu, and in this place he sculptured and designed on a great piece of stone, all the nations that he intended to create. . . .

Others affirm that this creation of Viracocha was made from the Titicaca site where, having originally formed some shapes of large strong men which seemed to him out of proportion, *he made them again of his stature which was, as they say, the average height of men,* and being made he gave them life. Thence they set out to people the land. . . . This was from the residence of Viracocha, their maker. . . .

[Viracocha—the God Creator—commanded the people], . . . saying with a loud voice, "Oh, you tribes and nations, hear and obey the order of Ticci Viracocha Pachayachachi, which commands you to go forth and multiply and settle the land."[13]

---

[13]Sarmiento, *op. cit.,* pp. 32-35.

Fig. 131: GOLD GOBLET IN NATIONAL
MUSEUM, LIMA, PERU

Observe the representation of a man wearing a
headdress of feathers carved on this goblet. Designs around the goblet are similar to those on a
palace at Mitla, Oaxaco, Mexico. This archaeological object was found in an ancient Peruvian burial.

—Photograph by Author

Sarmiento and other Spanish chroniclers were surprised and
perplexed to find that the American Indians already possessed many
of the teachings of the Bible when they first met the Spaniards.
Viracocha's command to the people is almost identical with the
command given by Jehovah when he created Adam and Eve.

In Genesis we read:

So God created man in his own image, in the image of God created he
him; male and female created he them, . . .[14]

It should be recalled that Indian tradition claimed that Viracocha "created men in his own likeness as they are now"; or again
we quote, Viracocha " . . . made them again of his stature which
was, as they say, the average height of men, and being made he
gave them life."

To continue with the Bible quotation:

And God blessed them, and God said unto them, Be fruitful, and multiply,
and replenish the earth, and subdue it: . . .[15]

SUMMARY—VIRACOCHA THE CREATOR

Practically every writer who obtained his information directly
from the Indians of the Andean region shortly following the Spanish

---

[14]Genesis 1:27.
[15]*Ibid.*, 1:28.

Fig. 132:   SERPENTS CARVED ON WALL IN CUZCO, PERU

This ancient Peruvian wall is claimed to have been erected approximately 900 years ago.

conquest maintained that there was a universal tradition crediting Viracocha with being the "Creator of all things." In order to summarize, perhaps we could do no better than to quote a summary of this subject found in a footnote of Sarmiento's *History of the Incas* (pp. 28-29):

> Uiracocha (Viracocha) was the Creator. Garcilasso de la Vega pointed out the mistake of supposing that the word signifies "foam of the sea." . . . Blas Valera said the meaning was the "will and power of God"; not that this is the signification of the word, but by reason of the godlike qualities attributed to Him who was known by it. Cieza de Leon says that Tici-Uiracocha was God, Creator of heaven and earth: Acosta said that to Ticci-Uiracocha they assigned the power and command over all things; Montesinos claimed that Illa-tici-Uiracocha was the name of the Creator of the world; Molina that Tesci-Uricocha was the Creator and incomprehensible God; the anonymous Jesuit maintained that Uiracocha meant the great God of "Pirua"; Betanzos stated that the Creator was Tici-Uiracocha.
>
> . . . *Ticci* or *Tici* is based on foundation, hence the founder. *Illa* means light. The anonymous Jesuit gives the meaning "Eternal Light" to *Illa-Ticci*. . . .
>
> Pachacamac and Pachayachachi are attributes of the deity. *Pacha* means time or place, also the universe, *Camac* is the Ruler, *Yachachi* the Teacher— "The Ruler and Teacher of the Universe."

It seems to the writer that a careful study of the part played by Jehovah (Christ) in creating the world and all that is in it as described in the Bible and the numerous statements regarding Christ's work as a Creator delineated in the Book of Mormon should give the reader sufficient evidence to convince him that Viracocha, as God and Creator, is the same person as Jesus Christ, our Creator, God, and Savior.

CHAPTER 12

QUETZALCOATL THE CREATOR
AND CULTURE GIVER

INTRODUCTORY STATEMENT

The previous chapter presented traditions and evidence to the effect that Viracocha, the "White and Bearded God" of the Andean region, was regarded as the creator of the heavens and the earth and of the human family. In this chapter we shall devote our attention to Indian traditions of Meso-America and examine the evidence given in Mexican and Maya documents pertaining to Quetzalcoatl as a creator and culture giver.

"SUN OF QUETZALCOATL"

Laurette Séjourné presents an elaborate and detailed discussion of the various Nahuatl and Aztec myths of the Creator-God, Quetzalcoatl; and then she expressed her viewpoint as to why the Indians considered him the creator of man. To quote:

The Meso-American people have pointed out the transcendence of his message. In most of their myths of creation, for instance, it is said that during the four eras previously destroyed the earth was populated only by animals, and it was not until the advent of the era of Quetzalcoatl that humanity was created. This suggests that it is only after the discovery of the spiritual principle as lived by Quetzalcoatl that man could be. This is doubtless the reason why Quetzalcoatl was considered as creator of the human being and all his works.[1]

Quetzalcoatl as "God of Wind" was accredited by the Indians as the deity who set the sun in motion, thereby becoming its creator. The Quetzalcoatl myth states that there had been four previous suns, each ending in disaster. Eventually, however, the "Fifth Sun" came into the sky; ". . . and when it . . . began to rise it seemed very red. It lurched from side to side, and none could look at it, for it took

---

[1]Laurette Séjourné, *Burning Water—Religion and Thought in Ancient Mexico* (London, 1956), p. 55.

sight from the eyes. It shone, and threw out rays splendidly, and its rays split everywhere; . . ."[2] However, the sun seemed incapable of movement and thereby was "no more capable of life than the previous ones that had been annihilated."

Thereupon the "God of Wind," Quetzalcoatl, breathed upon it and as a result of that dynamic spiritual breath, the Fifth Sun was set in motion in the heavens. "That is why the Fifth Sun (five is the number of the center) is the *Sun of Movement,* meeting in man. . . . The name of this Sun is Naollin (Four Movements), now it is ours, by which today we live . . . It was the Sun of Quetzalcoatl. . . ."[3]

QUETZALCOATL: CREATOR AND CULTURE GIVER

An Aztec document stated that Quetzalcoatl was ". . . *lord over all and maker of all creatures. . . .*"[4] He was regarded by those people as ". . . *an invisible god and creator. . . .* Moreover it is well known that the *maker of all creatures was none other than Quetzalcoatl.*"[5]

A Mexican archaeologist, Dr. Alfonso Caso, gives an excellent summarizing statement regarding the accomplishments of the Creator-God:

> . . . Quetzalcoatl appears as god of life, constant benefactor of humanity, and so we see that, after having created man with his own blood, he searches for a way to nourish him, and discovers the maize that the ants had hidden inside a mountain. He turns himself into an ant and steals a grain which he afterwards gives to men.

> He teaches them how to polish jade and the other precious stones and how to find where these stones lie; how to weave many-colored fabrics, with a miraculous cotton that existed already dyed in different colours, and how to make mosaics with *quetzal* plumes, from the blue bird, the humming bird, the parrot and other birds of bright plumage.

> But above all he taught man science, showing him the way to measure time and study the revolutions of the stars; he showed him the calendar and invented ceremonies and fixed the days for prayers and sacrifice.[6]

------

[2]Bernardino de Sahagún, *Historia General de las Casas de Nueva España* (Editorial Nueva España, S. A., Mexico, 1946), vol. 2, pp. 15-16.
[3]*Legendas de Los Soles* (tr. from Nahuatl by Angel Maria Garibay and cited in *Historia de la Literatura Nahuatl* (Editorial Porrua, Mexico, 1953), pp. 295-296, cited in Séjourné, *op. cit.*, pp. 72-73.
[4]*Anales de Cuauhtitlan* (Imprenta, Universitaria, Mexico, 1955), p. 61.
[5]Séjourné, *op. cit.*, pp. 35-40.
[6]Alfonso Caso, *El Pueblo del Sol* (Fondo de Cultura Economica, Mexico, 1953), p. 40.

—*Photograph by Otto Done*

Fig. 133:   QUETZALCOATL PLUMED SERPENT

This symbolic representation of the "White and Bearded God" is housed in the National Museum, Mexico City.

CHRIST THE CREATOR

Since at the time of the discovery of the New World the Indians of Meso-America had such a positive conviction that Quetzalcoatl was the creator of the heavens, the earth, and the human family, we shall now turn to the teachings of their forefathers, as recorded in the Book of Mormon, and study their claims regarding the Messiah.

Jesus Christ was known to the ancient Americans by numerous titles which connoted his divine nature or Godship. He played such a prominent part in the great creation program of the heavens, the earth, and man, that they regarded him as the omnipotent Creator of all things. He was the medium through which the Eternal Father did all his work. Christ was the Father's representative. So important was the Messiah's part in the creation program that he declared to the Nephites: "Behold, I am Jesus Christ the Son of God. I created the heavens and the earth, and all things that in them are. . . ."[7] An angel told King Benjamin that

. . . he shall be called Jesus Christ, the Son of God, the Father of heaven

---

[7] 3 Nephi 9:15.

and earth, the Creator of all things from the beginning; and his mother shall be called Mary.[8]

Samuel the Lamanite stood on the wall of the city of Zarahemla and called the people to repentance. He told them that he was preaching to them ". . . that ye might know of the coming of Jesus Christ, the Son of God, the Father of heaven and earth, the Creator of all things from the beginning; . . ."[9] Jacob reminded the Nephites:

Yea, I know that ye know that in the body he [Jesus Christ] shall show himself to those at Jerusalem, from whence we came; . . . for it behooveth the great Creator that he suffereth himself to become subject unto man in the flesh, and die for all men, that all men might become subject unto him.

For as death hath passed upon all men, to fulfil the merciful plan of the great Creator, there must needs be a power of resurrection, . . .[10]

We read (Jacob 2:5) that Jacob also informed his people ". . . that by the help of the all-powerful Creator of heaven and earth I can tell you concerning your thoughts, . . ." Another Book of Mormon writer named Amaleki claimed that the Jaredites were destroyed because ". . . they denied the being of their Creator; . . ."[11] King Mosiah II stated that: ". . . were it not for the interposition of their all-wise Creator [Jesus Christ], . . . they [the Nephites] must unavoidably remain in bondage until now."[12]

King Benjamin also instructed the Nephites as follows:

Therefore, I would that ye should be steadfast and immovable, always abounding in good works, that Christ, the Lord God Omnipotent, may seal you his, that you may be brought to heaven, that ye may have everlasting salvation and eternal life, through the wisdom, and power, and justice, and mercy of him who created all things, in heaven and in earth, who is God above all. Amen.[13]

The Prophet Jacob described the great and marvelous work accomplished by the Eternal Father through his Only Begotten Son Jesus Christ. He said:

Behold, great and marvelous are the works of the Lord. . . .

For behold, by the power of his word man came upon the face of the earth, which earth was created by the power of his word. Wherefore, if God being able to speak and the world was, and to speak and man was created, O then, why not able to command the earth, or the workmanship of his hands upon the face of it, according to his will and pleasure?[14]

---

[8]Mosiah 3:8.
[9]Helaman 14:12.
[10]2 Nephi 9:5-6.
[11]Omni 1:17.

[12]Mosiah 29:19.
[13]*Ibid.*, 5:15.
[14]Jacob 4:8-9.

Not only was Christ thought to be the Only Begotten Son and the Creator, but he was also regarded by the ancient Americans as man's constant and eternal enlightener. "The Light, the Life, and the Truth of the world," and "he that leadeth men to all good." This doctrine is taught very forcefully throughout the entire Book of Mormon.[15]

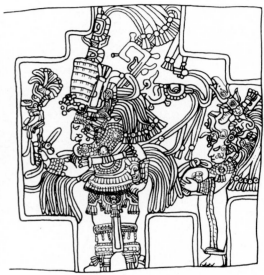

—Art Work by Huberta Berg Robison

Fig. 134: STELA 3, IXKUN, GUATEMALA

Fig. 135: LINTEL 1, YAXCHILAN, MEXICO

These ancient Maya carvings are beautiful examples of the extensive use made of quetzal plumes and jade, symbols of Quetzalcoatl, by the pre-Columbian peoples of Meso-America.

QUETZALCOATL THE CREATOR AND HIS EARTHLY ADVENT

Von Humboldt, an explorer, author, and collector of Indian traditions and old manuscripts, maintains that the Indians believed that Quetzalcoatl was originally a God and the creator of all things before his sojourn in mortality and his appearance to the inhabitants of ancient America. Von Humboldt wrote:

. . . authors might be adduced to show that the Mexicans believe that this Quetzalcoatl was both God and man; that he had previously to his incarnation existed from eternity, and that he had been the Creator both of

---

[15]Mosiah 16:9; Alma 38:9; 3 Nephi 9:18; 15:9; 11:11; Ether 4:12.

the world and man; and that he had descended to reform the world by endurance.[16]

The following is quoted from the Nephites' records to aid the readers in observing how accurately the Indians preserved in their traditions the story of Christ's position as a God, the Lord, and the divine Son, and of his crucifixion and resurrection, which events were followed by his descent from heaven to proclaim the gospel to the inhabitants of ancient America:

. . . they saw a Man descending out of heaven; and he was clothed in a white robe; and he came down and stood in the midst of them; . . .

. . . he . . . spake unto the people, saying:

Behold, I am Jesus Christ, whom the prophets testified shall come into the world.

And behold, I am the light and the life of the world; and I have drunk out of that bitter cup which the Father hath given me, and have glorified the Father in taking upon me the sins of the world, in the which I have suffered the will of the Father in all things from the beginning. . . .

. . . the Lord spake unto them saying:

Arise and come forth unto me, that ye may thrust your hands into my side, and also that ye may feel the prints of the nails in my hands and in my feet, that ye may know that I am the God of Israel, and the God of the whole earth, and have been slain for the sins of the world.[17]

Dr. De Roo summarized the work accomplished by the "White Bearded God," according to the traditions of the Indians of Mexico, as follows:

. . . They say it was Quetzalcoatl who effected the reformation of the world, but men had given themselves up to vice, on which account it had been frequently destroyed, but now had Tonacatecotl sent his son into the world to reform it.

Quetzalcoatl undertook the reformation of the sinful world through preaching, by word and example, the virtues of self-denial and fasting, of chastity and piety, of charity towards men, and of a pure religion towards the one true God. For a time he succeeded in Tula, where, according to some reports, his virgin-mother, Chimelma, lived; but in spite of all the wondrous good he did in that province, like Christ, he was persecuted, and finally driven out by the majority of the people. Carrying a cross, he came to the valley of the Zapotecs. . . .[18]

---

[16]Von Humboldt, cited in John Taylor, *Mediation and Atonement* (Salt Lake City, 1882), p. 202.

[17]3 Nephi 11:8, 10-11, 13-14.

[18]P. DeRoo, *History of America before Columbus* (Philadelphia, 1900), vol. 1, pp. 430-431.

Indians' Knowledge of Godhead Received from Quetzalcoatl

The early Spanish missionaries who labored in Middle America were greatly surprised to find that the Indians had an extensive knowledge of the Godhead or Holy Trinity. The natives made the claim that their knowledge had been given to them originally by Quetzalcoatl, which would be in harmony with the claims made by the Book of Mormon that Jesus Christ appeared to the inhabitants of ancient America and taught them his gospel in its fulness. Relying on the famous Catholic missionary, Padre Sahagún, for his information, Dr. De Roo wrote:

> The natives of Campeche assured the Spanish missionaries that their religious teacher, Quetzalcoatl, had given them images to explain his doctrine, and, in particular, a triangular stone, as an illustration of the Blessed Trinity, with which mystery they were well-acquainted, says Sahagún, and in whose name they were baptized.[19]

Hubert Howe Bancroft informs us that the Quiché Maya Indians in Guatemala also held in their traditions a belief in a Godhead, composed of three divine personages. The names by which they were known were Tohil, Awilix, and Gucumatz.[20]

Bishop Bartholome de las Casas, a famous Spanish Catholic priest who did extensive missionary work among the Indians of Chiapas, Mexico, and who recorded their traditions, reported that Francis Hernandez, a priest laboring under his direction, wrote him a letter in which he claimed that the Indians had a tradition of a Godhead, composed of three members, similar to the Holy Trinity worshiped by the Christians. The writer has found no statement among the Indian traditions which more clearly expresses this doctrine than the following which Bishop de las Casas attributed to Hernandez:

> . . . I found a good secular priest [Francis Hernandez], of mature age and honorable, who knew the language of the Indians, having lived among them several years; and because I was obliged to travel on to the chief town of my diocese, I appointed him my vicar, asking him and giving him charge to visit the tribes of the inland, and to preach to them in the manner that I gave him.
>
> The same priest, after some months, or even a year, as I think, wrote to me that he had met with a chief from whom he had made inquiries in regard to his ancient belief and religion, which they were used to follow in

---

[19]*Ibid.*, p. 372.
[20]Bancroft, *op. cit.*, vol. 2, p. 648.

that country. The Indian answered him that they knew and believed in God who dwells in the heavens, and that God is Father, Son, and Holy Ghost. The Father's name was Icona, and he had created man and all things; the Son had for name Bacab, and he was born from a maiden always virgin, called Chibirias, that lives in the heavens with God. The Holy Ghost they called Echuac. They say that Icona means the Great Father of Bacab, who is the Son. . . .

When the Indian was asked the meaning of Bacab or Bacabab, he said that it meant Son of the Great Father, and that the name Echuac signified Merchant. And, in fact, the Holy Ghost brought good merchandises to earth, since he satiated the world, that is, the people of the world, with his abundant divine gifts and graces.[21]

Hernandez also informed Bishop de las Casas that he had received the foregoing tradition from one of the old chiefs who claimed that that tradition had come to him from his ancient ancestors.[22]

CONCLUSION

The foregoing tradition of the Chiapan Indians gives a clear statement regarding the aborigines' knowledge of the Godhead, a doctrine thoroughly known by the inhabitants of ancient America, as is attested in the Book of Mormon. It seems evident that the basic ideas in the Godhead doctrine as proclaimed anciently by the Ne-

---

[21]*Las Casas*, cited in De Roo, *op. cit.*, pp. 373-374.
[22]*Idem.*, p. 373.

Fig. 136: PLUMED SERPENT AT TENAYUCA, MEXICO

Tenayuca is situated six miles northwest of Mexico City.

Fig. 137: SERPENT FRIEZE DECORATION OF BUILDING AT PALENQUE, MEXICO

phite prophets came down among the various Indian tribes from age to age to the time of the Spanish conquest.

It is also true that the knowledge of Christ's or Quetzalcoatl's work as the Creator and the knowledge of his contribution to the human family in giving them their religion and culture—truths originally proclaimed to the ancient Americans by Book of Mormon prophets and by the resurrected Messiah—came down through Indian traditions to the time of the discovery of America. The aborigines were as definite in their traditions that Quetzalcoatl was the Creator and culture giver as were their predecessors, the Nephites.

CHAPTER 13

QUETZALCOATL'S VIRGIN BIRTH

JESUS CHRIST'S VIRGIN BIRTH

Another significant historical event, the virgin birth of Jesus Christ, was thoroughly known by the inhabitants of ancient America, as is set forth in the plain teachings found in the Book of Mormon. A few examples of Nephite teachings will be quoted. Nephi saw in vision the following:

> . . . in the city of Nazareth I beheld a virgin, and she was exceedingly fair and white. . . .
> And he [the angel] said unto me: Behold, the virgin whom thou seest is the mother of the Son of God, after the manner of the flesh.[1]

It is also written in the Book of Mormon:

> . . . Behold, a virgin shall conceive, and shall bear a son, and shall call his name Immanuel.[2]

Alma informed the Nephites that it had been revealed to him that

> . . . the Son of God cometh upon the face of the earth.
> And behold, he shall be born of Mary, . . . she being a virgin, a precious and chosen vessel, who shall be overshadowed and conceive by the power of the Holy Ghost, and bring forth a son, yea, even the Son of God.[3]

Even before the time of Alma, another ancient American prophet, King Benjamin, knew of the virgin birth of the Messiah. As recorded in the Nephite records (Mosiah 3:3, 5, 8), one night an angel from the presence of God visited that prophet-king and said unto him:

> . . . Awake, and hear the words which I shall tell thee; for behold, I am come to declare unto you the glad tidings of great joy.

> For behold, the time cometh, and is not far distant, that with power, the Lord Omnipotent who reigneth, who was, and is from all eternity to all

---

[1] 1 Nephi 11:13, 18.
[2] 2 Nephi 17:14.
[3] Alma 7:9-10

eternity, shall come down from heaven among the children of men, and dwell in a tabernacle of clay, . . .

And he shall be called Jesus Christ, the Son of God, the Father of heaven and earth, the Creator of all things from the beginning; and his mother shall be called Mary.

INDIANS' TRADITIONS OF QUETZALCOATL'S VIRGIN BIRTH

With such doctrine being thoroughly taught among the inhabitants of ancient America, it is natural that those teachings would carry forward from age to age as part of the traditions of the "White Bearded God." History affirms that such was the case. Daniel G. Brinton commented on the wide dissemination of the virgin birth tradition as follows:

Many of the goddesses were virgin deities, as the Aztec Coatlicue, Xochiquetzal, and Chimelma; and many of the great gods of the race as Quetzalcoatl, Manibozho, Viracocha, and Ioskeha, were said to have been born of a virgin. Even among the low Indians of Paraguay, the early missionaries were startled to find this tradition of the maiden mother of the god, so similar to that which they had come to tell.[4]

In speaking specifically of Quetzalcoatl, Dr. Brinton wrote:

Quetzalcoatl was born of a virgin in the land of Tula or Tlapallan, in the distant Orient, and was high priest of that happy realm.[5]

Von Humboldt's statement regarding the tradition of the virgin birth of Quetzalcoatl is as follows:

How truly surprising is it to find that the Mexicans, who seem to have been unacquainted with the doctrine of the migration of the soul and the Metempsychosis *should have believed in the incarnation of the only Son of the supreme God, Tomacateuctli.* For Mexican mythology, speaking of no other Chimelma, the virgin of Tula (without man), by his breath alone, by which may be signified his work or will, when it was announced to Chimelma, by the celestial messenger, whom he dispatched to inform her that she should conceive a son, it must be presumed this was Quetzalcoatl, who was the only son.[6]

Dr. P. De Roo described Quetzalcoatl's virgin birth thus:

Both the mode and the object of our Lord's incarnation are represented in the rare and valuable Mexican codices, if we can believe the learned interpreters of their paintings. Quetzalcoatl is he who was born of the virgin, called Chalchihuitzli, which means the precious stone of penance, says the author of the "Explanation of the Codex Telleriano-Remensis." Tonacatecotl,

[4]Daniel H. Brinton, *American Hero-Myths* (Philadelphia, 1882), p. 172.
[5]*Ibid.*, p. 214.
[6]Von Humboldt, cited in John Taylor, *Mediation and Atonement* (Salt Lake City, 1882), pp. 201-202.

the Mexican supreme deity, begot Quetzalcoatl, not by connection with woman, but by his breath alone, when he sent his ambassador to the virgin of Tula.[7]

—Photograph by Author

Fig. 138:   SCENE FROM BONAMPAK MURAL

Observe the quetzal plumed headdresses and jaguar skins, symbols of Quetzalcoatl, worn by the men depicted on this ancient mural at Bonampak, Mexico, painted approximately A.D. 600.

Dr. De Roo also discussed the Indian traditions of the virgin birth of the "White Bearded God," as reported by the early Spanish missionaries who worked among the American aborigines. It is quite evident that the traditions are merely adulterated forms of the true story of Christ's birth. To quote De Roo:

. . . Mendieta states that according to other traditions, no mention is made of his father, but only of his mother, Chimelma, who, as she was sweeping the temple one day, found a small green stone, named chalchiuite, which she picked up; and through the virtue of this emerald she became miraculously pregnant.

Torquemada, relating still another version of the same original tradition, says, "The Mexicans knew of the visitation of the angel to Our Lady, but expressed it by a metaphor,—namely that something very white, similar to

[7] P. De Roo, *History of America before Columbus* (Philadelphia, 1900), vol. 1, p. 430.

a bird's feather, fell from heaven, and a virgin bent down, picked it up, and hid it below her cincture, and she became pregnant of 'Huitzilopochtli,' or better 'Teo-Huitz-lopochtli,' which name Borunda explains as meaning the Lord of the thorn or wound in the left side. It is always the same, . . . God the virgin's son."[8]

De Roo adds the following pertinent information:

. . . We have mentioned already the belief of the Chiapans, according to which the god Bacab was born of a virgin, Chibirias, who is now in heaven with him.

Sahagún relates that the Tlascaltecs designated one of their principal gods by the name of "Camaxtle," which means the Naked Lord. He was to them what Christ represents on the cross to us, for they asserted that he was endowed with both the divine and the human natures and was born from a devout and holy virgin named "Coatlicue," who brought him forth without lesion of her virginity, on the mount Coatepeo de Tula. All this information, says Sahagún, was first given to the Toltecs by Quetzalcoatl.[9]

Paul Gaffarel claimed that the Manica Indians of Brazil reported to the Catholic padres the following virgin-birth tradition of their "Fair God":

. . . a woman of accomplished beauty, who had never been wedded to man, gave birth to a most lovely child. This child, after growing up to man's estate, worked many wonders, raised the dead to life again, made the lame walk and the blind see. Finally having one day called together a great number of people, he ascended into the air and was transformed into the sun who enlightens this earth.[10]

No book, including the Bible, tells about the virgin birth of Jesus more clearly than does the Book of Mormon; and, since Christ is identified as Quetzalcoatl in the religion of the American aborigines, it was natural for the knowledge of that important event to become attached to him. History affirms that the ancient Americans' knowledge of the virgin birth of the "White and Bearded God" persisted in the New World to the time of the coming of the Europeans, as shown in this chapter; and that knowledge thereby serves as an additional witness that Jesus was resurrected from the grave and is the universal Savior.

---

[8]*Ibid.*, pp. 427-428.
[9]*Ibid.*, p. 427.
[10]Paul Gaffarel, *Histoire de la Découverte de l'Amerique* (Paris, 1892), cited in De Roo, *op. cit.*, pp. 426-427.

CHAPTER 14

QUETZALCOATL'S CRUCIFIXION, RESURRECTION, ASCENSION, AND SECOND COMING

KNOWLEDGE OF CHRIST'S CRUCIFIXION IN ANCIENT AMERICA

The knowledge of Christ's crucifixion was well known in Book of Mormon days. Nephi taught the people that

. . . the God of Jacob, yieldeth himself, according to the words of the angel, as a man, into the hands of wicked men, to be lifted up, . . . and to be crucified, . . .[1]

Nephi's brother, Jacob, told the Nephites of Christ's crucifixion. To quote:

. . . And he also has shown unto me that the Lord God, the Holy One of Israel, should manifest himself unto them in the flesh; and after he should manifest himself they should scourge him and crucify him, according to the words of the angel who spake it unto me.[2]

Somewhat later Jacob declared:

Wherefore, as I said unto you, it must needs be expedient that Christ— for in the last night the angel spake unto me that this should be his name —should come among the Jews, . . . and they shall crucify him— . . .[3]

King Benjamin gave a marvelous sermon regarding the Savior to the people in ancient America in which he made the following statement:

And lo, he [Jesus] cometh unto his own, . . . and . . . they shall consider him a man, and say that he hath a devil, and shall scourge him, and shall crucify him.[4]

INDIANS' KNOWLEDGE OF QUETZALCOATL'S CRUCIFIXION

With such an important event so thoroughly known among the Nephites and Lamanites, it would be natural for a knowledge of it to be carried down from age to age among their descendants, the

---

[1] Nephi 19:10.
[2] 2 Nephi 6:9.
[3] *Ibid.*, 10:3.
[4] Mosiah 3:9.

American Indians. History testifies that such was the case. Several Catholic padres were told by the Indians that Quetzalcoatl had suffered death by crucifixion. Von Humboldt, an important explorer and collector of Indian traditions during the past century, states that the "Fair God" ". . . was crucified for the sins of mankind, as is plainly declared in the tradition of Yucatán, and mysteriously represented in the Mexican paintings."[5]

Lord Kingsborough collected numerous Indian legends and writings of Catholic fathers and published them in nine massive volumes under the title of *Antiquities of Mexico*. In his famous collection he presents much evidence of the crucifixion of the "White Bearded God." Speaking of an early Mexican document, President John Taylor quotes Kingsborough as stating:

"Quetzalcoatl is there painted in the attitude of a person crucified, with the impression of nails in his hands and feet, but not actually upon the cross." Again: "The seventy-third plate of the Borgian MS. is the most remarkable of all, for Quetzalcoatl is not only represented there as crucified upon a cross of Greek form, but his burial and descent into hell are also depicted in a very curious manner."

----

[5]Von Humboldt, cited in John Taylor, *Mediation and Atonement* (Salt Lake City, 1882), p. 202.

Fig. 139:   PLUMED SERPENTS AND TIGERS, TEMPLE OF TIGERS, CHICHEN ITZA

In another place he observes: "The Mexicans believe that Quetzalcoatl took human nature upon him, partaking of all the infirmities of man, and was not exempt from sorrow, pain or death, which he suffered *voluntarily to atone for the sins of man*."[6] (Italics were Pres. Taylor's.)

In his book entitled *Monarquia Indiana,* first published in Spain in A.D. 1613, Juan de Torquemada wrote the following interesting report:

A friar named Diego de Mercado, a grave man and a dignitary of his Order, one of the most exemplary *religionists* of his time, told and wrote above his signature that years ago he had held a conversation with an Otomi Indian over seventy years old on matters relating to our holy faith. The Indian narrated to him how, long ago, the Otomis were in possession of a book, handed down from father to son and guarded by persons of importance, whose duty it was to explain it. Each page of that book had two columns, and between these columns were paintings which represented Christ crucified, whose features wore the expression of sadness; and such is the God who reigns, they said. For the sake of reverence, they did not turn the leaves with their hands, but with a tiny stick kept along with the book for that purpose. The friar having asked the Indian what the contents of the volume were and its teachings, the old man could not give the details, but said that, were it in existence yet, it would be evident that the teachings of that Book and the preaching of the friar were one and the same. But the venerable heirloom had perished in the ground, where its guardians had buried it at the arrival of the Spaniards.[7]

Bishop Bartholome de las Casas, a famous Spanish missionary, devoted most of his life to teaching the Indians of Chiapas, Mexico, and recording their beliefs. He received a letter from Francis Hernandez, a priest laboring under his direction, which stated that one of the old native chiefs claimed that the following story had come down to him from his ancient ancestors:

". . . They [the Chiapan Indians] tell that Eopuco put him [Bacab, the 'White Bearded God'] to death, had him scourged, placed a crown of thorns on his head, and hung him with extended arms from a pole; not meaning that he was nailed but bound to it; and to better explain, the chief extended his own arms. There he finally died, . . ."[8]

The foregoing tradition of the Chiapan Indians constitutes one more version of the crucifixion of the "Fair God." De Roo adds the following information concerning their tradition:

We have noticed before that the Chiapan son-god, Bacab, who had been scourged by Eopuco and crowned with thorns, had also been the divine son of the Mexican virgin goddess. This same son of Chibirias or Chimelma had

---

[6]Lord Kingsborough, *Antiquities of Mexico,* cited in Taylor, *idem.*
[7]Juan de Torquemada, *Monarquia Indiana* (Madrid, Spain, 1613-1732 ed.), *tomo,* p. 15.
[8]Las Casas, cited in De Roo, *History of America before Columbus* (Philadelphia, 1900), p. 373.

been put to death by crucifixion; and this sacrilegious crime had been perpe-trated on a Friday. So had the Chiapans been informed by bearded men who in ancient times had taught them to confess their sins and to fast every Friday in honor of the death of Bacab. . . .[9]

The foregoing quotations from several writers indicate that at the time of the discovery of America—even before the aborigines had had opportunities to receive information from European Chris-tians—the knowledge of the crucifixion of the "Fair God" was wide-spread. Since this event was thoroughly known by the inhabitants of ancient America, as is attested in the Nephite records, it is logical to conclude this event is the source of the Indian traditions.

DARKNESS AT THE TIME OF CHRIST'S DEATH

A graphic and vivid account is given in the Book of Mormon of the terrible destruction which took place upon the Western Hemisphere at the time of Christ's crucifixion and the excessive darkness that prevailed while the Master's body lay in the tomb.[10]

It is not strange that the knowledge of such momentous events would survive until after the discovery of America by Columbus, and documentary sources testify that this was the case.

As a result of his extensive study of the American aborigines, Dr. P. De Roo made the following statement:

Another circumstance of our Saviour's death seems to be remembered in Mexico, for it is related in its traditions that, at the disappearance of Quetzalcoatl, both sun and moon were covered in darkness, while a single star appeared in the heavens.[11]

Compare the following description from the Book of Mormon with De Roo's statement:

And it came to pass that there was thick darkness upon all the face of the land, insomuch that the inhabitants thereof who had not fallen could feel the vapor of darkness;

And there could be no light, because of the darkness, neither candles, neither torches; neither could there be fire kindled with their fine and ex-ceedingly dry wood, so that there could not be any light at all;

And there was not any light seen, neither fire, nor glimmer, neither the sun, nor the moon, nor the stars, for so great were the mists of darkness which were upon the face of the land.[12]

---

[9]Ibid., p. 431.
[10]3 Nephi, chapters 8, 9, 10.
[11]De Roo, op. cit., p. 190.
[12]3 Nephi 8:20-22.

APPEARANCE OF A NEW STAR

Students of the Book of Mormon readily recognize the fact that the Indians' tradition, mentioned by De Roo, that ". . . a single star appeared in the heavens" at Quetzalcoatl's death, confuses an event that took place at the birth of Christ with the events that occurred at his death; for the Nephites' records declare:

. . . Samuel, the Lamanite did prophesy. . . .
. . . Behold, I give unto you a sign; for five years more cometh, and behold, then cometh the Son of God to redeem all those who shall believe on his name.

Fig. 140:   PLUMED SERPENT HEAD IN NATIONAL MUSEUM, MEXICO CITY

—Photograph by Otto Done

And behold, there shall a new star arise, such an one as ye never have beheld; and this also shall be a sign [of Christ's birth] unto you.[13]

The fulfilment of this prophecy is recorded as follows: "And it came to pass also that a new star did appear, according to the word."[14]

The appearance of the new star affected the thinking of the inhabitants of Middle America so profoundly that the major Indian nations—such as the Toltecs, Aztecs, Zapotecs, and Mayas—regarded "Venus as the great star of Quetzalcoatl." The fact has already been mentioned that Venus played a prominent part in the religious life of the American aborigines; in fact, that star was one of the prominent symbols of the "White and Bearded God" at the time of the coming of the Europeans.

EVENTS AT THE TIME OF CHRIST'S CRUCIFIXION

A marvelous account of the destruction which took place on the Western Hemisphere at the time of Christ's crucifixion was recorded by Ixtlilxochitl, an Indian prince who lived near the city of Mexico (1600 A.D.).

To quote:

... the *sun and the moon eclipsed,* and the earth trembled, and the rocks broke, and many other things and signs took place, ... This happened in the year of *ce Calli,* which, adjusting this count with ours, *comes to be at the same time when Christ our Lord suffered, and they say that it happened during the first days of the year.* . . .

A few days after he [Quetzalcoatl] went from there, the *destruction and desolation* related of the third age of the world took place, and then was destroyed that memorable and sumptuous building and tower in the city of Cholula, which was like another tower of Babel, which these people were building almost with the same designs, it being destroyed by the wind. And later those who escaped the extermination of the third age built a temple on its ruins to Quetzalcoatl, whom they placed as god of wind, because the wind was the cause of its destruction, they understanding that this calamity was sent by his hand; and they likewise called it *ce Acatl,* which was the name of the year of his coming. And, *as it seems through the mentioned histories and annals, the aforementioned happened some years after the Incarnation of Christ our Lord.*[15]

Certain historians have maintained that Ixtlilxochitl received his information from the Catholic priests. It is logical to believe that

---

[13]Helaman 14:1-2, 5
[14]3 Nephi 1:21.
[15]*Works of Ixtlilxochitl,* cited in Milton R. Hunter and Thomas Stuart Ferguson, *Ancient America and the Book of Mormon* (Oakland, 1950), p. 190.

the Catholic fathers could not have given Ixtlilxochitl any information regarding the terrific destruction and unusual phenomena of nature on the Western Hemisphere at the time of Christ's crucifixion, since they knew nothing of those events. Such information could have come from only one of three sources, namely: first, from the Book of Mormon—not published until 230 years later; second, from the heavens through direct revelation; and third, from records handed down from his ancestors and traditions received from the old people. The third, Ixtlilxochitl claimed to be the source of the information he used in writing his marvelous account of the history of the American Indians. Thus it seems to the writer that the *Works of Ixtlilxochitl* must be taken very seriously by students and in general esteemed as genuine and authoritative.

Other Indian nations far removed from the Valley of Mexico also testify that, according to sacred records handed down from their ancestors, an unusual catastrophe occurred in ancient America. For example, at the time of the coming of the Spaniards to Yucatán, the Itzá Maya priests were well informed regarding a period of intense darkness in ancient times. The following marvelous statement, which appears on page 103 of his book *Kukulcan the Bearded Conqueror*, is quoted by T. A. Willard from an early Maya manuscript:

It was bitten, the face of the sun; and then it was darkened, the face of the sun; and then it was extinguished, its face. Then they [the people] were frightened. There it was burned [eclipsed] said their priests to them."

An even more amazing statement comes from far-off Peru. Cieza de Leon (a Spanish soldier who arrived in Peru in 1548 and published his book in 1553) was one of the first chroniclers to visit Cuzco, the capital of the Incas, and other important cities of the Andean region, and to obtain from the natives their traditions. His book, therefore, can be considered as very reliable. To quote Cieza:

. . . before the rule of the Incas in these realms, and even before they were known, these Indians relate other things much older than all that has been told.

They affirm that for a long time they were without seeing the sun, and that suffering a great deal on that account, they prayed and made vows to those of whom they looked as their gods, and begged them for the light which they needed. And while this was going on the sun rose in great splendour from the island of Titicaca, which is within the great lagoon of the Collao, so that all were delighted.

—Art Work by Huberta Berg Robison

Fig. 141: LINTEL 6, YAXCHILAN, MEXICO

Fig. 142: LINTEL 32, YAXCHILAN, MEXICO

Maya carvings. Beautiful representations of plumed headdresses, ornaments of precious stones, and elaborate clothing.

And immediately after this event there came and stayed a white man of tall stature, who, in his appearance and person showed great authority and veneration, . . ."[16]

The Indian legends as reported by the Catholic missionaries, the statements made by Ixtlilxochitl, and the story given in the Book of Mormon all agree on several important points relative to the events which occurred in America at the time of the crucifixion of Jesus Christ or Quetzalcoatl; for example, the *Works of Ixtlilxochitl* speak of a terrible "destruction and desolation" which took place in ancient America, and then the significant statement appears: "This happened . . . *at the same time when Christ our Lord suffered."* That statement is in complete agreement with the account given in the Book of Mormon. Ixtlilxochitl also wrote: ". . . *and it seems through the ancient histories and annals, the aforementioned happened some years after the incarnation of Christ our Lord."* As part of the Book of Mormon's detailed account of the terrific "destruction

---

[16]Cieza de Leon, cited in Thor Heyerdahl, *American Indians in the Pacific* (Stockholm, 1952), p. 715.

and desolation" which occurred on the Western Hemisphere, the Nephite historian placed the event at the time of the crucifixion of Jesus Christ.[17]

The records of the Itzá Mayas of Yucatán, Mexico, and Cieza's important account from the Andean region of South America—places separated by thousands of miles from each other—show how accurately the knowledge of the events that occurred at Christ's crucifixion and resurrection, including his appearance to the ancient Americans, was preserved by the aborigines. The readers should observe how closely Cieza de Leon's statement corresponds to the account given in the Book of Mormon. He makes it clear that immediately after the darkness dispersed a *"white man of tall stature, . . . showing great authority and veneration,"* appeared to the ancient Americans; and the Nephite record declares that the people saw a white man, clothed in a white robe, descending from heaven. This glorious personage told them that he was Jesus Christ who had been crucified for the sins of the world.

The Indian traditions quoted supply irrefutable evidence that the historical data relative to Christ's death, resurrection, and appearance to the ancient Americans, as recorded in the Book of Mormon at the time the events occurred, were widely disseminated anciently among the inhabitants of the Western Hemisphere, also that that information became a common heritage for numerous Indian nations. Thus all of these things bear witness that Jesus is the Christ and the universal Savior of man.

"THE CHANGING OF THE TIMES"

Another significant point is made by both Ixtlilxochitl and the Book of Mormon writers. Each account declares that Jesus was crucified during the early part of their year, which perhaps would be in early April according to our calendar. Ixtlilxochitl states, *"And they say it happened during the first days of the year"*; and the Book of Mormon declared that the event occurred, according to their system of reckoning time, *"in the first month, [and] on the fourth day of the month."*[18] (Italics supplied by author.)

----

[17]1 Nephi 19:8-13; Helaman 14:14, 20-24; 3 Nephi 8:1-6, 19-22.
[18]*Ibid.*, 8:5.

The parallels between these accounts are so remarkable that they indicate that the Indians of Mexico held in remembrance the Nephites' dating of events and the knowledge of what occurred down to the time of Ixtlilxochitl, which postdated the Spanish conquest. Therefore, the historical data relative to Christ's crucifixion and resurrection were recorded in the Book of Mormon at the time the events occurred, widely disseminated among the people, and then handed down from age to age among the Indian descendants of the Nephite-Lamanite peoples.

Not only did the people of Mexico retain the same system of reckoning time that the Nephites had established at Christ's birth,

Fig. 143:   ALTAR AT TZENDALES, MEXICO, DECORATED WITH PLUMED SERPENTS

but, according to Stacy Judd, the Maya Indians also retained in their traditions the knowledge of the fact that their ancestors—the Nephites—altered the point from which they reckoned time. This they termed "the Changing of the Times." To quote Stacy Judd's significant statement:

It will be remembered that in the answer to the questionnaire of King Charles V of Spain, the words, "the Changing of the Times," appear. The expression, "the Changing of the Times," indicated the period of the arrival of Kukulcan, or Quetzalcoatl, as he was known in Mexico, whence he came. Both names, Kukulcan and Quetzalcoatl, have the same meaning, "The

Plumed Serpent." "The Changing of the Times" was of vital importance to the Mayas.[19]

Students of the Book of Mormon know that "the Changing of the Times" took place in ancient America at the time of Christ's birth, and not at the time of his arrival in ancient America, as is suggested by Mr. Judd. The marvelous thing is that the tradition as handed down among the Indians until after 1500 A.D. should have been maintained as accurately as it was.

KNOWLEDGE OF CHRIST'S RESURRECTION

Ancient American prophets bore witness of Christ's crucifixion, and prophet after prophet throughout the entire course of Nephite history testified of his resurrection and ascension; in fact, no book gives one a stronger assurance of these facts than does the Book of Mormon.[20] Alma predicted the "resurrection of Christ, and his ascension into heaven,"[21] declaring that thereafter he would appear to the Nephites.[22] King Benjamin gave even a more detailed explanation of his resurrection, in which he predicted that ". . . he shall rise the third day from the dead; . . ."[23] Samuel, the Lamanite, also prophesied that following Jesus' death ". . . the space of three days" shall pass, and then "he shall rise again from the dead."[24]

Since these facts were widely disseminated among both Nephites and Lamanites, it was natural for them to be handed down through the ages in Indian traditions. During the early colonial period, Francis Hernandez, a Catholic priest, was sent by Bishop de las Casas to do missionary work among the Indians of Chiapas, one of the states in southern Mexico. He sent a detailed written report to Bishop de las Casas concerning the beliefs of the natives of Chiapas as they had been reported to him by one of their leading priests. Francis Hernandez's report concerning the natives of Chiapas shows how accurately this knowledge had been retained by these Indians to the time of the Spanish conquest. According to his report, Bacab, the "Fair God" of Chiapas

. . . remained dead three days, and the third day he came to life again and ascended into heaven, where he is now with the Father. Immediately

[19]Stacy Judd, *Ancient Mayas*, p. 54.
[20]3 Nephi 6:20.
[21]Alma 40:20.
[22]*Ibid.*, 16:20.
[23]Mosiah 3:10.
[24]Helaman 14:20.

after came Echuac, who is the Holy Ghost and who supplied the earth all that was needed.[25]

Dr. P. De Roo was of the opinion that "Our Lord's resurrection is plainly brought to mind by the [foregoing] statement of the venerable Chiapan chief. . . ."[26]

CHRIST'S BENEVOLENT WORK AMONG THE NEPHITES AND ASCENSION INTO HEAVEN

Following his resurrection and ascension, according to a beautiful account given in the Book of Mormon, Jesus Christ appeared

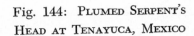

Fig. 144: PLUMED SERPENT'S HEAD AT TENAYUCA, MEXICO

to the inhabitants of ancient America and performed a mighty work. King Benjamin predicted these events as follows:

> . . . the Lord Omnipotent . . . shall come down from heaven among the children of men, and shall dwell in a tabernacle of clay, and shall go forth amongst men, working mighty miracles, such as healing the sick, raising

---

[25]Francis Hernandez's letter to Las Casas, cited in De Roo, *op. cit.*, p. 373.
[26]*Idem.*, p. 430.

the dead, causing the lame to walk, the blind to receive their sight, and the deaf to hear, and curing all manner of disease.[27]

After Christ had visited the Nephites and returned back into heaven, the historian summarized his benevolent works as follows:

. . . after having healed all their sick, and their lame, and opened the eyes of their blind and unstopped the ears of the deaf, and even had done all manner of cures among them, and raised a man from the dead, and had shown forth his power unto them, . . . [Jesus] ascended unto the Father—[28]

Compare Paul Gaffarel's report of the folklore of the Indians of Brazil with the foregoing quotations from the Book of Mormon. He stated that the "Fair God" had

. . . raised the dead to life again, made the lame walk and the blind to see.[29] Finally, having one day called together a great number of people, he ascended into the air and was transformed into the sun who enlightens this earth.[30]

According to the Nephites, after Jesus had accomplished his benevolent works he ". . . departed from them and ascended into heaven. And the disciples saw and did bear record that he ascended into heaven."[31] Mormon also wrote:

Wherefore, my beloved brethren, have miracles ceased because Christ hath ascended into heaven, and hath sat down on the right hand of God, to claim of the Father his rights . . . ?[32]

The legend of the Mixtec Indians of Mexico maintained that the "Fair God," Wixipecocha, ". . . first went off to the mountains on the summit of which he appeared to them for a few moments and then vanished. . . ."[33]

Christ's Second Coming

Before his final ascension, Jesus Christ informed the inhabitants of ancient America of his second coming. To quote: "And he expounded all things, even from the beginning until the *time that he shall come in his glory*—"[34] (Italics supplied by author.) The Master also declared:

---

[27]Mosiah 3:5-8.
[28]3 Nephi 26:15.
[29]Mosiah 3:5-6; 3 Nephi 17:7-10; 4 Nephi 1:5.
[30]Paul Gaffarel, *Histoire de la Découverte de l'Amerique* (Paris 1892), p. 428, cited in De Roo, *op. cit.*, p. 427; 3 Nephi 11:10-11; Mosiah 16:9; Alma 38:9; D & C 88:5-13.
[31]3 Nephi 18:39; 19:1; 26:15; Mosiah 15:9.
[32]Moroni 7:27.
[33]De Roo, *op. cit.*, p. 433.
[34]3 Nephi 26:3.

Fig. 145: THE CHICHAN CHOB, CHICHEN ITZA

This archaeological structure is sometimes known as the "Red House" or as the "House of the Three Brothers."

> And behold, this people will I establish in this land, unto the fulfilling of the covenant which I made with your father Jacob; and it shall be a new Jerusalem. And the powers of heaven shall be in the midst of this people; yea, even I will be in the midst of you.[35]

These predictions of his second coming and the promises that he would bless the people at that time were preserved also in the beliefs of the various Indian tribes; for example, Ixtlilxochitl reported Quetzalcoatl's prediction of his return to earth as follows:

> And at the time he went about taking leave of these people, he told them that in time to come, in a year which he called *ce Acatl, he would return, and then his doctrine would be received, and his children would be masters and would possess the land. . . .*[36]

---

[35]*Ibid.,* 20:22.
[36]*Works of Ixtlilxochitl,* cited in Hunter and Ferguson, *op. cit.,* pp. 214-215.

Regarding the second coming of Quetzalcoatl, William H. Prescott wrote:

. . . After presiding over the golden age of Anahuac, [Quetzalcoatl] disappeared as mysteriously as he had come, . . . As he promised to return at some future day, his reappearance was looked for with confidence by each succeeding generation.[37]

Prescott also wrote:

The Mexicans looked confidently to the return of the benevolent deity [Quetzalcoatl]; and this remarkable tradition, deeply cherished in their hearts, prepared the way . . . for the future success of the Spaniards.[38]

An archaeologist named A. Hyatt Verrill, speaking of the promise of Quetzalcoatl's second coming, wrote:

. . . before he disappeared [he] prophesied that long after his departure . . . eventually he would return and re-establish the Aztecs and their faith. . . . There are countless Mexicans today who are still expecting their Plumed Serpent God to reappear and they still superstitiously make offerings to him in the ancient temple of Quetzalcoatl.[39]

Dr. P. De Roo cites Father de Mercado, an early Catholic missionary, as claiming that he had obtained from the Totonac Indians who lived near Tampico, Mexico, the following legend:

Father de Mercado continues, telling what further discoveries he made in regard to the natives' dogmatic theology,—namely, that in some provinces of New Spain, as among the Totonacs, the people expected the advent of the Son of the great God into this world; and it was said he had to come in order to renew all things; meaning by this not a spiritual renovation, but an earthly material improvement, as they expressed it by saying that at his coming the loaves of bread would be much larger and everything else would grow better in like manner. With the intention of hastening the arrival of the Son of God, they celebrated a religious feast at a certain season of the year and sacrificed eighteen persons, men and women, whom they encouraged to die with the thought that they were to be messengers of the country to the great God, sent to ask and beg him that he would deign to despatch them his Son, . . .[40]

STONE REPRESENTATIONS OF THE "WHITE BEARDED GOD"

Near the close of the Book of Mormon period the inhabitants of ancient America apostatized from the true religion of Jesus Christ,

---

[37]Prescott, *Mexico and the Life of the Conqueror, Fernando Cortes* (New York, 1898), vol. 2, p. 388.
[38]*Ibid.*, vol. 1, p. 64.
[39]A. Hyatt Verrill, *America's Ancient Civilizations* (New York, 1953), p. 104.
[40]De Roo, *op. cit.*, pp. 425-426.

Fig. 146:   FERNE G. HUNTER BY STELA, TIKAL, GUATEMALA

retaining, however, many of the truths in an adulterated form. One of the pagan practices which developed among their descendants, the Indians, was the making and worshiping of stone statues of the "White Bearded God." The Catholic padres who first visited Indian tribes in various countries in Meso-America reported that they saw a number of these stone representations of the "Fair God." Some of the statues were destroyed by the Catholic *conquistadores*; others, however, have survived to the present time.

On each of the four trips that I have made to Guatemala, I have been intensely interested in a representation in jade of the "White and Bearded God," which is housed in the Guatemala National Museum, Guatemala City. A photograph of this jade figurine (Fig. 6) is found on page twenty-five of this book. The director of the Guatemala museum claimed that the figurine was a representation of Quetzal-coatl, and that as nearly as could be ascertained it would date during the early Christian period.

In December, 1954, only two or three days after visiting the museum in Guatemala City, the members of a touring party which I was conducting throughout Mexico and Central America and I visited Chichicastenango, Guatemala. There in a small museum we were shown a stone statue of the "Fair God," a rather grotesque representation, however. A photograph of this statue (Fig. 16) is found on page forty-three. The Quiché Maya Indians of Chichi-castenange paid unusual reverance to it.

Several other representations of "White and Bearded God" have survived until the present time. For example, a photograph of a jade head of Quetzalcoatl (Fig. 2, page 18) and one of an Aztec stone statue of the "Fair God" (Fig. 13, page 37), both from the Valley of Mexico, are shown in this book. Also, on page thirty-two (Fig. 11) a photograph of a Zapotec stone statue of Quetzalcoatl is reproduced. A photograph of the Haida Indians' "Fair God" is found on page fifty-eight and one of the youthful Itzamna—theItza-Maya Messiah—is reproduced on page forty-one. In addition to these, three photographs of Viracocha are reproduced in this volume. This makes eight statues of the "Savior God" of the American aborigines of which the writer has produced photographs and published them herein; and he knows of others which he has not photographed. Also, it is very likely that a number of other representations of the "White and Bearded God" have survived in Mexico, Central America, and South America to our day which have not come to the writer's attention.

Although these representations are somewhat crude, depicting a degenerated conception of the Savior, yet they are important, tangible evidence, showing that the Indians did have deep-rooted traditions of the "White Bearded God" long before Columbus discovered America.

BOOK OF MORMON TEACHINGS AND INDIAN TRADITIONS

It should be remembered that the central theme of the Book of Mormon is that Jesus Christ is the author of the plan of salvation and the Savior of the world, crucified and resurrected for the salvation of mankind; and the principal purpose in preserving the Nephites' ancient records was that they might come forth in the latter days ". . . to the convincing of the Jew and the Gentile that *Jesus is the Christ, the Eternal God, manifesting himself unto all nations—*"[41] It should be recalled also that in all their teachings the holy prophets and teachers of righteousness in ancient America proclaimed a similar central theme to that recorded in the Book of Mormon. Effectively they proclaimed Jesus Christ as the God who provided the gospel with its promised rewards for all mortals who will obey; and he who was crucified and broke the bands of death for every member of the human family.

All the Indian traditions presented in this book regarding Quetzalcoatl, the "Fair God," and many other legends not mentioned, show how effectively Jesus Christ was proclaimed to the inhabitants of the Western Hemisphere in ancient times. Although an apostasy from the true gospel occurred, Indians in all parts of the Americas retained the basic doctrines pertaining to the life, the crucifixion, the resurrection, and the mission of Jesus Christ— the "White Bearded God," generally known to the Indians in Meso-America as Quetzalcoatl.

---

[41]"Preface," Book of Mormon.

INDEX

A

Abinadi, quoted—atonement, 152 f.

Aborigines, Quetzalcoatl traditions of, 22.

Abraham, Jehovah's covenants with, 98.

Alma, quoted—Christ's resurrection, 274.

Alpacas, description of, 233 f.

Alpha, beginning, 97.

Amaleki, quoted—Christ Creator, 254.

America, ancient, Christ appeared in, 96; destruction in, 97; colonizing of, 86 f.

Americans, natives, 21.

Amulek, quoted—atonement, 151-152; quoted—immortality, 127.

Ancient Ones, Jaredites or early Toltecs, 61.

Andagoga, Pascual de, quoted—Viracocha visited Cuzco, 196.

Andes, stone work in, 238 ff.

Angels, visitation of, 126.

Animals, in ancient America, 228.

Apostasy, Nephites, 158 ff., 278.

Apostles, Jesus selects twelve, 99-100.

Aqueducts, Peruvian, 232.

Ascension, Christ's, 276.

Atonement, Book of Mormon teachings of, 151 ff.

Augur, Helen, quoted—"Mother Culture," 88 f.; quoted—Zapotec calendar dated, 90.

Aztecs, belief in immortal life of, 132 f.; belief of Father, 8; Christian doctrine had by, 46 f.; men becoming gods, 162; Montezuma not confused with emperor of, 39-40; poems — Heavenly Parents, 144; priests of, 185-186; Quetzalcoatl god of, 33; Quetzalcoatl redeemer of, 145 ff.; Quetzalcoatl worshiped by, 17, 20; Toltecs culture polluted by, 57; Quetzalcoatl creator, 252.

B

Babel, Jaredites from Tower of 56, 60 f., 85-86, 91 f., 106, 245.

Babylon, pyramids of, 106.

Bacab, resurrection of, 274 f.; the Son, 258; virgin birth of, 258, 263.

Bancroft, Hubert Howe, Ixtlilxochitl described by, 60; quoted—traditions regarding "Fair God," 19, 48; Quiché Mayas knowledge of Godhead, 257.

Baptism, necessity of, 100; Nephites practiced, 222.

Baptismal Font, at Pachacamac, 219 ff.

Bartholomew, claimed he brought Christianity to America, 48, 50.

Bath, Queen's, Peru, 220 f.

Benjamin, King, quoted—Christ's benevolent work, 275; quoted—Christ's crucifixion, 150, 264; quoted—Christ's resurrection, 274; quoted—Christ creator, 254; quoted—Christ's virgin birth, 260 f.; sermon of, 205.

Betanzos, Juan de, quoted—Viracocha the creator, 199 f.; quoted—Viracocha described by, 200.

Billeter, J. David, archaeological ruins of

Corinth, Greece, visited by, 233.

Bochica, Christ similar to, 204; culture giver, 202.

Book of Mormon, 83; account of Christ in, 21, 54, 193, 260; authoritative history of ancient America, 56; atonement teachings in, 151; claims in, 82; high culture of, 86; Mulekites discussed in, 57; Nephites described in, 64 ff.; new witness of Christ, 281; peoples discussed in, 23, 61 f.; quoted—Christ's appearance to brother of Jared, 85; serpent symbol in, 123-124; story of original American cultures in, 91-92; Christ's controlling nature in, 176 ff.

Books, in ancient America, 204-206.

Bountiful, City of, footnote, 28; Jesus appeared in, 98 ff.; meaning of, 27; not located, 157; Quetzalcoatl (Christ) visited people at, 27.

Bowman, Claudious, Teotihuacan visited by, 100.

Brinton, Daniel G., quoted—Andean culture giver, 203; Quetzalcoatl, culture giver, 38; quoted — plumed serpent symbol, 169; Quetzalcoatl a historical character, 33-34; quoted — Quetzalcoatl's virgin birth, 261; quoted—regarding Itzamna, 40 f.; quoted—sky serpent, 171; quoted—sky serpent and harvests, 172; quoted—traditions regarding "Fair God," 17; quoted—Viracocha described by, 191, 195-196.

C

Calendar, date of, 89-90.

Calmecac, religious college of Quetzalcoatl mysteries at, 165.

Candia, Pedro de, taken for Viracocha, 189.

Capac, Huayne, coming of white men predicted by, 189-190.

Capac, Manco, Cuzco founded by, 217.

Carranza, Jesus (Juarez), interpreted Quiché traditions, 111 ff.

Casas, Bartholome de, Catholic chronicler, 24.

Caso, Alfonso, "Mother culture," 92; quoted — early American culture, 88; quoted — origin of Indian culture, 83; quoted— Quetzalcoatl, Creator-god, 252.

Catholic fathers, Indian traditions had by, 17.

Chacmools, rain gods, 173.

Chacs, rain gods, 173.

Cheesman, Paul, photographing of, 240.

Chiapas, "Fair God" in, 19.

Chibchas, Bochica worshiped by, 202.

Chibirias, virgin mother, 258, 263.

Chichen Itzá, baptismal font at, 222; Itzamna worshiped at, 40 ff.

Chimelma, Quetzalcoatl's virgin mother, 256.

Chimu, culture, 216.

Chivin, culture, 216.

Cholula, Quetzalcoatl at, 19, 31; Quetzalcoatl worshiped at, 31; Toltec built, 62.